Ain't No Trust

The publisher gratefully acknowledges the generous support of the General Endowment Fund of the University of California Press Foundation.

Ain't No Trust

HOW BOSSES, BOYFRIENDS, AND
BUREAUCRATS FAIL LOW-INCOME
MOTHERS AND WHY IT MATTERS

JUDITH A. LEVINE

UNIVERSITY OF CALIFORNIA PRESS

Berkeley   Los Angeles   London

University of California Press, one of the most distinguished university presses in the United States, enriches lives around the world by advancing scholarship in the humanities, social sciences, and natural sciences. Its activities are supported by the UC Press Foundation and by philanthropic contributions from individuals and institutions. For more information, visit www.ucpress.edu.

University of California Press
Berkeley and Los Angeles, California

University of California Press, Ltd.
London, England

Library of Congress Cataloging-in-Publication Data

Levine, Judith Adrienne.
    Ain't no trust : how bosses, boyfriends, and bureaucrats fail low-income mothers and why it matters / Judith A. Levine.
        p.   cm.
    Includes bibliographical references and index.
    ISBN 978-0-520-27471-6 (cloth : alk. paper)
    ISBN 978-0-520-27472-3 (pbk. : alk. paper)
    1. Low-income single mothers—United States—Social conditions.
    2. Low-income single mothers—Employment—United States.
    3. Low-income single mothers—Services for—United States.   I. Title.
    HQ759.L4744   2013
    306.874'32086942—dc23

                                                        2013003307

Manufactured in the United States of America

21   20   19   18   17   16   15   14   13
10   9   8   7   6   5   4   3   2   1

In keeping with a commitment to support environmentally responsible and sustainable printing practices, UC Press has printed this book on Rolland Enviro100, a 100% postconsumer fiber paper that is FSC certified, deinked, processed chlorine-free, and manufactured with renewable biogas energy. It is acid-free and EcoLogo certified.

For my mother, Helene J. Levine, and in memory
of my father, Herbert S. Levine,
With appreciation for their love, support, insight,
and humor.

And for Edward Sobel and Julia Levine Sobel,
For making family life such a pleasure

I tell musicians, "Don't trust nobody but your mama, and even then, look at her real good."

—Attributed to Bo Didley

Contents

Acknowledgments

This book is based on two rounds of interviews that took place ten years apart. Given that time frame, I have racked up debts to several waves of advisers, research assistants, colleagues, and friends from different institutions. My first and greatest debt, however, is to the women who agreed to participate in the study. They generously told me the details of their lives, even though I could offer them little in return other than vague hopes that the research would help women like them down the road. Many of the women I met reported feeling mistreated by those who represented mainstream institutions, and their resulting suspicions, which are the subject of this book, kept them from interacting with too many like me—a graduate student and later a faculty member at large universities. Their willingness to give me their time, their thoughts, and sometimes their secrets was thus an enormous gift.

I thank Susan Lloyd, Rhonda Present, and Jody Raphael, who helped connect me to service providers through whom I might meet participants for the study. In addition, Susan Lloyd allowed me to identify several respondents through her own study in a Chicago neighborhood. I also thank all of the directors and staff members of various agencies who gave generously of their time and who allowed me to approach their clients with invitations for interviews. I regret that to protect the study participants' confidentiality, I cannot thank them by name.

I am deeply grateful to Rebecca Vonderlack-Navarro and Melissa Ford Shah for their hard work and great skill as they conducted almost half of the second round of interviews. They were also my partners in devising and implementing the coding scheme for the transcripts. Johanna Gray's quick mind kept us organized through the data collection and coding processes. Thomas Nigel Gannon helped me tackle the literature on trust, served as a sounding board for the book's major ideas, and was an insightful reader of drafts of most of the book's chapters.

For additional research assistance, I thank Adam Avrushin, Valerie Bonner, Abigail Coppock, Jessica Iselin, Amanda Naar, Neelam Patel, Yvette Pettee, Sarah Pollock, Lauren Ross, Jacqueline Singer, Christina Stewart, Rochelle Terman, Michael Tower, and Corey Waters. Kai Andersen-Guterman, Bessie Flately, and Tatiana Poladko conducted analyses of census data to produce the appendix's maps with advice from Melody Boyd and Richard Moye. Jorge Navarro translated research materials for Spanish-speaking research participants. Ellen von Schrott transcribed the majority of interviews for both time periods and encouraged me through her enthusiasm for the project.

I conducted the first round of interviews as a doctoral student at Northwestern University, where I had the dream team of dissertation committees. I am eternally grateful to Christopher (Sandy) Jencks, whose rigor made my work stronger, whose editing made my writing clearer, and whose warmth made my time in graduate school easier. I thank Art Stinchcombe for believing in this project, often seeing aspects of its conceptual significance that I was slower to discover. I thank Carol Heimer for her ability to advise on both the most abstract theoretical concepts and the most mundane tasks involved in conducting qualitative field research. One of the great rewards of academic life is that such relationships endure over the years. Even though my former committee members were not involved in the second half of the project's design and data collection, each continued to indulge my requests toward the end of the writing process. Rebecca Blank, Julie Brines, Kathy Edin, Roberto Fernandez, Mark Granovetter, Kathie Harris, Susan Mayer, and Mary Waters also provided valuable guidance during my graduate school career. Kathy Edin and Maureen Waller advised me on my successful application for a National Science Foundation (NSF) Dissertation Improvement Award. Fay Cook, Greg Duncan, and Mary Patillo invited me back to Northwestern for a productive year as a visiting scholar.

My many wonderful colleagues in graduate school provided support, but I want to especially acknowledge my dear friends Elizabeth Clifford, Brian Gran, David Shulman, and Christopher Wellin, who lent their encouragement and perceptive advice throughout the duration of the project.

During a Robert Wood Johnson Foundation Health Policy Scholars postdoctoral fellowship, I enjoyed the hospitality of Sandy Danziger, Sheldon Danziger, Ariel Kalil, and Catherine McLaughlin. Mary Corcoran read my work and promoted it enthusiastically. Denise Anthony, Betsy Armstrong, and Paula Lantz not only became good friends but also gave advice over the years at key moments. Denise, an expert on the trust literature, provided entrée into it, read most of the manuscript's chapters, and served as my go-to person for checks on how I was integrating concepts from the trust and poverty literatures.

Temple University has been a wonderful environment in which to bring the project to fruition. I treasure the support and insights of my colleagues here. Julia Ericksen, who (as chair at the time) recruited me to the department, read the manuscript in its entirety—including some chapters more than once. As both cheerleader and insightful critic, she was invaluable in helping me complete the book. Sherri Grasmuck and Matt Wray both read chapters and advised on how to make the arguments clearer and more engaging to readers. Conversations with Gretchen Condran, Kim Goyette, and Josh Klugman helped me hone my arguments. My current department chair, Bob Kaufman, is supportive in every way. Thanks are also due to Rebecca Alpert, Kevin Delaney, Rosario Espinal, Joyce A. Joyce, Laura Levitt, Peter Logan, and Heather Thompson.

I also benefited from the knowledge and supportiveness of a host of other colleagues. Evelyn Brodkin gave early encouragement to pursue this project, and her ethnographic work on caseworkers has been an invaluable resource for checking the validity of my respondents' reports. Susan Lambert was central to helping me see the consistency of the theme of distrust across the contexts I studied. Julia Henly is a steadfast friend who spent endless hours talking with me, reading my work, and generally being in my corner. Harold Pollack discussed the book's ideas with me and offered his support in multiple ways. Aimee Dechter has continually provided constructive criticism and equally enthusiastic support. Kate Cagney, Peter Conrad, Clifton Emery, Malitta Engstrom, Helen Levy, M. Katherine Mooney, and Bill Sites have given me both encouragement and insights. My students in both my graduate course on inequality and my undergraduate course on poverty have given me helpful feedback on the book's material. Susanne Rosenberg, my dear friend since childhood, proofread the manuscript meticulously.

Annette Lareau has long been a champion of this project. She read the entire manuscript twice. I thank her for her tremendous generosity and sage advice. Maia Cucchiara also read the entire manuscript and provided terrific insights on how to reshape several chapters.

The project was sustained through funding provided by a variety of sources. During the first round of interviews, I was supported by an NSF Dissertation Improvement Award; the NSF fellowship program in Poverty, Race, and Urban Inequality at Northwestern University; a Northwestern University Dissertation Grant; and a Northwestern University Alumnae Association Dissertation Fellowship. In later stages, I received funding from the Center for Health Administration Studies; the Center for Human Potential; the Sloan Center for Children, Families, and Work; a Temple University faculty summer research grant; a Temple sabbatical semester; and a Center for Humanities at Temple faculty fellowship.

It has been a pleasure to work with my editor Naomi Schneider, who has given me astute advice throughout, and with the editorial and production staff at the University of California Press. I thank the reviewers whose thoughtful suggestions benefited the manuscript greatly. I also thank Carolyn Bond for her keen editorial eye.

I was blessed with parents who considered it their job to provide unending support without ever expecting anything in return. It is painful that my father, who was in effect my earliest academic adviser, is not here to see the completed book. But I am comforted that he knew of my contract with University of California Press before his death. My mother's quiet sensitivity and insightfulness set a great example to try to follow in conducting qualitative work. I thank her for all the sacrifices she has made for me. No sister has ever had her sister's back better than Jan Levine has mine. And my brother-in-law Michael Zuckerman is right behind her. I thank them for all of the meals, conversations about politics, and encouragement. My brother Jonathan Levine died before I knew what profession I would pursue or that I would write this book. But the gifts he gave me while he was here—his confidence in me, his wisdom about what is important, and his example of how to tell a story well—will last my lifetime. My parents-in-law Shelly and Bob Sobel arrive for visits wanting to know what they can do to help and how my work is going. I thank them and my siblings-in-law Laurence and Joan Sobel and David Sobel for their wonderful support. I also have a rich network of aunts, uncles, cousins, and dear friends. I am deeply grateful to them all.

My daughter Julia has brought pure joy to my life. She has supported me in numerous ways, from decorating my office with signs, to coming up with ideas for the book's cover, to being more patient than children should have to be when their mothers are busy working. Writing the book would have been a much drearier experience without exposure to her cheery disposition. Ed Sobel has seen this project through from glimmer of an idea to completion. He has listened to me battle through the ideas, given me writing advice, and put up with my faulty estimations of when I would be finished. There are many positive adjectives I could use to describe Ed. If I were forced to pick one, though, it would be *trustworthy*. Now that I have written this book, I understand how valuable that is.

Introduction

One afternoon during the broiling hot summer of 1995, I sat in a tiny attic apartment on Chicago's West Side talking with Bethany Grant, a thirty-four-year-old divorced African American mother.[1] Bethany was living with the youngest three of her five children and, temporarily, with her friend Sheena and Sheena's children. The two-bedroom apartment was cramped for such a large number of people, and stifling hot, but the trees surrounding its windows made it feel like a tree house. Bethany's willowy frame and flair for creating fashionable outfits from even the simplest of clothes gave her a certain grace. Just like her tree-house home, Bethany seemed to float above the stark reality of her meager resources.

Bethany spoke calmly while reporting her struggles as a single mother experiencing financial hardship. By the time she paid for rent, gas, and electricity, she had almost no money left to get through the month. She had no cushion to soften the blow of any unforeseen setbacks. As a result, she was keenly aware of the risks involved if her navigation of the welfare system and the low-wage labor market went awry. On the basis of personal experience, she also had a deep skepticism of both the employers and the welfare caseworkers who guarded the gates of entry to resources. Bethany liked working, but whenever she took a job while she was on welfare she felt she risked that her caseworker would cut off her welfare benefits, even the ones to which she was entitled and on which she relied for survival.[2] Sometimes the hassle of "fighting to get them back" made her think working was "not worth it." Once, Bethany and her kids almost ended up homeless after she took a part-time job and reported it to the welfare office. Her earnings from the job were so low that she still qualified for a portion of her welfare benefits as well as food stamps and Medicaid coverage for herself and her children,[3] but her caseworker "messed up" her case by mistakenly cutting off the benefits she still was legally allowed.[4] "Every time I've worked, they wind up messing my whole case up. My case was messed up for like almost four months. I didn't know what I was going to do. It was just by luck I had a friend that gave me a place to stay because my gas was [shut] off during the winter. . . . If he hadn't been around, I don't know what, I probably be on the street."

Bethany also doubted that employers could be trusted to treat her fairly. This distrust, like her distrust of her caseworkers, kept her out of the labor market at times. For instance, her concerns about one work supervisor led her to leave the job and return fully to the welfare rolls before eventually cycling into another job. Bethany's brother had gotten her the job at the lobby concession stand in the downtown office building where he worked. At first Bethany enjoyed the position and appreciated the new skills it gave her, but as time wore on she became increasingly displeased with her boss's shirking of duties while talking on the phone and requests that Bethany run personal errands for her. Bethany was happy to work hard running the cash register and stocking the shelves, but she felt disrespected when her boss insisted that Bethany do tasks like picking up prescriptions for her at the pharmacy. The last straw came when Bethany was accused of stealing on the job.

People were stealing out of the safe. Things was missing out the storage room. People'd walk off with candy or whatever. . . . Then me and . . . this other coworker, we was like new to the job, so it was like . . . trying to point the finger at us. And it's like, "Wait a minute! Hold up, I'm not going through this!" I told my brother, "I'll leave the job before I sit up here and be ridiculed like that." And we come to find out it was two people that had been working there all along. We was like, "See?"

When the true culprits were apprehended, it was too late for Bethany. The incident cemented her belief that she would never be treated fairly by her supervisor. She quit. Bethany's distrust in people in two separate settings—the welfare office and the workplace—conspired to pull her out of steady employment and back toward the welfare system.

As the scholar Francis Fukuyama points out, trust is a "lubricant" for action, while distrust stalls it.[5] If persons or institutions are indeed trustworthy (a condition that often seems unmet in Bethany's world), trust in them opens up opportunities and distrust closes off opportunities. For low-income mothers like Bethany, distrust is a barrier to taking the actions the wider society wants them to take—voluntarily leaving welfare, finding work, using child care, getting married, involving their children's fathers in family life, and relying on kin rather than government for support. Low-income families who frequently face material and other hardships are in great need of the opportunities that trusting might bring, such as gaining a foothold in the labor market, accessing nurturing child care services, or partnering with those who may share the challenges of raising children in poverty. And yet, as it turns out, they find themselves in circumstances that do not promote trust. While they need trust's benefits, they are unlikely to trust. Distrust can be a powerful force in guiding key life decisions. But this factor, with its profound and wide-ranging consequences for low-income mothers, has been too long overlooked.

In 2005, ten years after my interview with Bethany, I visited Susan Schiller's brick row house in a Chicago low-rise public housing project. Her living room was painted a peeling dark greenish-brown. Its first-floor windows, which were immediately adjacent to the sidewalk and unadorned by curtains or shades, afforded no privacy. While Susan and

I talked, several neighbors stuck their heads right into one of the windows to say hello as they walked by. Susan, a white woman in her early forties and the single mother of four children (only two of whom were still under eighteen), had decorated the room with her children's sports trophies. At five foot ten, she was tall and attractive, though she complained about all the weight she had put on over the years. Her fourteen-year-old daughter, who was even taller than Susan, popped in and out of our conversation in order to affectionately tease her mom.

Susan, like Bethany, had a long work history interrupted by several stints on welfare. She had left her most recent job in a desperate but failed attempt to gain control over her fifteen-year-old son, who had gotten caught up in gang activity and was now incarcerated. She was looking for work and scraping by with help from her oldest son, a twenty-four-year-old who worked as a medical assistant and lived in his own apartment nearby, and her boyfriend, who made under $10 an hour as a forklift driver.[6] Luckily, since she lived in public housing, her rent was dropped to zero during the times she had no earnings.

Susan also did not place much faith in caseworkers. She suspected that a caseworker's main goal was to "cut [people] totally off," and since she felt caseworkers made it as unpleasant as possible to be on welfare, her wariness led her to try to avoid welfare as long as she could. She wanted to save the months she had remaining on her time-limited welfare clock because "Who's to say when hard times will come?" (She defined these potential hard times as worse than now, when she was "hurting" but still had "a roof over [her] head.") But that left her dependent on jobs in which she also at times distrusted both her supervisors and her coworkers and her supervisors distrusted her. As with Bethany, Susan's distrust in the workplace served to interrupt periods of employment. Susan had been fired from a job selling food at a large arena after being accused of stealing a hot dog. Susan denied stealing the hot dog and suspected that really her boss wanted to get rid of her after she had refused to spy on a coworker who she feared would retaliate.

> They don't screen their employees. Anybody can work there. You can just get out of prison and work there. . . . So they have a lot of people

who rob them. That's just constant. So, what they'll do is they'll spy on you. . . . [There was] this girl that was a couple registers down from me, and [my supervisor] said that she knows she's stealing and she wanted me to watch, and I said, "It is not my job. I'm not watching her and telling you nothing." That could cause a lotta stuff [meaning retribution]. Because, like I said, they'll hire anybody. "If you know she's stealing, then you have somebody else watch her. That's what you have . . . supervisors for. . . ." Then she got mad.

It is hard to know what exactly happened at the arena and who was at fault for what, but it seems fairly clear that mutual distrust played some role.

Bethany Grant and Susan Schiller are just two of the ninety-five women I spoke with about raising children and making do in poverty. Many of the other women also brought up the topic of distrust in case-workers and work supervisors and described how it related to their welfare and work outcomes. But lack of trust played a role beyond welfare receipt and employment patterns. Other women talked about distrust in relation to other outcomes, such as whether they signed up for child care, got married, allowed their kids' fathers into their kids' lives, or relied on their family and friends for help. In fact, there did not seem to be any important outcomes in their lives that the women discussed without referencing how their trust or distrust in others played a role.

When I interviewed Bethany in the mid-1990s, I was a doctoral student writing a dissertation on how attention to the full context of low-income mothers' lives helps us understand how women in poverty make decisions about welfare use and getting jobs. I explored women's experiences not only in welfare offices but also in workplaces, and with child care providers, boyfriends and husbands, and family and friends. When I conducted these mid-1990s interviews, I was not looking for the presence of distrust and I did not ask specifically about it. I simply wanted to know how various settings, such as welfare offices or child care markets, influenced women's choices about welfare and employment. But once the interviews were completed, I was struck by how many women talked about their suspicions of others' unreliability and by how these suspicions arose in almost every area of women's lives.

While each of the contexts I studied had its particular impact on the women's experiences, I came to see a familiar pattern: the women distrusted many of those whom they encountered, and their distrust was a key ingredient in shaping their behaviors.

A year after I completed the 1990s interviews, and hence between the time I talked with Bethany and the time I met Susan, a major piece of federal legislation designed to change low-income women's decision making was passed. The Personal Responsibility and Work Opportunity Reconciliation Act (PRWORA), or welfare reform, as it is more commonly known, was signed into law by President Bill Clinton on August 22, 1996, and was implemented in 1997. Its goals were (and continue to be) to promote quick exits from the welfare rolls, employment, marriage, paternal involvement, and reliance on kin rather than government. To do so, it created time limits on welfare benefits (hence Susan's concern over her welfare "clock"), work requirements, and funding streams for child care subsidies and marriage promotion programs. It removed disincentives to marry and made paternity establishment mandatory for the receipt of benefits.

In the immediate post-reform era, a flurry of research activity sprang up to examine welfare reform. Although I had moved on to work on other topics, I followed the new welfare reform literature with interest, eager to see how the experiences of women navigating the worlds of welfare and low-wage, work since reform differed from those of the women I had studied before reform. As time wore on, however, I came to see that little comparable work was being produced. There were many quantitative studies designed to identify the effects of reform,[7] and some key qualitative studies had looked at specific aspects of reform—how post-reform welfare offices delivered services or how low-income mothers patched together child care services, for instance[8]—but with only one or two notable exceptions, little qualitative work had examined low-income women's lives holistically in the post-reform era.[9]

In the mid-2000s, I decided to write a book on the subject, and in order to do so I set out to conduct a new round of interviews with a different group of women now living in the post-reform world. These women were at a similar stage in their life course to that of the women I had interviewed ten years earlier, meaning that they had children young enough to be eligible for welfare and that they either were receiving welfare or had received it in the past few years. The interviews with this new group of women coupled with the interviews conducted with the other group of women interviewed earlier would form the basis of the book.

While of course it would be interesting to know how my original interviewees were doing, they most likely had long moved on from straddling the border between welfare and work—either because their children would now be too old to be eligible for welfare or simply because only a tiny minority of women use welfare benefits for that long. In the pre-reform era, the average woman who entered the welfare system received assistance for just about four and a half years before stopping.[10] Reinterviewing the original group of women would thus have entailed major problems. It could not have addressed the question that interested me, namely how women at the same point in their lives (i.e., with minor children and current or recent welfare usage) were faring after reform and whether distrust in each of the contexts I had studied earlier still played a role in the actions of women at this life stage.

I expected to see enormous differences after reform, and of course, I did see some. Welfare reform heralded important changes. These changes are reflected in the fact that Bethany faced no work requirements and hence could hesitate to take a job and keep getting welfare benefits. By contrast, Susan was driven to eschew welfare in order to save the limited time she could draw on benefits for when "hard times" might strike. The women I interviewed in the mid-2000s knew they would have to find child care and try to find work or make do without the welfare benefits, which required work activity. Most of the women I interviewed, like so many other low-income women in America since reform, tried to stay off welfare as much as possible. Indeed, the mass exodus of low-income mothers from the welfare rolls in the aftermath of reform represents the near elimination of one piece of the U.S. welfare state.[11]

But my other expectations about differences across the two time periods were not met. I had assumed that after reform women would no longer feel they could afford the luxury of acting upon their suspicions of others. For instance, I thought that no mother would leave a job because of questions about her supervisor's fairness, since she could no longer count indefinitely on welfare to support her. Nor did I expect distrust to play as much of a role in blocking women's actions in any of the contexts I studied. The new policy gave women voluntary incentives to leave the welfare rolls before mandatory ones hit, to find and stay in jobs, to find and maintain child care arrangements, to get married, to get help from children's fathers, and to rely on friends and family for support, and I had presumed that these would override mothers' feelings of distrust when they made decisions. But instead, I was mostly struck by the similarities across time. Women interviewed in the mid-2000s described the same problems and the same distrust in much the same ways as women interviewed in the mid-1990s. In fact, until I became so familiar with my interview transcripts that I immediately recognized the details of a case, I often could not tell whether I was reading one from the pre- or post-reform time period. They did not really differ. Yes, the details of how welfare policy operated had shifted, but the women's struggle to keep their families afloat and the impact of their lack of faith in others in the five contexts studied remained remarkably stable.

The post-reform interviews echoed the theme of the pre-reform interviews: the contexts I studied and the interactions within them were often marked by distrust. And that suspicion, the wariness that so many women described, functioned in the same way at both time periods: it kept women from taking risks. Distrust kept them from believing that the "carrots" in policies designed to voluntarily entice them into the labor market were real (though it also led them to be certain that the mandatory "sticks" that forcibly pushed them to work were real). It led them to quit jobs at the first sign a boss might not treat them fairly. It encouraged them to yank their children out of child care arrangements they questioned. It made them hesitant to marry or to become too close to their romantic partners. It gave them pause about involving their children's fathers in their lives. And it kept them from exchanging goods and support with certain friends and family members. In other words, it kept them from doing many of the very things welfare reformers wanted them to do.

The more I compared the interviews conducted at the two different time periods, the more the book became about continuity rather than change. What started as a book about how welfare reform played out in the lives of low-income mothers became a book about the consistency of distrust in low-income mothers' lives as they managed the same old struggles. Despite the controversy and hyperbole that accompanied the development and passage of welfare reform of the 1990s, the legislation fell short of addressing root causes of many of the problems of those in poverty.[12]

Welfare reform strove to "fix" the individual behavior of low-income mothers, who were seen as unduly dependent on government funding and personally averse to mainstream family norms. Reform held such mothers accountable for their own plights and aimed to encourage their "personal responsibility" by creating a set of incentives and mandates designed to promote behaviors such as welfare exit, employment, and avoidance of nonmarital fertility. These incentives achieved some success for some groups of women but left other women's lives unchanged or changed for the worse.[13] Reform had a greater impact on outcomes related to work and welfare use than on those related to marriage and childbearing.[14] And the initial positive effects of reform slowed over time both as economic recession hit and as the most advantaged recipients left the rolls, leaving behind those who were less likely to fare well without more support.[15]

Why were reform's benefits limited in these ways? One reason is that basing reform legislation on a single-minded conception of low-income women as autonomous actors ignores the ways low-income women's actions are constrained by their social environment. This approach fails to grasp a fundamental social science finding: social contexts profoundly influence individuals' behavior. A host of social experiments make this fact abundantly clear. For instance, the Asch conformity experiments show that people will correctly answer questions about the lengths of lines drawn on cards if they are alone but will answer incorrectly if they are in a group of people who give incorrect answers.[16] They succumb to peer pressure and conform to others' answers even when they know the answers are incorrect. An even more dramatic example is the Stanford prison experiment conducted by Philip Zimbardo.[17] In this study, Stanford University students were randomly assigned to perform the role of either "guard" or "prisoner." In the course of just a few days, the simulated prison context of the experiment led the guards to behave sadistically toward the prisoners, and the prisoners, traumatized by the experience, to become submissive to the guards' authority and depressed.

It is not enough to try to change individual behaviors; we also need to understand the individual's reaction to her surrounding contexts. Contexts where key people—such as caseworkers, employers, or boyfriends—act in erratic, irresponsible, or untrustworthy ways can produce a form of distrust in individuals that in turn affects their behavior. Distrust and the behaviors influenced by distrust were often a *response* to the conditions the women I interviewed found (or expected to find) in various social contexts.

If we really want to understand low-income mothers' welfare, employment, and family choices and outcomes, we need to look beyond the mothers themselves to the social contexts in which mothers find themselves.[18] These contexts affect low-income mothers' impressions of what will happen if they take the actions the reformers hoped for. The women I interviewed reported that they did not trust the people and the institutions in their environment to follow through on promises and to treat them with respect. This lack of trust constrained their actions. It protected them when people around them proved untrustworthy, but it could cause them to forego or misperceive potential opportunities that would improve their situations. No policy that ignores the forces that produce distrust will truly change the lives of low-income mothers and their children.

These women's distrust appeared to arise from several sources. They learned it through direct experience with those who prove untrustworthy. Experiences with one caseworker, boss, or romantic partner taught them that others were not reliable, and they then carried over that distrust to new caseworkers, bosses, and boyfriends. They absorbed wariness from others in their community whose experiences taught them to be suspicious of the motives and reliability of various actors and institutions. They used distrust as armor to preemptively protect themselves from those who might disappoint or mistreat them.

In all of these situations, the women's subordinate position in contexts such as the welfare office and the low-wage workplace—and even sometimes romantic relationships marked by violence or intimidation—was likely to be at the root of their distrust. This structural position brought with it a degree of powerlessness. Relative powerlessness vis-à-vis those around them made the women vulnerable to mistreatment by those who did not share their interests.

The women's limited power also left them with few tools in their arsenals, other than distrust, with which to confront the indignities of their position. Others might be in control, but the women retained the power to withhold trust. Without deep changes—much deeper ones than those offered by welfare reform—that would actually alter their relative position of power in interactions or at least provide some guarantee that others would share their interests or would reliably make good on promises, distrust and the barriers to action it creates would prevail.

The women I interviewed were not only in a disadvantaged position in welfare offices, workplaces, and similar local contexts, they were also at the bottom of the hierarchy in U.S. society more broadly. Most notably, they were at the very bottom of the income distribution. In 2005, during my second round of interviews, a single mother of two children in Illinois with no other income than welfare received $4,752 in income for the entire year, unless of course she did not manage to retain benefits for the whole year, in which case she received less. If instead of receiving welfare she worked for minimum wage, which was $5.15 in 2005, she would still make only $10,712. And that would be if she worked forty hours a week, fifty-two weeks a year, without missing a single day. The poverty line for a family with one adult and two children in 2005 was $15,735. Thus the welfare recipient's income was less than a third of those living at the poverty line figure, and even a full-time minimum-wage worker's income was only about two-thirds of the poverty line amount.[19]

Many of the women I interviewed faced other disadvantages in addition to low income that relegated them to the bottom of the U.S. stratification system. They lived in neighborhoods of concentrated poverty with high crime rates. Their children attended low-performing schools, much like the ones they themselves had attended. Often the men in their lives were incarcerated. They did not have the political voice to sway politicians to address their concerns. The women's disadvantage and relative powerlessness were thus twofold: they were in subordinate positions both in several of the contexts I studied and in U.S. society at large. These positions of subordination fed their suspicion that others did not share their interests and that it was up to them to protect themselves.

AIN'T NO TRUST'S MAIN FINDINGS AND ARGUMENT

The study documents that most of the low-income mothers interviewed experienced feelings of distrust. This distrust surfaced, not in just one setting, but in all of the arenas studied: welfare offices, workplaces, child care markets, romantic unions, and social networks. The presence and nature of distrust did not change across the two time periods studied. Distrust inhibited the actions of the women during both the pre- and post-welfare reform time periods. Most notably, it often kept women from taking the very actions that welfare reform was designed to promote. These four findings—most mothers experienced distrust, mothers experienced distrust across multiple arenas, distrust did not change across the time periods, and distrust inhibited action at both time periods, even those actions welfare reformers intended to promote—are the main findings of this book.

On the basis of these findings, *Ain't No Trust* argues that welfare reform's effects would have been larger if distrust had not limited women's response to the incentives that reform created. Other researchers, discussed further in chapter 1, have indeed found that despite the impact of welfare reform, it fell short of achieving all its intended effects and did not universally improve the lives of low-income families.[20] Indeed, the stories told by the women interviewed for this study support these findings in that they talked about having nearly identical problems whether they were interviewed before or after welfare. The daily struggles of low-income mothers' lives sounded no different across time periods.

Welfare reform did not attempt to reduce distrust. It did not address any of the elements that produce distrust in the five settings this book investigates. As scholarship described in chapter 1 shows, it did not change the incentives for caseworkers, working conditions in low-wage jobs, the supply of high-quality child care, the opportunities for low-income men, or the resources to communities in which the members of women's social networks live.[21] These are "structural" elements of the five settings. It also did not change the fact that low-income mothers, especially single mothers, still occupy a disadvantaged position in the U.S. social structure at large. For instance, single-mother families have the highest poverty rate of all family types in America.[22] William Julius Wilson defines social structure as "the way social positions, social roles, and networks of social relationships are arranged in our institutions, such as the economy, polity, education, and organization of the family."[23] These patterned arrangements affect both the relationships people have with each other and the opportunities (or barriers to opportunity) people have.

The research is based on a study of low-income women and hence does not directly study these structural factors themselves.[24] But we know from the studies discussed in chapter 1 that welfare reform did not make changes in these structural factors. We can see the women reacting to these factors in their reports of why they distrust. As they detail events, we see that the women learn to distrust through direct experience. They learn to distrust because they interact with people they deem untrustworthy. The women report that these people can be unreliable, abusive, unsafe, disrespectful, or destructive in other ways. This perceived untrustworthiness in turn relates to the structural factors that welfare reform left in place. For instance, some mothers share Bethany's claim that caseworkers cut them off from benefits to which they are entitled. This complaint relates to a structural element of the welfare office: in both time periods, caseworkers have been strongly encouraged to reduce the size of their caseloads and have not been penalized for making bureaucratic errors that cut benefits to eligible recipients.[25] It is true that at times some mothers appear to enter into interactions already distrusting. But this preemptive distrust is still structurally undergirded by either the women's past experiences or their knowledge of others' experiences.

This book is about the prevalence of distrust in low-income communities. Women of different races, ethnicities, ages, educational levels, and employment histories and from different time periods all report high levels of distrust. The book is about how distrust guides behavior. It is about the costs of learning to distrust the hard way: by placing trust in those who prove untrustworthy. In short, *Ain't No Trust* argues that we cannot understand life in poverty without attention to the production and consequences of distrust.

The book uses the case of welfare reform to illustrate the role of distrust in low-income life and to highlight the persistence of distrust when the structural factors that produce it do not change. And by using the case of a policy reform, the book also shows that policies that do not attend to the structures that produce distrust may be able to achieve certain effects but that these effects will be limited in scope.

CONTRIBUTIONS TO TRUST, POVERTY, AND SOCIAL POLICY RESEARCH

The findings in this book contribute to several different literatures. Overall, they suggest that these literatures should incorporate the lessons learned by each other. In this section, I discuss each of these literatures in turn.

Ain't No Trust argues that the literatures on poverty and social policy would benefit from paying more attention to the literature on trust. The trust literature tells us that distrust is more common among low-income and minority populations than other populations.[26] It establishes that people are less likely to trust those who hold power over them.[27] It shows us that distrust dissuades action.[28] Each of these findings has great relevance for understanding both life in poverty and the workings of social policies. And yet these insights are often ignored in scholarship on poverty and social policy. I find that low-income mothers feel plagued by those they believe to be untrustworthy and that their resultant distrust undermines key goals of welfare reform policy. These findings bring home the value of heeding the trust literature's lessons when studying the struggles of low-income families and the policies that affect them.

At the same time, this book's findings suggest that the trust literature would benefit from paying more attention to the real-life trust problems that low-income populations face. Much of the trust literature is based on experiments or is theoretical. Actual field-based studies are few and far between.[29] The investigation reported here of distrust in a natural setting shows the development and implications of distrust for real lives outside the laboratory.

In addition, the trust literature finds that powerlessness is a barrier to trust, but it has little to say about how powerlessness creates a trust barrier or how that barrier might be overcome.[30] Karen S. Cook, a leading scholar on trust, has written about this limitation of the trust literature.[31] The women interviewed for this book often experienced relative powerlessness vis-à-vis those with whom they interacted. Caseworkers had the power to deny them needed benefits. Bosses had the power to fire them from needed jobs. Boyfriends exerted power over them through physical intimidation or other means. This study provides insights into how the women's relative powerlessness in these realms produced distrust and what would be needed for them to trust. For instance, women would have greater trust in their caseworkers if they knew that caseworkers were rewarded for avoiding bureaucratic errors and treating them with respect. Women do not trust caseworkers because they do not believe they share their interests. Changing the incentives for caseworkers would realign caseworker interests so that clients would begin to believe their interests were shared, which in turn would promote trust. The detailed examples from this study and similar field studies can begin to move the trust literature toward a theory of trust and powerlessness.

Another lesson of the book for the trust literature is the importance of maintaining a distinction between trust and trustworthiness. The political scientist Russell Hardin makes clear that one's choice to place trust in another is related to but different from whether the other is indeed worthy of trust.[32] Despite Hardin's highlighting of the importance of the trust versus trustworthiness distinction, much of the trust literature focuses on trust rather than trustworthiness. When the trustworthiness of interaction partners is ignored, it is easy to focus solely on those who do not trust and see "fixing" their inability to trust as the solution. Instead, I attend at all times to the potentiality of untrustworthiness in interaction partners as a producer of distrust. Many of the contexts in which low-income women find themselves are structured in ways that promote the untrustworthiness of others. (The discussion above of caseworkers being rewarded for getting clients off the welfare rolls, even if they do so by making errors, is just one example.) Consequently, getting women to be more trusting is not the solution. Getting their interaction partners to be more trustworthy is.

A final implication for the trust literature relates to a debate in the field over whether trust and distrust stem from a personality trait, set of moral values, or from learned experience in social contexts.[33] This study provides evidence that people learn to trust or distrust through experience. Many women interviewed described trusting, getting burned, and learning to distrust as a result. Women also told stories of not knowing what to expect in a situation and being surprised by the behavior of others, behavior that eventually taught them to distrust. These narratives of learning distrust through experience support experimental evidence that trust and distrust cannot be attributed to a personality trait wholly unrelated to experience and social context.[34]

The findings in this book also have implications for research on welfare usage and poverty. Many of the quantitative studies of low-income parents' movement off the welfare rolls look at the impact of individual traits on outcomes. They consider the role of education, work experience, physical and mental health, drug use, car ownership, and similar factors on women's outcomes in the reform era.[35] However, the quantitative literature pays less attention to the role of social context—which this book shows is crucial for understanding low-income women's behavior and outcomes.

The qualitative literature on welfare reform, and low-income mothers more generally, pays much more attention to social context, but most studies focus on a single context. For example, there are excellent studies of what happens in welfare offices or between romantic partners.[36] Some of these studies identify distrust as an important explanation of behaviors. But few studies take a holistic approach and look across multiple settings, as this book does. Others have made important contributions by showing the role of distrust in romantic relationships or child care choices or job referrals.[37] But in these studies, the investigator is narrowly focusing on the particular context of interest and, in trying to understand women's experiences in that context, discovers distrust to play a role. This study extends such findings and shows that distrust exists in these isolated settings and more—distrust can be everywhere and has the potential to block action in every direction. Furthermore, the study provides evidence that distrust operates in similar ways in each setting. Since this book takes a more holistic approach and studies multiple contexts of women's lives, it can create a more generalized view of how distrust and stalled action recur as a social process in almost every area of low-income women's lives. The problem is not only that distrust blocks action when it comes to interacting with caseworkers or boyfriends. The problem is that distrust blocks action in multiple key arenas of policy concern in which low-income mothers find themselves.

This study also contributes something new to the qualitative literatures on welfare reform and low-income mothers by drawing on interviews from two time periods. Because of this, it is able to show the consistency of distrust in low-income mothers' lives despite the introduction of a major policy change.

Ain't No Trust also contributes to the literature on poverty more generally. It is a counterargument to a culture of poverty perspective. Culture of poverty theories posit that low-income populations respond to structural barriers, such as lack of political power or access to education, by adapting their cultural values to match their lack of opportunity. Most importantly, culture of poverty theorists suggest that these altered, and now deficient, values are passed down from parents to children across generations.[38] Policy makers or taxpayers who complained that welfare had become "a way of life" and that single mothers lacked "family values" and who looked to welfare reform to change a "welfare culture" were implicitly arguing that welfare programs had unwittingly created or enabled a "culture of poverty."

My argument joins the early work of Elliot Liebow, who forcefully argued against a culture of poverty in his study of low-income African American men who spent time on a street corner in Washington, D.C., in the 1960s.[39] He asserted that the men he observed were not taught by their fathers a pathological set of cultural values that crippled their aspirations for middle-class life. Instead, Liebow argued, these men experienced the same structural barriers that their fathers had encountered, and they adapted to them over time in the same way their fathers had. Kathryn Edin and Maria Kefalas concluded similarly that low-income women's failure to marry the fathers of their children is not based on a set of values about marriage different from middle-class values; rather, it reflects low-income women's strict adherence to middle-class marriage values. Edin and Kefalas argued the women feel they cannot afford marriage because they cannot afford a traditional wedding and because their potential husbands, who face both high unemployment and high incarceration rates, cannot fulfill the traditional male breadwinner role. Although they cannot achieve economic stability in time to marry before having children, they hope to marry one day.[40]

My findings suggest that the structural arrangements of welfare offices, of workplaces and labor markets, and of other contexts in which low-income women interact with others produce their distrust and its resultant stalled action. Many of my respondents indicated that they had at first trusted various others, only to learn themselves through experience over time that this trust was unwarranted. This process indicates that they had not inherited cultural values that led them to reject these outcomes. Instead, they reported that their experience of the structural contexts of the welfare office and other settings had produced their skepticism about whether they could count on caseworkers, bosses, boyfriends, and others to come through for them. Like Liebow's "streetcorner men" and Edin and Kefalas's single mothers, for these women structural forces and not cultural values appear to guide the behaviors that those observing from afar have deemed undeserving.[41]

THE STUDY AND THE ORGANIZATION OF THE BOOK

The findings in this book are based on a total of ninety-five interviews with two different sets of women in Chicago, one before welfare reform and one after.[42] I interviewed twenty-six women in 1994–95, before reform was passed. Another sixty-nine women were interviewed in 2004–5, after reform was fully in place.[43] All of the women had at least one child under the age of eighteen and either were receiving welfare or had received it in recent years. The women varied in age, race and ethnicity, education level, marital history, and number of children. Some had received welfare for long periods, some for only quick stints. Some seemed to have made stable transitions into the labor force, some had made initial forays that seemed less assured of permanence, and for some, finding employment appeared to be only a distant hope. In short, while my qualitative nonrandom samples cannot represent the full population of low-income women in Chicago (and, while one might expect some similarities to other large urban areas, Chicago cannot represent other geographical locales, especially rural ones), I was careful to include a wide variety of women from different backgrounds who were at different points in making welfare-to-work transitions.[44] This latter variation allowed me to hear about both current welfare and current employment experiences from the women I interviewed. I thus feel confident that I have tapped the experience of a varied group of women in each time period.

I draw primarily on the interviews themselves, but to provide additional information that might help to interpret findings, I and my graduate student assistants did spend more informal time with a handful of women in each time period, allowing for follow-up and more in-depth observation of the challenges they faced in daily life. I was also able to conduct some informal observation at some of the job-training sites and welfare offices where respondents received services and where I also spoke with personnel.[45]

Chapter 1 provides a more in-depth overview of how U.S. policy has addressed low-income mothers over time, what welfare reform actually did, and what we know about reform's effects. It then moves on to treat trust and distrust in more detail. It concludes by discussing the role of structural factors in creating the circumstances that produce distrust.

The detailed findings of the study are given in chapters 2 through 6, each of which covers one of the five contexts in which I studied distrust. Chapter 2 focuses on women's interactions with caseworkers in the welfare office. It is through caseworkers that women learn welfare rules and access welfare benefits. The nature of a woman's relationship with her caseworker determines in part her understanding of welfare rules and whether she believes they will be followed reliably. While some women praised supportive caseworkers, most described caseworkers who paid inadequate attention to their needs and treated them with hostility. As a result of these difficult interactions, many women in both time periods either did not know official welfare rules or suspected that caseworkers honored only the rules that were not in a recipient's favor. Both the lack of communication of welfare rules and the distrust that they would be properly implemented undermined voluntary incentives designed to entice recipients into the labor market. Distrust thus inhibited women's positive response to voluntary incentives. Mandatory policies such as time limits, however, were more effective, since they were in line with women's view of caseworkers as unsupportive.

Chapter 3 explores women's experiences in the workplace as they interacted with supervisors and coworkers. The workplace is an arena in which both employers and employees face uncertainty. As other scholars in the sociology of work have suggested, but as is not sufficiently recognized in studies of policy, employers do not know which employees will perform reliably and be trustworthy and which will not.[46] Similarly, employees do not know whether employers will treat them fairly. Women in low-wage jobs often feel their supervisors (and sometimes their coworkers) mistreat them and thus do not trust that they will get a fair shake at work. Surprisingly, this distrust led women to quit their jobs not only before welfare reform, when they could reliably replace wages (at least in part) with welfare benefits, but also after reform, when no such financial guarantee was in place. Quick turnover in jobs was thus due not only to factors outside the workplace, such as insufficient child care or transportation challenges, but also to traits of the workplace itself—in this case, the conditions that produced employee distrust of supervisors.

Chapter 4 investigates the arena of child care. The post-reform group described the same inability to trust the quality of child care providers available as the women interviewed before reform. Women after reform sometimes felt forced by work mandates to use care providers they did not trust, but they tended to stop these arrangements eventually. Women in both time periods interrupted their labor market participation because of their distrust in their children's care providers.

Chapter 5 treats women's relationships with the fathers of their children and other romantic partners. Many women reported they could not trust the fathers of their children or other romantic partners. Even though some women were romantically involved with men, they often kept partners at arm's length, and their suspicions kept them from marrying the men in their lives. Despite welfare reform's removal of several marriage disincentives and its rhetoric about the value of marriage, distrust still forestalled marriage.

Chapter 6 addresses women's relationships with members of their kinship and friendship networks. This was the arena in which women trusted people the most. Many women considered family members and friends priceless allies. Still distrust was present. Some friends and family members used drugs and alcohol to excess, others promised to take care of children but went out to party instead, while others constantly asked for money or food or, worse yet, took it without asking. Women who felt they could not trust network members went to great lengths to keep such people out of their lives and away from their children. Untrustworthy network members not only represented a lost source of potential support but could drain households of resources, time, and peacefulness. Chapter 6 also explores whether the kinds of resources that kinship and friendship networks provide women have changed since welfare reform. It shows that women interviewed before reform drew more on their networks for job information that helped them get ahead, whereas women interviewed after reform were more likely to draw on their networks for resources like money or child care that helped them survive day to day. In both time periods, there was a relationship between women's trust in their networks and their ability to draw support from their networks.

The Conclusion urges reformers to think more broadly and deeply than they have about how distrust is produced and what its consequences are for low-income mothers. It pays particular attention to the ways in which policies designed without regard to the importance of building trust (such as welfare reform) may fall short of their intended goals.

Each of the book's chapters tells a story of distrust. The details differ depending on the particular arena of low-income women's lives examined in that chapter, but the general process is strikingly similar throughout. By watching this process play out five times in five separate contexts, we begin to see clues that something about the structure of the context itself—about the incentives and constraints that other people and institutions in it were facing—made the women keenly aware that their interests were not the same as the interests of these others and made them deeply suspicious of the others' trustworthiness. The women were not uniform in their distrust. Some distrusted only some people in each arena, or only people in certain arenas. And certainly many women did experience trust in others at times. But across all the women and all the contexts, there were distinct patterns of distrust. Welfare reform certainly made changes, but it did not change the circumstances that produced distrust or the inhibiting effects of distrust described by women in poverty.

ONE Welfare Reform and the Enduring Structural Roots of Distrust

A BRIEF HISTORY OF CASH ASSISTANCE FOR LOW-INCOME MOTHERS AND THEIR CHILDREN

PRWORA was not the first time the United States attempted to reform the way it delivers cash assistance to low-income families. In fact, just a mere eight years earlier, the Family Support Act of 1988 had made similar, though smaller, changes. Both pieces of legislation echo themes that run throughout the history of the American welfare state. Since the beginning of this history, politicians and the public have been concerned that "hand-outs" in the form of cash assistance would create a dependent population and undermine the value of work.[1] Additionally, policy makers have resisted rewarding the "wrong" sorts of people—those deemed undeserving or unworthy of help either because they are able-bodied but are not employed or because their moral character is considered lacking in other ways.[2] Those deemed deserving benefit from more generous social programs and those deemed undeserving receive less generous benefits or, sometimes, none at all.[3] Popular resentment of welfare recipients, considered undeserving by many citizens, has played an important role throughout this history. This theme continues in the most recent reforms. In fact, one can interpret the welfare reform of 1996 as an aggressive attempt to promote "deserving" behavior (welfare exit, employment, marriage) and to transform the welfare population from an "irresponsible" and "undeserving" crowd to a responsible and deserving one.[4] After all, the words "Personal Responsibility" appear in the name of the legislation that ushered in welfare reform.

While all forms of government social spending can be considered "welfare," when people refer to welfare they typically mean cash assistance to low-income families. These families usually, but not always, consist of single mothers and their children. At the time the 1996 changes were being debated, the program that issued such assistance was called Aid to Families with Dependent Children (AFDC). The earliest precursors of AFDC, which were instituted even before the United States had a federal system of social welfare policies, were the Widows' Pensions, a set of state-level pensions designed to support Civil War widows, enabling them to continue raising their children rather than losing the children to orphanages. Widows, especially those who had lost their husbands in wartime military service, were considered a group particularly deserving of government assistance. Furthermore, staying home to raise their children was accepted as the appropriate role for women. This sympathy for war widows supplied the needed political will to pass the Widows' Pensions. In doing so, state governments were willing to act as a substitute for an absent breadwinner in the family by replacing his earnings, at least in part.[5]

The concept behind Widows' Pensions became the basis for a national program of cash assistance to low-income families when Franklin Delano Roosevelt passed his main New Deal legislation, the Social Security Act of 1935, in response to the Great Depression.[6] The Social Security Act created a two-tiered national welfare state in which employed Americans receive social welfare benefits, such as disability and retirement payments, through a set of universal, employment-based, contributory *social insurance* programs, while those out of the labor market whose income falls under a defined eligibility level receive benefits through noncontributory *public assistance* programs. Roosevelt initially conceived of cash assistance to low-income families and similar public assistance programs as equal in importance to employment-based social insurance programs, but they quickly became less favored and less generous. Even Roosevelt feared that cash relief without work requirements would become a "habit with the country."[7]

The two-tiered welfare state not only resulted in an uneven welfare state in terms of generosity but also divided the population into those eligible for the more generous programs and those shuttled into the less generous ones. Since women, racial minorities, and members of the lower classes have had less stable attachments to the labor force, the division has largely been based on gender, race, and class lines.[8]

These lines became even clearer in the 1960s when civil rights legislation and President Johnson's "War on Poverty" and "Great Society" programs (inspired by President Kennedy's antipoverty efforts cut short by his assassination) gave political voice and equal access to welfare benefits to many African Americans for the first time. Suddenly the welfare rolls swelled and those receiving cash assistance benefits were increasingly African American. In addition, the single-mother recipients of benefits were increasingly never-married women rather than widows. Coupled with the 1960s' racial unrest in many cities, these changes made middle-class Americans less likely to view single mothers as a group deserving of government aid. While African Americans still constituted a minority of those on the welfare rolls, a public perception of welfare recipients as primarily African American probably decreased support for social welfare spending.[9] Welfare served as a convenient focal point for white America's anger at and judgment of African Americans. As Jill Quadagno writes in her book *The Color of Welfare: How Racism Undermined the War on Poverty,* "No program better exemplifies the racially divisive character of the American welfare state than Aid to Families with Dependent Children (AFDC). Conservatives attack AFDC for discouraging work and family formation and for rewarding laziness. Such comments are really subtly veiled messages about family structures and employment patterns among African Americans. However, often the attacks are neither veiled nor subtle."[10] These racially tinged reactions to welfare largely spelled the end of the Great Society efforts to eradicate poverty.

As time wore on through the feminist movement of the 1970s and the increasing labor market participation of mothers in the 1980s, the idea that women should be home with children, and that those without a husband's paycheck to enable them to do so should be paid by the government instead, lost support.[11] Cash assistance to low-income mothers and their children was no longer seen as a benefit that appropriately replaced an absent male breadwinner's earnings so that women could fulfill their duties as mothers and children's basic needs could be met; instead, it was viewed as one that rewarded recipients who were undeserving on account of their lack of a work ethic and their sexual immorality. Attitudes gradually shifted from a "maternalist" welfare state, or one designed to support women's roles as mothers, to a "universal worker" welfare state, or one that encouraged men and women alike to provide for children not through stay-at-home care but through paid employment.[12] Some argued that the cash assistance program created perverted incentives that discouraged both work and marriage, creating a pathological "dependency."[13]

The 1980s ushered in the transition from the "War on Poverty" to the "War on Welfare." President Reagan used the image of the "Welfare Queen," always depicted as an African American woman and often as one who picked up her welfare check in her Cadillac and fur coat, to drum up (or tap into) animosity toward welfare spending. In Reagan's view, the biggest problem with welfare was the fraud it bred, and he used racial tensions to add fuel to the public's anger over paying taxes for a program that, in many people's eyes, benefited only the undeserving. In 1981, he passed the Omnibus Reconciliation Act, which began to chip away at welfare benefits. The Family Support Act of 1988 mandated that each state institute a welfare-to-work training program for welfare recipients and allowed states to require recipient participation, created work supports for recipients transitioning to work, and stepped up efforts to establish the paternity of children receiving benefits in order to increase enforcement of child support payments to reimburse the state for welfare expenditures.

But it was the Democratic president Bill Clinton who took welfare reform across the finish line. Polling during his 1992 presidential campaign bid indicated that his line promising to "end welfare as we know it," which was written by a young aide the night before he first used it, was one of the most popular phrases he uttered on the campaign trail.[14] Once elected, he set out to make good on that campaign promise. He brought top social policy experts from Harvard University and Washington, D.C., think tanks to help develop the right mix of programming. Then the Republican-led Congress drafted its own versions of a bill. Twice President Clinton vetoed these versions, arguing that they placed too much burden on recipients without enough support. When the third version came to his desk in August 1996, he signed. Mary Jo Bane and Peter Edelman, two of the experts he had brought to his administration to work on welfare reform, resigned in protest, claiming the new law would drive many additional families into poverty.[15]

Fears of rewarding the undeserving have been with us since the beginning of our welfare state. Over time, single mothers and their children have lost their status as a deserving group and have been seen increasingly as unworthy of our support. Coupled with frustrations with the cash assistance program on all fronts, including among recipients of benefits themselves, this shift led to increasing demands for welfare reform and, ultimately, to the passage of reform in 1996.

WHAT POLICY CHANGES DID WELFARE REFORM MAKE?

While the 1996 legislation made many changes to AFDC and other programs (such as Food Stamps), I outline here the key changes it made to the AFDC program, since, as the main cash assistance program to low-income families, AFDC is often what people mean when they refer to "welfare." Before reform, women like Bethany Grant, whom we met in the Introduction, received monthly cash assistance through AFDC, but reform replaced AFDC with a new program called Temporary Assistance for Needy Families (TANF).[16] The word *temporary* underscores the idea that women like Susan Schiller, whom I interviewed after reform and whom we also met in the Introduction, should see the program as an emergency, short-term source of support between periods of employment or marriage to an employed spouse. Unlike Bethany, who had no limit on the amount of time she could receive cash assistance, Susan faced a lifetime limit of five years of receipt.[17]

Susan had received cash assistance, or "welfare," four times in her life. Three of these were before reform and began when she gave birth to each of her first three children. These three times totaled about five years. Susan then remained off welfare for almost a decade until after reform, in 2001, when she was between jobs, was suffering from depression, and went back on welfare for about four or five months to get herself together before finding another job. Had reform's time limits been in place during each of the times Susan received welfare, she would have reached her time limit before this last time. Though she had not used welfare in close to ten years, was out of work, was severely depressed, was the single mother of three minor children at the time, and received no child support from the fathers of any of her children, she would not have been eligible. For this reason Susan considered returning to welfare a last resort. However, since only her 2001 short stint was after reform, Susan actually had over four years before she would hit her time limit. If Susan's trouble finding a job or the pressures of her son's legal issues led her one day to return to welfare, she might end up reaching that limit. If so, then Susan would never be eligible for cash assistance again in her lifetime, no matter what financial disaster might befall her. Neither the loss of a job, a new baby in the house, a medical emergency, nor any other circumstance would allow her to be eligible.[18]

Unlike Bethany, who was encouraged but not required to find a job, when Susan was receiving cash assistance in 2001 she did face work requirements.[19] The exact nature of these requirements differs across the states, but in Illinois, for a woman like Susan who was not caring for an infant at the time, was not in a domestic violence crisis, did not have a health condition deemed severe enough to warrant an exemption, was not caring for someone else with a severe health condition, and was not over the age of sixty, these requirements began immediately.

Like most Illinois welfare recipients since reform, Susan spent the first thirty days after she filed her application "working for her check," meaning she had to do volunteer work cleaning, carrying boxes, and filing papers in a welfare office from 9 a.m. until noon five days a week to "earn" the $342 she received in cash assistance for the month.[20] She was then sent to a job-training program that sent her out on job interviews. These interviews gave her little control over the kind of job she might get, her hours, or the job's location. Luckily for Susan, she found a job that suited her needs through her own efforts and left the welfare rolls. It was this job that she left when she was trying to gain control over her son, leaving her in her current situation of getting neither welfare benefits nor earnings from work.[21]

Before reform, Bethany was guaranteed access to welfare benefits. The Social Security Act of 1935 made cash assistance a federal entitlement for low-income families. This meant that as long as a family met the eligibility criteria, it could not be denied benefits even in times of budgetary stress on the government. Susan enjoyed no such guarantee. Now the federal government gives each state a block grant to cover its cash assistance program for low-income families. If there is high demand for welfare benefits—for example, during a period of economic recession—the block grant could run out of money.[22] If so, the state is allowed to say that it will no longer pay welfare benefits because welfare reform has taken away the federal entitlement to those benefits. Many critics of welfare reform point to this ending of entitlement as the most audacious change reform made because it undoes what Roosevelt did when he established a right to benefits under the Social Security Act of 1935.

To discourage nonmarital childbearing, reform also allowed states to decide not to give welfare benefits to new babies if their mothers were already receiving cash assistance. Illinois initially decided to take this option to impose what is called a "family cap," but it then reversed its decision and began to phase out the family cap provision in August of 2003.[23] If Susan had been a welfare recipient when the family cap was in place and had gotten pregnant, she would not have received any cash assistance benefits for her new baby.

Undocumented immigrants have never been eligible for cash assistance benefits. The 1996 law extended limitations on immigrants' eligibility by allowing states to bar documented immigrants from cash assistance benefits. Both Bethany and Susan were U.S. citizens; several of the other women interviewed after reform were not, but since their children were U.S. born, the children could receive benefits.[24] Reform also allowed states to deny eligibility for benefits to those with a drug felony record.

Mothers are now required to establish officially the paternity of their children before they can receive cash assistance so that states can attempt to reimburse their welfare programs with child support payments from absent fathers. When Susan applied for cash assistance in 2001, she was given an appointment with a separate child support office in order to establish paternity. She named the father of her children who were still minors at the time, and the court awarded child support, even though he never paid. Some fear that this provision puts women and children in harm's way by reinitiating their contact with potentially abusive or hostile men. Provisions have been made for exemptions for women fearing violence, though critics remain concerned that exemptions are too difficult to get. While child support enforcement serves the financial goal of paying back the state for welfare outlays, proponents also argue that it encourages the reintroduction and involvement of fathers with their children. Welfare reform legislation also encourages states to promote marriage in a variety of ways, including "relationship-training" programs whose goal is to teach parents constructive ways to interact with each other. President George W. Bush was particularly supportive of the marriage promotion aspects of welfare reform.

The post-reform changes in welfare rules are enforced through a system of "sanctions" that remove benefits from recipients who fail to comply with rules by not attending required appointments, failing to file paperwork, not meeting job search and work activity requirements, or committing other similar infractions.[25] Reform also enhanced work supports for low-income parents. It increased money available for job training, child care, and transportation subsidies. The Clinton administration fought for additional work supports as well. It succeeded in decoupling eligibility for Medicaid from the receipt of welfare so that families with income low enough could maintain Medicaid coverage even if they were not current or recent cash assistance recipients. Reform also was accompanied by a substantial increase in the Earned Income Tax Credit (EITC), which rewards low-wage and even working-class families for being employed with a tax credit that can be sizable.[26]

WHAT EFFECTS DID WELFARE REFORM HAVE ON LOW-INCOME FAMILIES?

The literature on the effects of the landmark 1996 welfare reform legislation has focused largely on assessing whether reform met its goals of reducing the size of the welfare rolls and increasing the employment rate, earnings, and marriage rate of welfare recipients.[27] In general, this research has reported that in the early years following reform welfare caseloads plummeted, poverty rates declined, and recipients entered the labor force at rates exceeding expectations.[28] Investigators, however, caution that it is difficult to disentangle fully the separate effects of policy and economic changes, especially since reform was implemented during a period of great economic prosperity.[29] Also, despite welfare reform's goals of decreasing the nonmarital fertility rate and increasing marriage, analysts have found reform to have virtually no effect on marriage and childbearing patterns.[30] Even so, early studies celebrated what seemed to some like enormous positive effects of reform or, to those more skeptical, at least much less disastrous effects than originally predicted.[31]

These findings at first seem to throw into question the validity of my assertion in the Introduction that the struggles of the women I interviewed after welfare reform do not look very different from those I interviewed before reform. Adding to the confusion, I am not the only one to make this assertion. Other investigators similarly find that reform did not change the qualitative nature of life for low-income mothers. In her book *Flat Broke with Children: Women in the Age of Welfare Reform,* Sharon Hays asserts that reform did not help the women she interviewed because of its contradictory messages. She argues that it simultaneously urged mothers to follow "the Work Plan," which promotes single-minded independence, and "the Family Plan," which encourages marriage and commitment to others. Hays concludes that following both at once is nearly impossible and that her respondents were consequently unable to succeed or benefit from reform's initial promise.[32]

In *American Dream: Three Women, Ten Kids, and a Nation's Drive to End Welfare, New York Times* journalist Jason DeParle suggests that welfare recipients are too busy trying to keep their heads above water either to pay attention to welfare policy or to feel any impact of it. As Angie, one of his three main informants, told him when asked about welfare reform, "I don't pay no attention to that crap!" DeParle goes on to write, "With welfare or without it, Angie said, 'you just learn how to survive.'"[33]

While the initial quantitative evaluations of welfare reform showed great promise for the effectiveness of the policy and improved outcomes for low-income families, later work began to question how far-reaching and long-lasting these effects would be. These later quantitative studies are more in line with the results that Hays, DeParle, and I discuss.[34]

For example, one study questioned the standard practice in early studies of focusing on average effects.[35] Results based on what happened to families on average mask variation across families and thus hide the fact that some families may not be helped by reform and may actually be hurt by it. To address this problem, analysts investigating a Connecticut reform program examined effects separately for welfare recipients in the top half of the income distribution (among program participants) and those in the bottom half of the income distribution. They discovered opposite effects of reform measures for the two sets of recipients.[36] While the relatively advantaged recipients experienced earnings gains as a result of reform, the more disadvantaged women experienced no earnings gains and often even had earnings losses. These findings suggest that many current and former welfare recipients may not be sharing in any of reform's potential benefits and may instead even be financially suffering as a result of reform.

Another study showed that while reform might have reduced poverty rates, it did not actually change low-income mothers' standard of living or lower their levels of hardship.[37] Between 1997 (the year reform was implemented) and 2003 (the year before I conducted my second round of interviews), low-income single mothers were no more likely to obtain health insurance coverage or establish their own households than before. They were also no less likely to worry that they would run out of food by the end of the month or to have a child go hungry for an entire day in the previous twelve months. In other words, while officially their rates of poverty might have gone down, their standard of living remained the same. The study authors explain that going to work probably raised the women's incomes but that employment entailed work expenses. The increase in their incomes was spent on transportation, child care, and uniforms, leaving no money to actually make life easier. Since work expenses are not calculated in determining the federal poverty line, increased work hours and income translate into lowered poverty even if employment entails expenses that actually mean lower discretionary income for a family.[38] No wonder my post-reform respondents described the same struggles as the women I interviewed before reform.

Additionally, studies found that as the years wore on, those who left the welfare rolls began to experience less positive outcomes than those who had left shortly after the implementation of welfare reform.[39] This was so in part because the most employable recipients left the rolls early (or chose not to apply for welfare in the first place given the new requirements), leaving behind those less likely to do well. One clear indication that the welfare rolls are increasingly filled with families with more problems is that the number of families on welfare with active involvement with child welfare services has increased significantly since welfare reform.[40]

The increasingly less optimistic findings on reform's effects are also due to the fact that the robust economy of the late 1990s gave way to a recession in the early 2000s.[41] It is too early for a complete analysis of the much more dramatic "Great Recession" that began in 2008, but it undoubtedly has eroded the well-being of families who leave or decline to take up welfare, and it threatens to drive poverty rates to their highest levels since the 1960s.

Today's low-income families also face an environment of budget cuts to a variety of programs from which they might receive support. Since welfare reform ended the federal entitlement to cash assistance, state governments are free to make cuts to their TANF programs. Many in fact are taking money from their TANF budgets to fill other budgetary needs.[42] Mary Jo Bane, who, as noted above, resigned from the Clinton administration in protest of the version of reform that was passed, writes scathingly in a 2012 article of the damage welfare reform did to the safety net that the poor need in recessionary times.[43] She cites that between 2007 and 2011 the number of children in poverty went up by three million, but the number of children receiving cash assistance through TANF went up only by half a million. In 2010, this meant that of the 16.4 million children in poverty only 3.2 million were being served by the cash assistance program meant to address "needy families" in times of economic crisis. She concludes, "I continue to believe that the moral measure of a society is the way it cares for its poor and vulnerable. By that measure, we should all be ashamed."[44]

The later quantitative findings are sobering. Welfare reform coincided with a dramatic decline in the caseload (70 percent between 1994, when the rolls started to decline, and 2008),[45] but how long term and how far-reaching any actual improvements are in low-income families' lives is much less clear. The studies I have discussed provide evidence that many families have not seen positive changes as a result of reform and some have seen negative ones. There are multiple reasons for why that would be so, including the declining economy and a host of barriers low-income mothers face in successfully transitioning to work. This book argues that an additional important, yet mostly overlooked, reason is that welfare reform ignored the sources of distrust in low-income women's lives and hence was not able to overcome distrust's effects.

WHY TRUST AND DISTRUST MATTER

The more mothers like Bethany Grant and Susan Schiller trust others with whom they interact (their "interaction partners"), the more willing they are to take risks like responding to welfare policy's employment incentives, taking a job, leaving their children with a child care provider, marrying their romantic partners, involving their children's fathers in their children's lives, and relying on network members for help. The more they distrust their interaction partners, the more hesitant they are to take such risks.[46]

In this way, they must make choices about trust in the face of risk, as did the diamond merchants in James Coleman's classic article on social capital.[47] For the diamond merchants it was an efficient business practice to allow other merchants interested in buying their goods to take stones home to examine them. It saved time compared to having to conduct all such examinations in person. However, this practice risked the possibility that the diamonds would be stolen. The diamond merchants that Coleman describes trusted other merchants not to steal because they all came from the same, tightly knit ethnic and religious community. If their shared values were not enough to ensure ethical behavior, the substantial power of the community to impose sanctions was. The fact that the merchants trusted each other allowed the business of buying and selling diamonds to proceed unfettered by expensive insurance arrangements that would be needed in the absence of trust.

Coleman's study shows us that trust eases cooperation and the achievement of outcomes. Without it, the diamond merchants would not cooperate with each other.[48] By extension, distrust can thus be a barrier to both cooperation and action and might block business opportunity for the merchants.[49] Francis Fukuyama captures these ideas when he describes trust as a "lubricant."[50]

Such lubrication is particularly valuable when taking action entails risk in the face of uncertainty.[51] Whenever Coleman's diamond merchants were correct in their assessments of others' trustworthiness, the risks they took by allowing others to take home stones paid off by making their work lives more efficient. If, however, they were ever wrong in their assessments and misplaced trust in the untrustworthy, trust would not have paid off. They would begin to practice distrust instead. Trust eases action, distrust blocks action, and trust may pay off—but *only* if one's partners in the interaction are trustworthy.

Surprisingly, when policy makers discuss the actions of low-income women, they consider a host of factors about the women such as their skills, their access to child care, and their work ethic, but they do not consider the role of trust. Yet trust operates for low-income mothers like

Bethany and Susan in the same way that it does for diamond merchants. Unlike the diamond merchants, however, who know that the buyers have an interest in behaving in a trustworthy way (since they would be shunned by the community if they did not), the low-income mothers rarely feel that their interaction partners have an incentive to behave in a trustworthy way. As a result, the mothers are more distrustful than the diamond merchants. When they are right, their distrust protects them. When they are wrong, their distrust may cost them opportunity.

Uncertainty is ever present, and thus almost all action entails risk of some kind. It is the near-constant presence of risk that creates the need for trust in order for action to smoothly take place. One might argue that low-income parents face a particularly risky and uncertain world. This is especially true for low-income parents who live in neighborhoods of concentrated poverty, as many of the women I interviewed do. For one thing, the neighborhoods where they live and raise their children pose certain dangers. In Chicago (and cities as different from Chicago as Stockholm), rates of violence go up as the level of concentrated poverty in the neighborhood goes up.[52] Gang activity and drug dealing may lead to acts of violence that affect bystanders. Children may be pressured to join gangs or to get involved in other potentially unsafe activities.[53] As we saw in the Introduction, local gang members' grip on her son led Susan to quit her job. Another mother, Dolores Rios, pointed to recent shootings on the main street around the corner from her apartment as one of the primary reasons she did not want a job that would interfere with her ability to walk her children home from school.

The mothers I interviewed talked a great deal about their concerns over the safety of their children. Many other aspects of their lives were riddled with risk. When one lives in tight financial circumstances, any false move that results in a loss of income or similar setback is devastating. While the same uncertain behavior in a middle-class family may cost savings, upward mobility, or the ability to pursue opportunities for children, it can cost low-income families shelter, having enough to eat, or the ability to pay for heat. As we saw, Bethany lost her heat in the middle of a Chicago winter and almost became homeless after she risked taking a low-wage job and her caseworker "messed up" her case.

The sheer magnitude of the potential ill effects inhibits low-income mothers' risk taking.[54] The existence of trust thus is particularly crucial for low-income families to take risks. Low-income families are also especially in need of the potential benefits that accrue to risk takers. However, the above discussion suggests that low-income families are less likely to trust those in their environment.[55]

The assertion that trust and distrust are related to social advantage and disadvantage is supported by the research literature. Investigators have shown that those who have low levels of income and education, who live in communities that have high levels of income inequality, who are members of racial minority groups, who are women, or who have experienced trauma in recent years are less likely to trust.[56]

In addition, trust is greater between partners who are on an equal footing.[57] Familiarity breeds trust.[58] Even if one is not personally familiar with an interaction partner, one may trust that partner if he or she is an agent of a trusted institution.[59] But government institutions are less trusted by the disadvantaged—especially if they are deemed unresponsive.[60]

Clearly, then, low-income mothers are less likely to find themselves under the circumstances that promote trust. Most notably, given their disadvantaged position, many of their interactions, especially those in the welfare office and the workplace, are with people with whom they do not enjoy equality. In fact, they are with people who hold substantial power over them. Even if they are familiar with their interaction partners, they appear less likely to trust the institutions that their partners represent, especially if these are associated with the government.[61]

Their distrust in the government probably reflects in part the fact that low-income people have less power and ability to get the state to be responsive to their needs. It probably also reflects the more dire consequences of not getting the government to respond. Middle- and upper-class citizens also experience great frustration with an unresponsive state, but those interactions tend to result in high tax bills, minor unsuccessful battles with bureaucracy, and other such annoyances. When low-income people are unable to successfully interact with government agencies, they may lose the resources needed for their very subsistence, lose custody of their children, or face other extreme outcomes. Again we see that the precarious nature of their lives leads low-income people to become more distrustful and less willing to take the risk of trusting in the face of uncertainty.

In the women's interviews, trust and respect were closely intertwined. When the women were asked why they did not trust various others, perceived disrespect was one of the major answers they gave. The importance of respect cut across almost all of the five social settings studied. Rude caseworkers, rude bosses, unfaithful boyfriends, and gossiping friends and family members were all deemed disrespectful. The child care market was the only setting in which respect did not appear salient for the women.

One might think of respect as an outcome one wants delivered from an interaction partner. If one has reason to suspect that respect will not be delivered, perhaps from past experience, one will not trust that interaction partner. Alternatively, if a low-income mother's growing up as a member of a marginalized group has taught her to see the world as a place that treats her with suspicion and that is best approached skeptically, she may be quick to interpret actions as disrespectful and to distrust that disrespectful interaction partners will deliver on any kind of promises. Thus respect, though not the same as trust, is closely tied to it either as an outcome that one trusts will be delivered or as a trait of interaction partners that suggests whether they can be trusted to deliver other outcomes.[62] Other researchers have similarly argued that for low-income and marginalized groups who are shut out of mainstream material success, respect takes on heightened meaning.[63]

THE KEY ROLE OF STRUCTURE

Many of the women I interviewed encountered interaction partners with an open mind, sometimes even a trusting mind, and learned through direct experience to distrust that partner. It was their direct encounter within a particular structure (such as a welfare bureaucracy, a low-wage workplace, or a child care market) that taught them their distrust.[64] In *Tally's Corner*, discussed in the Introduction, Elliot Liebow writes,

Each man comes to the job with a long job history characterized by his not being able to support himself and his family. Each man carries this knowledge, born of his experience, . . . It is the experience of the individual and the group; of their fathers and probably their sons. Convinced of their inadequacies, not only do they not seek out those few better-paying jobs which test their resources, but they actively avoid them, gravitating in a mass to the menial, routine jobs which offer no challenge . . . to the already diminished images they have of themselves.[65]

The distrust exhibited by the women I interviewed both before and after welfare reform similarly stemmed from "the experience of the individual and the group." Sometimes the experience was direct experience with the potential trustee. Sometimes it was experience not with the potential trustee but with people in the same role as the potential trustee (different caseworkers or different boyfriends, for example). Sometimes it was the experience reported by others in the community, such as mothers or friends. Sometimes it was experience reported more distantly in news media or rumor. Sometimes, it was a self-protective approach that mothers drew upon preemptively to combat potential disrespect or mistreatment—a worldview or strategy based not on first-hand experiences or others' reports about the specific current situation but more generally on collective experience about how things go for those in poverty. But even in this latter circumstance when the women's distrust was not based on specific experiences, it was very much rooted in structural circumstances. The mothers I interviewed sat at the bottom of the U.S. stratification system, in terms of both their material resources and their prestige. Coming from that position, they pulled distrust out of their "toolkits" to defend themselves against the stigma of their position and the threat of further material deprivation.[66] A distrustful stance served as an armor to shield them from a world in which they had little other protection. And sometimes, perhaps, the power to withhold their trust was their one and only means of wielding power when they controlled so little else.

Many trust theorists argue that trust or distrust comes from calculating expectations about potential outcomes of an interaction.[67] That is, people take into consideration what they know about their interaction partner's interests in the particular social context and what they have observed about the partner's behavior in order to calculate the chances that the partner will reliably come through for them. In other words, they make calculations about whether their interaction partner is trustworthy. These calculations dictate whether a taxi driver decides it is safe to pick up a particular fare or whether a bank gives a particular client a loan.[68]

Much of the distrust that the women I interviewed expressed was indeed based on their collecting information about their interaction partners and, from it, making the calculation that their partners were not trustworthy. This information might be based on direct interactions themselves, similar past experiences, or the experiences of others they knew.[69]

One of the key factors on which people base expectations about trustworthiness is whether they believe their interaction partners share their interests.[70] Because of the women's disadvantaged structural position both in several of the contexts I study and more generally in U.S. society at large, their interests were often at odds with those of their interaction partners. In the five settings studied, low-income women found themselves interacting either with people who held power over them or with people who shared their powerlessness. When interacting with those who held power over them, they rarely felt they shared interests. For example, caseworkers' interest was in moving them off the rolls as quickly as possible while theirs was in maintaining benefits or in moving off only when stable jobs could be found. Similarly, employers' interest was in maintaining a flexible, cheap, and easily replaced low-wage labor force while theirs was in securing stable employment with advancement opportunity.

When the women were interacting with those who were in a more equal structural position (informal child care providers, boyfriends, friends and family), the likelihood that they would share interests was greater and thus the potential for trust was greater. However, their shared powerlessness in relation to the outside world, that is, their mutual relegation to the bottom of what I have called the U.S. stratification system, often meant that their interaction partners were scrambling to survive and hence could not be relied upon to take their interests to heart. The desperation that powerlessness creates means that everyone must be out for him- or herself at times. For example, the workers in Sandra Smith's book *Lone Pursuit* did not help their unemployed peers find jobs at their workplaces for fear that if these peers did not perform well it would reflect badly on them and they would risk losing jobs they needed to survive. As much as they might wish to help their friends and family members, they did not trust these others to behave acceptably at work.[71]

THE STRUCTURES THAT WELFARE REFORM DID NOT FIX

I have described the women I interviewed as disadvantaged in two different kinds of structures. In U.S. society at large, what we might call "macro-level structure," they were at the bottom end of the class system. They had very little income, lived in dilapidated apartments in neighborhoods of concentrated poverty, had few options but to send their children to underfunded schools, and mostly had education levels below those required for jobs that pay a living wage. Welfare reform did not change these facts. The women I interviewed before reform did not differ on these dimensions from the women interviewed after reform.[72] The quantitative studies reviewed above provide evidence that welfare reform did not change these facts for many other low-income women as well.

Welfare reform changed policies about the delivery of cash assistance. It did not ameliorate the forces that create inequality on the macro level. Most notably, it did not change the fact that globalization and increasing technological skill demands have eroded wages for low-skill workers.[73] Income inequality has grown dramatically since the late 1970s. The rewards of economic growth have been concentrated primarily on those at the top of the income distribution.[74]

Low-wage jobs do not provide enough income to lift families out of poverty. When I conducted both my pre- and post-reform interviews, if a woman worked full time and full year in a minimum-wage job, she would still be significantly under the poverty line. This was true not only for a mother of one or more children but even for a single adult. In 2004, 60 percent of families below the poverty line contained at least one worker, and 28 percent contained at least one full-time, full-year worker.[75] Low-wage work is not an automatic ticket out of poverty.

Welfare reform also did not adequately address insufficient labor demand. While many assume that anyone can always get a job "flipping burgers," that is untrue, especially in urban areas of concentrated poverty. Anthropologist Katherine Newman discovered that in central Harlem there were fourteen applicants for every opening at the fast-food restaurants she studied.[76] Even those who find jobs may discover that their employers do not reliably offer enough weekly hours to guarantee stable income or to allow welfare recipients to meet their required number of work activity hours.[77]

In addition to not addressing these macro-level structures, welfare reform brought no change to the structure of the contexts in which women must choose whether or not to trust—often called meso- (or middle-) level structures.[78] Here too the women I interviewed found themselves, at both time periods, in a disadvantaged position. Welfare reform established financial incentives for low-income mothers to find jobs and provided for a limited number of subsidized jobs, but it did not create any substantial changes in the way workplaces operated. Since low-wage jobs usually require few hard skills, low-wage workers are easily replaced. Their dispensability gives them little power to demand fair treatment.

Some night-shift employees of Walmart and Walmart's subsidiary Sam's Club, for instance, have been locked in stores overnight, in part to inhibit theft by employees. As a result, workers have been unable to escape even during emergencies. Sam's Club worker Michael Rodriquez learned of this problem when his ankle was crushed by a fellow employee driving an electronic cart. It took over an hour for a manager with a key to arrive at the store and release the pain-wracked Rodriquez. Similar events have involved a worker having a heart attack and expectant fathers delayed from attending their children's births.[79] Academic researchers have further documented the poor conditions and indignities of low-wage work.[80]

Welfare reform did not restructure workplaces. It did more directly affect the organization of welfare offices, but it left key problematic structures in place. Most notably, it added job tasks and responsibilities for caseworkers, but it did not make significant changes in the size of caseloads or training to absorb these enhanced workloads. Nor did it create incentives for caseworkers to treat recipients respectfully or fairly. Evelyn Brodkin's studies of Chicago-area welfare offices show that caseworkers routinely denied or terminated benefits for which recipients were eligible before reform and that these practices continued after reform.[81] In support of Brodkin's findings, another study shows that administrative hearings before termination of benefits are often successful, demonstrating the illegitimacy of some terminations.[82] Several additional studies show the difficulty post-reform welfare recipients have in working with the welfare bureaucracy to get the work supports that would ease transitions off the rolls.[83] Another study finds that post-reform battered clients often do not receive the domestic violence services stipulated by reform measures.[84]

Caseworkers have not faced a penalty for these types of errors either before or after reform.[85] Instead, caseworkers have incentives to shed clients from their caseloads. One can hardly blame overworked and underpaid caseworkers from responding to such incentives. In her study of Boston-area welfare offices, Celeste Watkins-Hayes finds post-reform caseworkers under enormous pressure to meet the demands of welfare reform.[86]

Studies have also shown that clear communication between caseworkers and welfare recipients was a problem before reform when recipients had trouble understanding welfare rules.[87] A post-reform study finds that one of the reasons recipients are sanctioned (penalized through benefit cuts for not meeting requirements) is that they do not understand, and hence do not appropriately follow, welfare rules. This finding suggests continued problems in the communication of rules.[88]

Reform similarly fell short in making structural change in the child care market. It created child care subsidies that made it somewhat easier for mothers to afford child care, but it did not address either the supply or the quality of child care services. Instead it has focused almost exclusively on giving low-income mothers subsidies so that they can go out and buy child care of the same quality that existed before reform, when mothers claimed that care of acceptable quality was nearly impossible to find in their neighborhoods. In fact, in the period between reform's passage and my last interviews, funding for child care doubled but only 4 percent of that funding went into quality improvements in the supply of child care.[89] The other 96 percent went toward helping mothers pay for the same low-quality care that had existed prior to reform. And since the subsidy levels are dramatically below the market rate for many child care providers, it mostly only helps mothers buy the least expensive forms of care.[90] Researchers have found that low-income mothers' lack of confidence in the quality of child care they can access has limited their ability to go to work since reform.[91]

Reform removed some disincentives and created some incentives to marry. As long as their family income is low enough, married couples are now eligible for the main cash assistance program. Prior to reform, they were not eligible. Welfare reform also created a small pool of money for marriage promotion programs, including relationship-training classes that strive to teach low-income people the value of romantic unions and strategies for preserving them. Finally, by removing the permanence of cash assistance, which gave women some small degree of economic independence from men, welfare reform increased the value of marriage if a potential spouse can provide income to the family.

But despite these changes, welfare reform did little to change relationships between men and women (and boys and girls). Multiple researchers have documented that relationships between low-income men and women, including those in the post-reform era, can be marked by distrust and hostility.[92] These characteristics of gender interaction can start as early as adolescence.[93] Several studies show a relationship between women's distrust in men and women's choice not to marry.[94]

Reform also did not change the structural circumstances of low-income men's lives, particularly the inhospitality of the labor market and the ever-present enticement of the drug trade and other illegal activities. It is thus not surprising that welfare reform has had little or no effect on marriage rates.[95] As low-income women's education and employment levels rose over the 1990s, low-income men's actually fell.[96] Women were pushed into the labor market by welfare reform and were also told that marriage was a solution to poverty. Yet as women pursued employment as a means to self-sufficiency, marriage appeared a less promising route given the declining economic prospects of men. Both men and women consider men's employment a precondition for marriage.[97] Unemployment rates are particularly high for low-income African American men, as are incarceration rates.[98] In 1999, for instance, the risk of imprisonment for African American men who left school before getting a high school degree was 60 percent.[99] Having a conviction record creates additional barriers to labor market entry, and incarceration itself removes men from family life. In addition, men's incarceration lowers the probability of marriage.[100]

Women's social networks were a key source of support for them both before and after reform.[101] However, the need to care for network members also drains women of time and resources, making it harder to maintain a foothold in the labor market. Researchers have shown this to be true both before and after reform.[102] Reform was accompanied by rhetoric about transferring responsibility for poor families from the government to their own communities, but as a policy focused on individual low-income parents it did not invest in those communities. Thus the structure of communities themselves and the resources within them were untouched by reform. In addition, by treating welfare recipients as individuals rather than as members of social networks, reform missed an opportunity to capitalize on the potential power of networks to share resources.

What do these policy shortcomings have to do with the trust levels of low-income mothers? The answer is, a great deal. Because welfare reform did not make fundamental structural changes on either a macro or a meso level, the social contexts in which low-income women's social interactions occur have remained relatively constant before and after reform. So, for example, before reform, Bethany probably went to caseworkers who had caseloads that were too big to manage effectively. These caseworkers were not sanctioned for being uncommunicative or for inappropriately denying benefits.[103] The caseworkers Susan met after reform were, if anything, more burdened than they had been before reform. Now caseworkers face increased pressures and have greater incentives to get people off the rolls, even if this happens because of poor communication regarding benefits or inappropriate denial of them.[104] In short, for both low-income mothers today and their counterparts in an earlier policy regime the structural setup is one in which caseworkers and recipients have opposite interests and probably feel equally (although differently) oppressed. These conditions produce hostile relationships between caseworkers and recipients. The nature of these relationships creates distrust of caseworkers on the part of recipients (and, undoubtedly, vice versa).

Social interactions in workplaces are similarly shaped by structural conditions. Bethany and many other women before reform held low-pay, low-autonomy jobs that often led them to feel mistreated by—and therefore distrustful of—their supervisors. For some women, this dynamic led to quick turnover. Susan's experience in post-reform workplaces was no different.

Similar stories, detailed in the chapters to come, characterize each of the five settings I discuss. The creation of distrust is related to how the interactions between actors are structured in the specific setting, and none of the settings I examine has changed dramatically since the implementation of welfare reform in the 1990s. Mothers struggling to raise children in poverty today are thus just as likely as similar mothers in an earlier time period to distrust and shy away from potential opportunities in almost every setting in which they find themselves.

TWO

"The Way They Treat You
Is Inhumane"

CASEWORKERS AND THE WELFARE OFFICE

It was forty-five minutes of hell. It was terrible. She doesn't
like the people that need the help.

—Julie Callahan

'Cause, like Public Aid kind of makes you feel like you just
panhandling almost, might as well say. The way they treat
you. They just don't treat you right. You go up to them office and they all cold . . .

—Danielle Adams

For several cold winter months in 2005 after reform, I spent a lot of time
talking with Julie Callahan, a white mother of two whose freckles and
strawberry blonde ponytail made her look even younger than her twenty-
three years. Two days after I first met Julie, she applied for cash assistance
through the Temporary Assistance for Needy Families (TANF) program. We
then spoke after each of her appointments in the process of her qualifying
for benefits. Julie had been on TANF briefly when her five-year-old daughter was born but had quickly gotten back to work as a waitress in a restaurant managed by her family members and had left the rolls. She was reap-
plying because she had had a second child, a son who was now just under
a month old. Julie was not married, but she was very close with her son's
father even though the two did not live together. Her five-year-old had a
different father who was no longer involved with Julie or Julie's daughter.

Julie was apprehensive about having to go to the welfare office, and she was unprepared for what happened during her first meeting with her caseworker. As she explained on the phone that same evening in an agitated voice when I asked her how it went, "Oh, it was a big problem. The caseworker, Ms. Driscoll, was very mean and she was very disrespectful. She said she doesn't care what happens because . . . she's tired of young women coming to her asking for welfare. She said she's going to retire soon and she's settled, but my life's just beginning and I'm already asking for welfare."

Julie was clearly very upset and spoke quickly and forcefully, repeating over and over, "She was so degrading" and "She acted like the money is coming out of her pocket." Julie reported that Ms. Driscoll had just started attacking her at the beginning of the meeting, saying, "Why can't you get a boyfriend who has a job?" When she first started the meeting and was looking over Julie's case file, Julie reported, Ms. Driscoll said, "What's changed since the last five years [the last time Julie was on assistance]? Oh, I know, you have another kid—and you can't even support the one you have." Julie was speechless. "I don't know why she has to get into my personal life—who my boyfriend is and what I do with my spare time. It's almost like they want to know when I go to the bathroom." Julie's final summary of the meeting was simply, "It was forty-five minutes of hell. It was terrible. She doesn't like the people that need the help."

Throughout the long application process, Julie dealt with others in the Public Aid office.[1] She found some to be just like Ms. Driscoll and others refreshingly pleasant. But as Ms. Driscoll remained Julie's caseworker, Julie's overall impression of social interaction at the office was that it was belittling and uncooperative.

Like Julie, most women interviewed for this study perceived the majority of social interactions between themselves and caseworkers in the welfare office to be adversarial. Women at both time periods reported that caseworkers did not take the time to explain rules clearly and that they treated recipients disrespectfully. Many women said they had trouble getting or keeping benefits to which they believed they had a legal right. Such experiences engender distrust.

This distrust interferes with the intended incentives of specific welfare policies. Not only the specifics of welfare benefits and rules but also the philosophy of welfare policy is communicated through caseworkers.[2] Since the women receiving welfare in my study tended to see these messengers as the enemy, they tended also to report to me that they were suspicious of welfare policy's promises and intentions. Thus they did not trust that promised benefits would accrue in practice. They believed that their interests were directly at odds with those of the welfare office—that is, that their own interest was in retaining benefits, while the main motivation of the welfare office and its personnel was to move them off the welfare rolls.[3]

I begin this chapter with an overview of how welfare offices and welfare policies differed before and after welfare reform. What did not change was the fact that the women I interviewed reported hostile relationships with their caseworkers at both time periods. I then discuss two reasons why these hostile relationships are a breeding ground for distrust. First, communication in the client-caseworker relationship is poor, resulting in women not knowing or understanding official welfare rules and benefits. This is a problem because even when caseworkers follow rules appropriately and cut a woman's benefits legitimately, a woman who does not understand the rules will feel she has been treated unfairly and, as a result, will distrust her caseworker. Poor communication about rules and benefits also generates distrust because it leads women to feel that their caseworkers are holding out on information they should be giving them, for instance about available work supports like transportation subsidies. Second, even when women do know about rules and benefits, they do not believe that the caseworkers with whom they have hostile relationships will actually follow the official rules and deliver benefits appropriately. Hostility leads to distrust that caseworkers will make good on the welfare office's promises. As a result, women are less responsive to voluntary incentives to enter the labor force than they would be if they believed promised benefits would be delivered. I conclude with a discussion of how the structure of the welfare office, particularly the lack of shared interests between caseworkers and clients, promotes distrust and how such distrust might be addressed.

Today's low-income women who receive cash assistance interact with a welfare office and with caseworkers who must operate under the goals and incentives set forth by the 1996 reforms. For a long time, welfare policies have been trying to move recipients into the workforce, leading caseworkers to stress that benefits should be seen as temporary supports. The welfare reform act of 1996 dramatically stepped up such efforts.

A Preference for Sticks over Carrots

The 1996 welfare reform legislation was not the first policy with the goal of moving low-income women into the labor market, but it shifted the. emphasis from encouragement to force. As discussed in chapter 1, less than a decade before welfare reform was passed, the Family Support Act (FSA) of 1988 attempted to reform welfare as well. As implemented in some states, the FSA did create work requirements for certain groups of recipients, but they were not applied as broadly and were not as onerous as those created by the 1996 policy. Most importantly, the FSA did not impose time limits on benefits. Hence, the 1996 reforms focused more on mandatory "sticks" to force recipients to find jobs, whereas implementation of the 1988 legislation, especially in certain states, relied more heavily on voluntary incentives, or "carrots," to draw recipients into the workforce. Two of the voluntary work incentives instituted by the FSA were to provide low-income mothers who left welfare for work with a child care subsidy for one year and to grant continued Medicaid coverage, also for one year, after the transition to work. Before the passage of the 1988 legislation, Medicaid had been available to low-income families only if they fell into certain categories, one of which was being a cash assistance recipient. As a result, most parents who left welfare for low-wage work, which rarely provides insurance benefits, were faced with immediate loss of medical coverage for themselves and their children. FSA's transitional Medicaid benefits thus removed one disincentive for welfare recipients to find employment.

Another major voluntary incentive, called the Work Pays program, was instituted in the state of Illinois in 1993. Prior to the implementation of Work Pays, a welfare recipient's monthly assistance grant was docked one dollar for every dollar that she earned through employment. This effectively meant that earnings were taxed at a rate of 100 percent, which created a disincentive to enter the labor force.[4] The Work Pays program changed this rule, instead allowing recipients to keep two out of every three dollars of earned income. Illinois was able to supersede the federal dollar-for-dollar reduction rule because in the early 1990s, before the 1996 welfare reform bill was penned, President Clinton liberally granted states waivers to experiment with welfare rules. This state-level experimentation provided ideas for policy innovation and evidence of policy effects that were eventually used as support for federal reform. Illinois received a waiver in 1993 to run Work Pays, and the program has been in place ever since.

Several carrots still exist (and existed at the time of my post-reform interviews) in Illinois alongside reform's new sticks. In addition to the Work Pays program remaining in effect, eligibility for Medicaid was decoupled from the receipt of cash assistance by federal decree at the time reform was passed. This means that as long as a family's income is low enough to be eligible, the family can receive Medicaid benefits. Eligibility for Illinois's child care subsidy is also decoupled from cash assistance receipt. This decoupling of child care subsidies and Medicaid replaces FSA's transitional child care and Medicaid benefits. Now income-eligible families can receive these benefits no matter how long they have been off cash assistance.[5] Illinois also provides additional work supports for women transitioning from welfare to a job, such as money for both transportation to work and clothing required for work. These remaining and additional voluntary incentives, however, are overshadowed by the dramatic coercive measures that reform instituted.[6] For example, women cannot receive cash assistance without participating in an approved work activity, there is a lifetime limit of sixty months of assistance, and those who do not meet requirements are "sanctioned" by having their benefits reduced or even eliminated.[7] The guiding belief of reform is that carrots alone cannot be effective and sticks must be increased to get welfare mothers to work.

The welfare department has been successful in communicating the "sticks" of welfare reform, partly because this message is drummed into the heads of recipients during almost every interaction with the welfare office in a way that the more nuanced messages about "carrots" are not. As we will see below, recipients are often unaware of the carrots but clearly know the sticks. The sticks have also been emphasized in communications by other outlets, such as the news media, during reform's passage and implementation.

Reform's requirements that state governments reduce their cash assistance caseloads and produce near-universal employment among welfare recipients trickle down to the structural arrangements of local welfare offices. Caseworkers must reduce caseload size and increase employment among their clients in order to perform well in their jobs. These structural forces encourage caseworkers to focus on coercive measures, which are more easily communicated and delivered than the more complex voluntary incentives. And this focus promotes welfare recipients' distrust.

Changes in the Role of the Caseworker

As welfare policies changed after 1996, so did the job of the caseworker. Before reform, the main job of caseworkers was to "cut checks." In other words, it was their job to assess applicants' eligibility for benefits, to give applicants the appropriate amount, and to make sure that clients were not doing anything (such as receiving unreported income) that changed their eligibility status.[8] Yes, caseworkers were supposed to encourage clients to move off the rolls through employment or other routes, and they had some role in helping clients do so, especially after the passage of reform's precursor, the FSA, in 1988. But it was not their job to systematically assess and address recipients' barriers to employment and to make sure that all cases got off the rolls within a set period of time.

Since reform, the job has been different. Caseworkers are now case managers whose job is not just to encourage but to actually shepherd clients' movement into the labor force. They now are supposed to address clients' issues with job skills, domestic violence, substance use, child care, transportation, and a host of other factors that interfere with employment.

It is their job to connect clients with a separate government office that manages paternity establishment, with another office that manages Medicaid, and with job-training programs (usually separate not-for-profit agencies or for-profit businesses that contract with the state to provide job training to welfare recipients). When it is appropriate, they also are supposed to help transfer clients with disabilities from TANF onto Supplemental Security Income (SSI), a federal assistance program for the physically and mentally disabled.[9]

Moreover, reform did not just create new requirements for welfare recipients. It also created new requirements for state governments. States that do not meet work participation targets for their caseloads are penalized by the federal government by being given less funding to run their cash assistance programs. States are also rewarded through increased funding if they do various things such as lower their nonmarital fertility rate (without raising their abortion rate). These federal penalties on and rewards to state governments translate into increased pressure on caseworkers to meet goals for clients. Needless to say, being a caseworker in the post-reform world is not an easy job.

In an informational interview with a manager in a Chicago welfare office, I learned of the difficulties welfare offices face in making the transition needed to meet these new demands. One challenge is shifting caseworkers to doing tasks that require both a new set of job skills and a new mind-set toward the goals of the job. The manager described this shift as a work in progress, even though I interviewed her eight years after the passage of welfare reform.

Little Change in the Quality of Interactions in the Welfare Office

Most women interviewed both before and after welfare reform described their experiences interacting with caseworkers in negative terms. Women reported that caseworkers were impatient, rude, and disrespectful while simultaneously being incompetent. Common images emerged across women's narratives in both time periods. In fact, it is striking how often women used similar words to describe these interactions. Common phrasings included that the caseworkers "treat us like children," were "snotty," had a "bad [or nasty] attitude," and "act like the money is coming out of their own pocket." This common language was used by a striking number of women.[10]

There was, however, some variation in the reported quality of caseworker interactions within each time period. Some women reported that, while they knew others who had had bad experiences, they had been lucky to have had neutral or even highly positive relationships with their caseworkers (though only women after reform identified specific positive experiences). There was also variation in the experiences of individual women across reported interactions with different caseworkers, some seen as supportive and others as hostile. Despite this variation, the overwhelming assessment by women in both time periods was that their interactions with caseworkers were fraught with tension and disrespect. Studies of caseworkers indicated that they too experienced frustrations in communicating with clients and pointed to the structural arrangements of the workplace as a major source of their difficulties.[11]

Most women before reform consistently reported negative interactions with caseworkers. A handful spoke neutrally or in nonspecific positive terms about their interactions with welfare office personnel, but none of the pre-reform women spoke enthusiastically about a caseworker or gave a detailed story of how a caseworker had helped them. Instead, they simply commented that they had had a helpful caseworker here and there.

Juanita Soto, interviewed before welfare reform, was a thirty-eight-year-old Puerto Rican woman with a quiet, thoughtful, and warm demeanor. Her long dark hair framed a strong, attractive face and deep brown eyes. She lived with her twelve-year-old son and eight-year-old daughter. She also had a twenty-one-year-old son by the same father, but he had been raised mostly by her parents since she had had him when she was fifteen. He was now living with Juanita's sister, attending community college, and about to enter the National Guard. Like many women I interviewed, Juanita was short a bedroom or two in her apartment, so the living room served as her bedroom and the one small bedroom was shared by her children, who slept in bunk beds that took up almost the entire room. Juanita said it was not an ideal situation, especially for a twelve-year-old boy to have to share a room with his younger sister, but that she had "no choice."

One evening, we sat folding laundry together on the small Formica table in her kitchen while she explained what it was like to have to engage with caseworkers. It was difficult to imagine Juanita being anything but polite, since she displayed a gentle and mature personality with me. She had none of the toughness or hostility in her tone that some of the other women exhibited, especially when they spoke about their caseworkers. One would expect she would elicit courteous treatment, but she reported a different story.

Juanita had received cash assistance for eight years, starting when her oldest child was two, during a period when his father went to jail and stopped contributing money to the household. When she finally got a job working as a receptionist, she was immediately cut from the welfare rolls. While she was surprised to lose her benefits so quickly, she did not miss the treatment she reported receiving at the hands of her caseworkers. "I mean . . . they disrespect you. They make you feel stupid. They treat you like you're . . . you know, nobody. Terrible. I had so many caseworkers that did . . . that. . . . Just because you're on the other side and you're making your check does not give you the right to down-talk us or to embarrass us or make us feel dumb. . . . Oh, I hated it."

During a brief, more recent stint on welfare when Juanita was between jobs, she found her caseworkers to be no better, and she was relieved when she found a job and was again free of them. Many other women echoed Juanita's words. Nakida Brown bluntly stated, "They got a nasty attitude, a shitty attitude, like that money that they giving us is coming out of they pocket." Tahiera Jackson complained, "They so snotty up there. Just the way they talk to people. They just have a bad attitude."

Danielle Adams, a thirty-five-year-old African American mother of a thirteen-year-old and a five-year-old, was one of the most successful of the women in the labor market. While wages earned by most of the rest of women interviewed before reform ranged from $4.25 to $8.00 an hour (or roughly $6.50 to $12.00 in constant 2012 dollars), Danielle was making $16.77 an hour ($25.92 in 2012 dollars) as a seasonal sanitation worker for the city of Chicago. She had to work for five years from April to

November before she could be hired as a full-year worker. The winter before our first interview, she returned to welfare for the second time in her life until the job began again in April. She explained that she greatly preferred being independent from the welfare system. "'Cause, like Public Aid kind of makes you feel like you just panhandling almost, might as well say. The way they treat you. They just don't treat you right. You go up to them office and they all cold."

Since Danielle was an extraordinary success compared to most of the women—she was in line for a relatively highly paid permanent job—one might expect caseworkers would appreciate that she was on the brink of a stable employment history. But she did not describe any difference from other women in how she was treated. For example, Grace James, who differed greatly from Danielle in that she had been out of the labor market for many years and had no plans for reentry, reported similar treatment: "They act as if they're giving you so much. But actually, they're not giving you barely enough to live on."

It is hard to argue with Grace. At the time of the pre-reform interviews, a single mother in Illinois with two minor children received $377 a month in cash assistance. Benefit levels have always been set by the states, and this Illinois rate was just above the national average of $367— above the lowest rate in Mississippi of $120 but below the highest rate in Alaska of $923. The Illinois cash assistance rate, which translated into $4,524 per year, did not bring a mother's income anywhere near to being over the poverty line. By the time of the post-reform interviews, Illinois had raised its rate but only to $396. This increase was also not nearly enough to keep up with inflation. Once these figures are adjusted for inflation, we see the Illinois benefit actually went down between the two interview periods. Converted to constant 2012 dollars, the pre-reform benefit was $568 per month, whereas the post-reform benefit was $465.[12] Thus women after reform had to do more to get less.

Women also stated that instead of helping them gain confidence to enter the workforce, caseworkers often demeaned them. Luisa Estevez, who eventually achieved success in a salaried job with benefits at a job-training center after leaving welfare, felt that her caseworker regularly belittled her. During one appointment, he had her take a written test. "I gave him the test back and . . . he goes, 'Oh, you're a doofus.' And I don't know what the word meant, but I knew I didn't take it well. It just so happened that there was a dictionary there and I looked up the word, and the word mean 'stupid.'" Luisa learned from this incident that her caseworker was not supportive. In fact, she came to see him as someone who pulled her down.

Many women had similar stories, but Dolores Rios summed up the general reaction to caseworkers quite simply: "They're all full of shit. . . . Oh man, they're real bitches, real bitches." While not every woman spoke as forcefully, and some pointed to a humane interaction here and there, most women agreed with Dolores's general sentiment. In the eyes of most women, caseworkers were not allies. They were not supporters. They were hostile and disrespectful gatekeepers that one had to endure in order to get public assistance benefits.

Given the new tasks that welfare reform required of caseworkers, the women interviewed after reform had much more contact with caseworkers than women did before reform. They were also more likely to interact with several caseworkers. This increased contact exposed women to the possibility of both more negative interactions and more positive ones than women had had before reform, when they simply picked up checks from caseworkers. Perhaps not surprisingly then, women after reform reported both extremely negative interactions and (though rarely) extremely positive interactions with caseworkers. The increased pressure on caseworkers to move clients into the workforce also probably contributed to the increased incidence of both negative and positive interactions. Clients who felt that caseworkers' only interest was in pushing them into the labor market were likely to feel mistreated. But a few reported encountering caseworkers who really took an interest in them in order to help them find jobs, with the result that the women had positive feelings about interactions. The general tone of the post-reform women's descriptions of their interactions, however, was similar to that of women before reform. Overall, they too saw caseworkers not as helpful agents but as hostile gatekeepers.

Most women after reform reported that caseworkers were rude and treated clients unprofessionally. Many women complained that caseworkers did not take the time to treat them as individuals, an approach that was considered demeaning and meant that women's particular needs were not addressed. The increased demands on caseworkers after reform may make it difficult for caseworkers to take the time to give each recipient what she needs.

As Wanda Bailey explained,

> You can find out a lot about a person if you just talk with them instead of treating them like a piece of paper. And we just a name on a paper with a number to them. . . . And it's like, "I just want to deal with her and get her outta here" and "I just want to see the next person." . . . I speak for most young ladies that's on aid. All of us are not unruly and just angry all the time. There's a lotta people who are very intelligent, have been in college and have held jobs for . . . years. And the way they treat you is inhumane. . . . They try to belittle you with their words and . . . there's never a please or thank you.

Another common complaint was that caseworkers asked very personal questions, often about sexual relationships, and did not respect women's privacy or appear to have any code of confidentiality. This particular concern was much more common among the post-reform women, probably because welfare reform's new paternity establishment requirements had led to this line of questioning. It was these types of questions that made Julie Callahan complain that she felt as if caseworkers almost wanted to know when she went to the bathroom. Julie did not seem to realize that the questions might have been about trying to figure out the identity of her baby's father so that child support could be collected. Furthermore, she did not recognize that many citizens probably felt that the father's identity was legitimately the state's business once a mother was asking for financial assistance. Instead, the questions simply seemed invasive to her. The fact that she felt that way indicates that her caseworker did not explain why the questions were necessary and did not ask them in a suitably delicate way given their sensitive nature.

Adriana Marquez, the mother of an infant son, was appalled at how insensitively she was treated when she applied for TANF after her son was born. She reported that personal information such as her welfare history and the fact that she was not together with her baby's father was publicly shared. "I went to try to apply when my son was first born and they tried to embarrass me in there, the caseworkers. . . . When I went the second time, I [asked to talk] to a supervisor and [my caseworker] started hollering all my business out in the room [when] it's supposed to be private."

Like women before reform, what women after reform considered most difficult about interacting with caseworkers was simply how rude they found them to be. Dionne Anderson, a tall and stately thirty-eight-year-old African American woman, was unusual among those interviewed in that she did not have her first (and only) child until age thirty-six. In a sense, Dionne was not unlike upper-middle-class professional women who delay childbearing as they pursue careers. Dionne, however, had been side-tracked from motherhood because she was busy "in the life," otherwise known as the drug trade. Her ability to "gain authority" (rise above the level of street dealers) had protected her from the police, who were never able to pin anything on her. But Dionne eventually left dealing when she sensed the police were beginning to close in on her. She was tired of it anyway. After leaving the life, she became involved with her church and regretted that she had spent so much time "in the streets" rather than pursuing the education she quit after eleventh grade. "I could have had a degree and gotten somewhere by now," she sighed with resignation.

Dionne described everything about parenting as new to her since she had spent so many years childless and had not spent much time around children. Having earned a sufficient living selling drugs, she was also not familiar with the welfare system. She thus found the interaction style of caseworkers a shock when she started receiving benefits after her son's birth. "I'm not comfortable at all because . . . they don't know how to talk to you. They don't know how to present theirself to you. So I am sitting here nicely—just like I'm sitting here with you, you know. It's like they holler at you like you some kind of little kid, you know. I'm looking at this lady like 'Is you crazy?' . . . The caseworkers, they are very snotty. Some of them, you can't talk to them."

Dionne really had no preconceived notions of what it would be like to interact with caseworkers. She had applied for welfare expecting help and not the treatment she described. Dionne had been no saint, for sure. But, as she indicated in her quote above, she did indeed speak with me in a calm and professional manner—or "nicely," to use her words. She also did not have children young or have a lot of children, conditions that might raise the hackles of caseworkers tired of doling out aid. But she described the same treatment that Julie Callahan, mother of two at twenty-three years old, described.

Though most women after reform reported negative interactions with caseworkers, some had positive interactions in welfare offices. In contrast, no women before reform described specific incidents of positive interactions with caseworkers, though a few made general statements about some caseworkers being helpful. Caseworkers after reform earned praise when they treated the women respectfully, when they followed through on what they had promised to do, when they were flexible, when they went out of their way to help, or when they cheered on women who were trying to transition to work.

Georgia Burke, an African American mother of seven children, liked her caseworker's reliability. "Say like the food stamps don't be on your card when they supposed to be there. He, instead of letting his paperwork pile up, he puts it in that same day as he tells you. He don't wait. When he say he's gonna do it, he does it."

When caseworkers let their "paperwork pile up," the cost for recipients is high. They may have to wait to receive benefits that they desperately need. By doing his paperwork right away, Georgia's caseworker showed that he recognized how important the food stamps were to her family's well-being. He was thus not only serving her needs but showing her respect.

Melissa Jacobs, a married twenty-eight-year-old white mother of three, was happy with one of her caseworkers for the same reason. As we sat at the dining room table in her apartment with her children loudly playing around us and her husband in and out, she described her experiences. "The caseworker was very respectful. She did everything like it was supposed to be. I didn't have no interruptions on my case. I didn't have no problems until she retired and then they switched me [to another caseworker]." Note that Melissa appreciated that she had "no interruptions" in her case, and remember that a main frustration that Bethany Grant, whom we met in the Introduction, had with her caseworker was that she "messed up" Bethany's case and that Bethany was without benefits for several months during the cold Chicago winter as a result. Melissa's new caseworker was less reliable than the one she appreciated, and she had complaints both about the way she was treated and about the difficulty of getting her benefits consistently. The difference between her actual experiences with each caseworker was what taught her who could be trusted to deliver and who could not.

Monisha Hall, an African American mother who at twenty-six was busy managing three children under the age of five, was grateful that her caseworker was willing to be flexible in the bureaucratic process of assessing her eligibility for cash assistance. Otherwise, she would have had to wait longer for her check to come through. Monisha lived in her sister's apartment, and her sister charged her rent. Monisha's caseworker had told her that she needed a notarized letter from her sister stating the amount of the rent so it could be included in a calculation of Monisha's expenses and hence her needed income. Many women described caseworkers who were sticklers about every rule, but when Monisha forgot to bring the letter, her caseworker did not demand that she get it. "I was supposed to bring in . . . a notarized letter from my sister about the rent 'cause she was charging me like a hundred dollars. And I had forgot to get it. And [my caseworker] was like, 'All right.' She just let it go. She was like, 'I know you say it's your sister, I know what's going on, I know how much you give her, so you don't have to bring it back.'" From this experience, Monisha learned she could trust her caseworker to be on her side.

Still, many of the positive descriptions were coupled with statements about how rare such caseworkers were. Kala Amos, a twenty-five-year-old African American mother of three who hoped to be a police officer and had held two jobs as a security guard, appreciated her caseworker because she did "what [she] say [she]'ll do." Also, her caseworker would call her to remind her of appointments or paperwork she needed to bring in, which Kala said the caseworker was not required to do. Kala did not think her caseworker is typical, however. "She real nice. You gotta have a good relationship with your caseworker in order to get your paperwork done. You can't have no attitude. But some of the caseworkers down at the Aid office, they'll make you have a attitude 'cause some of 'em so snide. They don't know how to talk to you. And you grown. And you down there trying to get yourself together and they be having attitude. Not all of 'em, but some of 'em do. But the caseworkers that I've had, I never had a problem with mine."

Kala's comments are interesting for several reasons. First, she was saying that getting "your paperwork done," by which she meant completing all the bureaucratic requirements to apply for benefits and to keep them coming, could not be done without a good relationship with one's caseworker. Second, she was acknowledging that not all clients exhibited a good attitude, but she attributed that to the belittling attitudes of caseworkers who treated clients like children even though the clients were "grown" and were trying to "get themselves together." Third, she felt she had had good caseworkers but said she had observed bad ones.

Even women who reported positive interactions with a caseworker explained that in addition to their positive experiences, they had had negative interactions with other caseworkers or had observed negative interactions between other caseworkers and other clients. Unlike most women who had much shorter periods on welfare, Alpha Walker, a mother of seven, had been on AFDC and then TANF for a total of seventeen years. She had certainly seen her share of caseworkers. With a resigned sigh, she said, "Some of them are all right. I mean, they know how to talk to you and they try to help you. But some of them, they talk to you snotty and they act like it's they money coming out they pocket." Here Alpha's reference to "money coming out they pocket" echoes Julie's use of the same phrase when describing Ms. Driscoll's attitude. Similarly, Kala's comment above about caseworkers treating "grown" clients inappropriately harkens back to Dionne's surprise at caseworkers who treated clients like children. As I mentioned earlier, often women who did not even know each other observed the same behaviors in their caseworkers.

Edwina Bright was an African American mother of four children—two grown daughters who were married and lived with their husbands and two teenage sons. Edwina was particularly thoughtful, often took time to really think before answering a question, and exhibited no active hostility about her time on welfare. Edwina had held many jobs and had stably transitioned from welfare shortly after reform policies began. At the time of our interview, she had held her current position for four years. Her job, as a janitor who also did a lot of the landscaping at her building, was unionized, which was very rare among the women in either time period. Back when she had received welfare, Edwina had had both good and bad interactions with caseworkers. "Throughout the times that I was on aid, I could say it was kind of like a mixed thing. Some of the caseworkers that I had were really good. Really interested in your well-being. Trying to help you as much as they can. Then, I found some that was just little dooky-heads . . . really didn't care what happened, you know, and would tell you. I had one tell me, 'Oh, I don't care . . . I don't care what happens.'"

One caseworker, however, stood out in her memory for having really taken an interest in encouraging her to stick to her goals. Edwina had left welfare for work but had lost her job. When she went to reapply for welfare benefits, she met a caseworker who dissuaded her. Edwina listened to her, returned to searching for a job, and eventually found a job she liked. She had not been on welfare since. Normally, Edwina said, she might complain that the caseworker was not being cooperative, but there was something about her warmth and respectful tone that Edwina found sincere. "But what she told me was, 'You have made a [transition] from being on public aid [to] having a job. Don't fall back into the hole again. Try to find something else. You know, we have programs. Try to get into a program. Don't go back. You took two steps forward. Don't take twelve steps back, you know. You owe it to yourself and your children.' . . . I appreciate her giving me that talk. There are a lot of people who don't take the time out to do that."

One might interpret Edwina's story the same way she did, that the caseworker was going out of her way to help her. Of course, one might also see the caseworker as guided by her new post-reform job requirements of deterring applicants from joining the rolls and encouraging them into the labor market instead. What made the difference for Edwina was the respectful tone the caseworker used. Many women felt like cogs in the large machine of the welfare office. Making a human connection with a caseworker was rare, but when it happened it was valued.

Caseworkers, of course, have their own perceptions of their actions and their interactions with clients. In several informational interviews that I held with caseworkers, they expressed a great deal of frustration with clients who did not follow procedures or were nonresponsive in other ways. It is impossible to know from interviews with recipients whether their perceptions accurately reflect what happened during their visits to the welfare office. Other researchers who have studied caseworkers themselves, however, do find evidence in support of my respondents' reports.[13]

My own observations also lend some support to the women's claims. In multiple visits to welfare offices, I observed caseworkers and other office personnel speaking to recipients in impatient and demeaning ways. At one office, I sat on a bench in front of a reception counter waiting to meet with a member of the staff with whom I had an appointment. Several clients were sitting on the bench with me. The woman working at the long counter began barking at them as if they were naughty schoolchildren.[14] With a stern expression and in an angry voice, she began yelling orders that were difficult to interpret. I was not sure whether she was trying to tell them they should not be waiting there, they should be coming up to her, or some other directive. She treated them as if they were doing something wrong before ascertaining why they were waiting. The clients looked shocked and confused. It seemed to take them a minute to realize the woman was speaking to them, presumably because they could not figure out what they had done wrong or what she wanted them to do to fix it. The woman's approach to the clients—scolding them like children, assuming they were doing something wrong before finding out the facts, and not explaining calmly what she needed them to do— illustrated many of my interviewees' comments about welfare office personnel.[15]

Caseworkers and counselors in job-training programs may themselves be of two minds about reform's requirements. In informal interviews with one caseworker and three different job-training counselors, I asked about the challenges of dealing with clients under the post-reform regime. All four stressed the importance of clients' following rules and expressed frustration with clients who did not meet reform's requirements. They said they had no patience for certain clients, especially those who did not bring required paperwork, who missed meetings, or who were evasive when asked questions. As they spoke, they exhibited the harsh tone of which clients accused them.

But then I asked them a different kind of question. I asked what they thought of reform itself. Each of the four surprised me. Each said that they thought the policies reform had put in place were too harsh. They agreed with reform's goals, but they did not think it was flexible or forgiving enough for women who needed more time to find stable employment that allowed them also to care for their children. Most of the women I interviewed said the same thing. They too thought they should not rely on welfare long term and should find employment, but they thought they needed more support, more time, and more understanding when it could not happen immediately or when crises intervened. Thus caseworkers, job-training counselors, and clients may think similarly, but their different roles force them into adversarial positions. Caseworkers' and job-training counselors' job is to enforce reform's mandates, and that required task overrides their personal views of reform. Clients get to see only the person fulfilling that job task and rarely the person who has a more humane understanding of a client's challenges.

We see here how the structure of the welfare office, and of job-training programs to which welfare offices send welfare recipients, shapes the nature of interactions between low-income mothers and caseworkers or job-training counselors. Because caseworkers and counselors are rewarded for moving clients from welfare to work and not for treating them sensitively, making sure they understand policies, or making sure they get all of the benefits to which they are entitled, their jobs are structured so that they have interests at odds with those of welfare recipients who are trying to retain benefits and who wish for sensitive treatment.

ISSUES OF DISTRUST IN THE WELFARE OFFICE

The dynamics described in this chapter, in which welfare recipients often view their caseworkers as disrespectful and uncaring, have profound consequences for their experiences on welfare. After all, it is the caseworkers who must help the women navigate the complex rules and procedures of the welfare system.

These dynamics also have implications for how welfare policies play out. If welfare recipients are not aware of or do not understand welfare rules and the work incentives they contain, they cannot take advantage of such incentives. And even when the women do know the rules, if they do not trust their caseworkers they may not believe that these incentive policies truly will be applied. As a result, they may not take the steps necessary to receive them. This was equally true for the women I interviewed in both time periods.

Knowledge of the Written Rules

It may at first seem that it should be easy for welfare recipients to grasp what welfare policy rules are. However, the rules that are written in legislation, the rules as they are actually implemented by caseworkers, and recipients' interpretation of the written and implemented rules all differ from each other. The gaps between these three things lead to difficulty in caseworker and client communication about policies. Often the women I interviewed described welfare rules differently than they were written up officially. As we will see below, they might say that they would be cut off Medicaid benefits if they got a job, when the written rules said this would not happen. When women did not describe rules in the same way as they were written, I say they had "a different understanding of the rules" rather than an "incorrect understanding." This is because it is possible that rules were not implemented according to how they were written. The women's understandings of the rules would be "wrong" if indeed rules were implemented as written. However, if they were not, then the women might have a correct understanding of the rules as implemented, even though that understanding was different from the rules as written. As we shall see, many of the women at both time periods reported that the rules as written were not the same as the rules as practiced.[16] As described in more depth below, I myself found a brochure in a welfare office informing clients of a policy that the state had voted to discontinue a year and a half earlier. Clearly, the written legislation (that this particular policy should be stopped) and the policy implemented, or at least communicated, in the welfare office were in conflict with each other.

The rules themselves, of course, differed before and after reform, which somewhat affected the interviews' content. Even so, many of the women in both time periods either stated that they did not know particular rules or gave descriptions of the rules that were different from the official descriptions.

Pre-reform interviews focused on how women perceived two different kinds of "carrots" to entice them into the labor market. The Work Pays program, described above, allowed (and continues to allow) employed welfare recipients to keep two out of every three dollars of their earnings instead of having their welfare grants reduced a dollar for every dollar earned through employment. The transitional medical and child care benefits set up by the earlier reform measures of 1988 allowed women to keep both Medicaid coverage and child care subsidies for a year after they exited welfare for work.

If properly applied, Work Pays would allow women who work for minimal pay and limited hours to retain eligibility for cash assistance and to raise their income levels. The transitional benefits, if granted as indicated in written policy, would ensure that families would not lose medical coverage for at least a year after a mother became employed.

I asked each respondent detailed questions about each of these welfare rules. Fewer than half of the women described the Work Pays program or the transitional benefits as they were laid out in written materials at the welfare office. Most women assumed that they would be cut off from all benefits as soon as they took a job. They did not realize that the written regulations stated that, on the basis of the Work Pays program, they should have been able to keep a portion of their cash assistance grant (unless their earnings were so high that they were no longer income eligible) and that, on the basis of the FSA of 1988, they should receive transitional child care and Medicaid benefits for one year.

When she was a teenager, Pauline Garett worked in a fast-food restaurant. Fast-food jobs are low-paying and often part time. They are thus exactly the type of employment Work Pays and transitional Medicaid and child care benefits were designed to encourage by subsidizing the low wages and adding work supports. However, Pauline did not see this potential, as her response demonstrated when she was asked if she would take a fast-food job at age thirty-three after years of not being employed:

> No, I would take something that would give me a little bit more money to pay my bus fare to get there. Really, I would have to be careful what kind of job I take. I know right now, if I took a job and it didn't work out and [had] no kind of [medical] coverage for my kids—'cause Public Aid, they gonna snatch that right away as soon as I report it to them—they take that from me, and say a job paying like five or six dollars, it's not gonna make it. 'Cause I got to pay my own expenses on my own, pay for me to get to the job. Still, I need something to cover me, some kind of [medical] coverage for my kids, so I don't know.

Ironically, the problems Pauline cited as preventing her from taking a fast-food job were the very problems Work Pays was intended to solve: she did not think the job would pay enough to cover the expenses it would entail, and she was certain that immediately upon acceptance of a job she would lose Medicaid coverage for herself and her children. Again, if the policies were implemented as they were written, she should have retained a portion of her welfare grant, Medicaid, and child care benefits, which presumably could have made working financially worth it. Pauline, however, may not have been wrong. If caseworkers did not follow the rules as written, either intentionally or through oversight, then indeed Pauline might have ended up getting cut from the welfare rolls and might not have received transitional benefits even if she took a job that paid very little.

Other women before reform showed a similar lack of knowledge of the existence of Work Pays and transitional benefits. When I asked Estrella Cervantes what she would do about child care if she got a job, she made it clear that she was not familiar with the idea of Work Pays or transitional benefits. She said, "That would be kind of hard. I have to pay the babysitter. That's why I can't get a job that's going to pay four dollars [roughly minimum wage at the time] . . . because you have to get off public aid right away, right?"[17]

Allison Smith was much more confident in her response to a question about whether she would be able to keep any of her welfare grant if she worked: "No, they just cut you." Nakida Brown echoed this response: "They just cut you, and you never know why." Clearly, Nakida did not know, understand, or, perhaps, believe that the Work Pays policy would allow workers with wages low enough that they remained income eligible to continue on welfare.

Women after reform understood Work Pays and other work incentives in similar ways to women before reform. In addition, they felt that they did not have adequate information about the new or enhanced work supports that welfare reform had put in place to encourage employment and quick welfare exits. The majority of the women interviewed after reform also either were unaware of some welfare rules or understood them differently from their official version. A third of the sixty-nine post-reform women had never heard of the concept of Work Pays, and only a fifth described how it worked in the same way it was described officially. Fewer than half of the women described the details of time limit rules as they were legislated. On the other hand, a full three-quarters of the post-reform respondents described the spirit of time limit regulations as the welfare department intended them, meaning that recipients should think of welfare as a temporary source of income to be used in emergencies. Half of the women, however, did not know how many months remained on their own time clocks.

The women's belief that benefits would indeed be time limited and contingent on work (as opposed to their lack of belief in other aspects of welfare policy) was in keeping with their general distrust of the welfare bureaucracy. Recipients believed that caseworkers did not really want to help them but were instead always motivated by the goal of moving them off the welfare rolls. Thus recipients' lack of trust in the welfare department led them to believe that welfare's time limits and work requirements were real, whereas program components designed to entice recipients into jobs were not credible in the women's eyes.

Wakeisha Jefferson, a twenty-four-year-old mother of two who had been on TANF three separate times since first becoming pregnant in 1998, expressed her frustration that her caseworkers did not tell her about work supports to which she was entitled. She learned of her eligibility for these benefits from other recipients and then asked her caseworker about them. "They should tell us this stuff when we're applying for it. Why we gotta get all this information from some outsiders when they supposed to be telling us? . . . And they look at me like, 'Oh yeah, we do this, yeah.' I'm looking at them like, 'Okay, you all . . . why you didn't tell me this when I was filling out the application?' 'Oh yeah, we do this, we do the uniform, transportation, we do all this.' They don't tell us."

Alpha Walker, a mother of seven with a particularly long history of welfare receipt, had similar complaints. She too felt caseworkers were much better at telling clients about work requirements than at explaining and actually providing work supports. She was not given transportation benefits to which she believed she was entitled (and which she eventually got), and she had to fight to prove that her lack of transportation funding meant her absence from job training should be excused. When asked whether her caseworkers had explained policy rules well to her, she replied,

> Well the things they tell us about . . . the things we're going to have to start doing for our check. Things like that, basically they tell us. But some of the things, like right now I'm waiting on some information . . . about the transportation situation I was telling you about. And then when you try and call them . . . if you mention it they'll be like, "Well I got so many clients, . . . I got a lot of work to do." So I'll be like, "Well, sometime we have the same problem. We got so many kids or we got so many problems, but you don't give us a chance, you know, to get things together."

Wakeisha's and Alpha's view that it is difficult for recipients to get full and accurate information from the welfare department is supported by one of my observations in the waiting room of one of Chicago's largest welfare offices. As I observed interactions between clients and staff at the front desk of the office, my eye settled on a prominently displayed brochure on a table just to the left of the main reception counter. At first I could not figure out what I found strange about the brochure, but then I realized it was advertising a policy "stick" that did not exist any longer. The brochure was informing clients about the family cap, a policy designed to discourage nonmarital fertility by denying welfare recipients who got pregnant access to any additional assistance for the new child.

The state of Illinois had dropped the family cap provision eighteen months previously, citing its lack of effect on fertility. The failure to remove the brochure that greeted clients right as they entered the office may have simply been an oversight. But at the very least it showed a lack of attention to clear and accurate communication of rules. It also showed a gap between policy set at the state level and policy as practiced (or at least as communicated) on the street level of a particular welfare office.[18]

There were also indications that only those who acted as their own advocates got what they needed. For example, Gabriela Garcia, who had attended college for several years and had served in the army, entered the welfare system for the first time shortly before our interview because her husband had left her and she was having trouble finding a job. Like Wakeisha and Alpha, she also felt that available work supports were not voluntarily offered. Instead, she suggested that welfare recipients needed to gather their own information from unofficial channels that they could then use to request benefits themselves. "Most of the time it seems like if you don't know about the benefits that they have, they don't really tell you. You . . . find out because you sit there [in the welfare office] and you hear everybody talking [about] what they find out or what they [get], and if you ask a specific question you get the answer. But there's no volunteering any information when it comes to these programs." Marisela Suarez, who differed from Gabriela in that she had little education and had spent many years on welfare while her three children were young, had the same impression. "They haven't explained nothing to me. I guess they don't explain to nobody the benefits that . . . are out there for them because they don't want them to get it. Maybe they think we gonna get used to it. But if you realize that we are working people, we don't get used to that little where we can make more." Marisela's comment links the lack of communication about benefits to the lack of trust that benefits will be delivered. This distrust is the subject of the section below.

Distrust in Delivery of Benefits

Many women interviewed both before and after welfare reform did not trust that policies meant to benefit them would be delivered as they were officially described. In other words, they were skeptical that the promised carrots would really be made available to them.

For some women before reform and the institution of work requirements and time limits, the unreliability of the welfare department was enough to pose a disincentive to work. Knowing that working was an invitation to have their cases reviewed and altered, some women avoided the hassle by declining work. We saw this clearly in the case of Bethany Grant, who appeared in the Introduction. Bethany complained that she had spent four months fighting to get back benefits to which she was entitled after her case was "messed up" when she took a job and reported it to her caseworker.

Some women who received child care money before reform were disappointed in the benefit. A major concern was that the benefit was not enough to pay the market wage for a babysitter. Despite the subsidies, women still needed to find day care programs or babysitters (often family or friends) willing to accept a below-market wage. In addition, the child care money was paid directly to the provider but was often greatly delayed, sometimes by several months.

Faith Stubbs tried to enroll her children in a local day care center but was told that it had stopped accepting payment through Public Aid because the bureaucracy involved was too difficult to manage.[19] Linda Waters lost her babysitter because of the payment delay. She described her frustrations with the system. "I said, 'Well, you all don't send the checks on time for the babysitter, and the babysitter said, "I'm tired of babysitting for you."' It takes them two to three months to get paid. Two to three months! And then you get on the phone, you talk to them and they put you on hold. You know, listen to this music. I'm tired of listening to this music!"

The women's suspicions stemmed from a combination of their past experiences with the welfare department and the experiences of other women in the community. Many of these women had tangled with the welfare department before. Many were used to hearing a promise, only to find out later that it would not be honored. Bernice Alexander, an African American mother of a thirteen-year-old girl and a twelve-year-old boy, was another one of the more successful mothers in the labor market. When I interviewed her before reform, her typing skills were earning her $6.00 per hour (or $9.28 when adjusted to 2012 dollars) as a temporary clerical worker in the police department. Minimum wage at the time was $4.25 (or $6.57 in 2012 dollars). Bernice had shown a lot of initiative by trying to pursue her education and staying in the labor market more consistently than other women. She was vaguely aware of Work Pays but was dismissive of its possible benefits.

> I read [about it] in the paper, and when I called them of course it's like, "Are you from Mars?" You know, it's like they put [out] this stuff, and when you call and request it, "Oh, you don't qualify for that." Yeah, like, "I just wanted you to [get] the paper, you know. I didn't actually want you to call and request for this!" So, it's like that. . . . Once I heard that they was giving bus fares to go to school [and] child care [money]. Well, when I called, "Oh, I'm sorry, but you don't qualify." . . . That's something that they put out to get you to make that move, but they cannot make it up once you need that help.

Bernice's skepticism was also based on the fact that she had once tried to take a GED class at a local community college. When she went to the class, the instructor did not show up. Demoralized, she went home, and the seeds of her distrust in agencies that promise to help began to grow. She continued to attend the class, which entailed both transportation and child care costs, even though the instructor frequently did not appear.

Grace James also learned from experience that not everything she understood the welfare office to offer was actually delivered. She began working before Work Pays went into effect, but she was told by the department that she would still receive her welfare grant for six months. And even though I could not find any rule on the books that indicated she was owed this extension of welfare funds, she said she did indeed receive the six months of benefits. However, she then received a letter saying that her continued receipt of the benefits had been an error and that she now had to repay the department for them. "Oh yes, they tell you you can draw this money for six months, you know, . . . but they'll send you a letter telling you owe them for six, because they overpaid you for these six months. They be lying, tellin' you you can keep this money and food stamps. I don't understand why they would tell you that. Or why they would keep sending you checks and then penalize you for it later. You know, it just didn't make sense."

Since Grace had only enough income to scrape by, she certainly did not have any savings. In addition, she soon lost her job and became officially eligible for welfare again. The department thus deducted the close to $2,000 ($3,092 in 2012 dollars) from her future cash assistance payments, creating great hardship for her and her son over a period of several months. Grace's voice broke and her eyes became moist as she discussed the difficulty of that time.

Because of these experiences, neither Grace nor Bernice believed that Work Pays truly existed or could have any effect on them. Grace assumed that if she got a job she would lose all benefits since that was what had happened to her the last time she worked.

Bernice also claimed that that was what had happened to her when she got her job. When Bernice began her job a year before our interview, she was immediately cut from the welfare rolls. She lost her Medicaid card and her full cash grant days after starting to work. Because she could not afford child care and received no transitional child care assistance, she had to routinely leave her children unattended overnight while she worked a night shift. She kept working because she preferred to be active, to set an example for her children of what she termed "independence," and to be free of the welfare bureaucracy. If she had left or lost her job and had returned to welfare, however, she would not have trusted that transitional benefits would ease a reentry into the labor market, since she had not received the benefits during her most recent transition to work, even though she could not figure out why.

Juanita Soto was similarly surprised by an abrupt cessation of welfare benefits two weeks after she became employed. Like Grace, she had become employed before the more generous Work Pays program went into effect. Nonetheless, her counselor at a job-training program had told her that she would continue to receive aid. "Janis came out and said, 'Well, you know, you've been on welfare for so many years and they're not going to leave you out in the cold. They're going to give you for six months, you know, you still going to get food stamps . . . , they'll cut half of the check and they'll apply for a day care center.' None of that happened. All she did was made a phone call [to report the job], boom, the next thing you know, everything was cut off."

Bernice, Grace, and Juanita learned to distrust any promises made by the welfare department through their own experiences being denied benefits they expected to receive. Marguerite Guerrera's story suggests that women learned their pessimism from the experiences of others as well. When I asked what a job would have to pay for her to take it, she replied, "I hope it's not $4.25 [minimum wage at the time]. I cannot do nothing with that." I then asked whether she would take a job that paid $4.25 an hour (or $6.57 in 2012 dollars) if she was offered one. She said, "My Public Aid says that they're gonna help me, but I was talking to a lady, she said she was working for $4.50 [and] Public Aid just cut her off. She's gone back here on public aid again. Who could make it with $4.50 an hour? Not me."

Marguerite herself did not have experiences demonstrating that the welfare department did not make good on its promises to offer help during the transition to work, but she took the experiences of the other woman she met into her consideration of whether to trust the system. Most of the recipients who began to work, whether under Work Pays or the previous policy regime, were surprised when the department eliminated or greatly reduced their grants or failed to provide transitional medical and child care services. We cannot know whether these policy outcomes were due to mistakes on the part of caseworkers or to caseworkers' failure to communicate the legitimate reasons behind their actions. Either way, the women's experiences made them wary of the potential financial advantages of work. Past experience with what they perceived as the unpredictable nature of the welfare department led them to distrust the credibility of work incentive programs.

In the post-reform period, the women's distrust did not keep them from working; they were convinced that the sticks of the current policy were real. Yet they doubted the delivery of benefits just as the women interviewed before reform did. That is, for them the promises of work supports remained an illusion.

Michelle Brewer, an African American mother of two, who at the time of our interview was living in a shelter after her apartment was destroyed by fire, also believed that the welfare department was most interested in cutting off recipients' benefits. When asked if she had found that what the welfare office told her generally came true, she answered, "Any little thing that you don't follow up on, you will lose your benefits. It's very easy to get cut off. . . . One little slip-up or one little missing an appointment, no identification and you can easily lose your benefits."

The way Michelle interpreted the interview question reveals just how much she distrusted the department. The question was intended to determine whether she had found that the welfare department delivered on its promises of benefits. Instead, Michelle interpreted the question to be asking whether the welfare department delivered on its threats of denying benefits.

Women could be suspicious of the department's activities and doubt that benefits would be delivered whether or not they understood the benefits rules. The following exchange indicates that Renee Steele, another respondent interviewed after reform, had an understanding of how time limits worked that was very different from the written policy. It also shows that despite this difference, she clearly believed that the threat of forcing recipients off the rolls would be implemented.

Renee: [When I had] one child, I was only getting $292 [a month]. Now people are getting three hundred dollars and four hundred dollars. I think they give you all that money to rush you, to get you a job, to make your clock run out. That's why I think they raise the grant up . . .

Interviewer: Wait, why do you think they would raise the grant up, so that you get a job?
R: Yeah, because your time is running out quicker like that.

I: So if you, the more money they give you, the more quickly your time runs out?
R: The more money you're using up.

I: Did someone tell you this or . . .
R: This is just something I'm figuring out because all of a sudden it has changed now. . . .

No other woman interpreted time limits as related to the dollar amount of a cash assistance grant. Since Renee's unique understanding of the time limits was so dramatically different from how time limits are supposed to work—they are based on months of receipt, not amount of cash assistance received—this exchange appears to indicate that Renee actually misunderstood the rules (rather than that she was just reporting on how a rule was implemented). It also demonstrates that Renee believed that all of the welfare offices' practices were guided by the desire to move people off the rolls and into work. Hence, her distrust about the department's activities led her to believe in the department's goal of forcing welfare-to-work transitions.

An exchange with Flor Ramero, after she was asked what would happen to her welfare money if she got a job, perhaps illustrates best the nature of distrust many women voiced in the welfare department's promises. Even though her understanding of official rules matched the way they were written, she still doubted that benefits will be delivered.

Flor: They talk about, okay, if you do get a job they say they cut off like out of every three dollars you make, they cut off a dollar of what your TANF cash is, so that sounds good, but in reality we all know they ain't gonna do that. No, they lie.

Interviewer: They lie? And what are they gonna do?
F: They're gonna cut you off completely. The second they know you are working, they cut you off completely.

I: No matter what you're making?
F: If you're working fifteen hours, twenty hours, they cut you off completely.

As Flor was fully aware and understood, official Work Pays rules indeed stipulated that any low-wage woman working part time should lose from her welfare grant only one out of every three dollars she earns. But clearly, Flor did not trust that the Work Pays policy was ever carried out. She had no problem believing, however, that the welfare department's primary motive was to move clients off the welfare rolls.

Women in both time periods were unaware of certain official welfare policies, such as Work Pays, transitional benefits, or various post-reform work supports. Their lack of awareness of official policy could relate to several factors. Caseworkers might do a poor job of communicating official policies, whether because of incompetence, their own ignorance of complex and frequently changing rules, or subterfuge. If, however, as many clients suspected, official rules were not followed, then the street-level practices of caseworkers became the rules in practice.[20] Clients then had no incentive to learn official rules, which existed on paper only. Instead, they were motivated to learn only the procedures enacted at the street level. They learned these rules through their own experiences and through the stories shared by others in their social networks.

It is unclear from the women's interviews whether they were denied various benefits inappropriately, as many of the women assumed, or whether benefits were denied legitimately because of eligibility rules women did not know or understand. Both probably occurred. Welfare rules are so complex that many recipients may not be aware of rules that render them ineligible for a particular benefit. Other researchers, however, have indeed found that cash assistance clients have difficulty getting benefits, work supports, and services to which they are entitled.[21]

Again, whether recipients are denied benefits legitimately or illegitimately, if they *perceive* that they have been treated unfairly, they learn to distrust the welfare department. Regardless of what actually happens between caseworkers and clients, low-income women's *perceptions* of their interactions with caseworkers determine how they respond to work incentives. The question addressed here is whether low-income women perceive the welfare office to be trustworthy and thus work incentives to be credible. The answer, for many of the women interviewed in both time periods, was no.

Some may conclude that the dramatic decline in the welfare rolls and increases in employment since reform indicate that the new coercive measures are necessary and that the previous reliance on voluntary incentives was ineffective. The problem with that conclusion is that we do not know if the voluntary incentives alone could have worked in an environment where low-income women trusted their caseworkers and thus trusted that the incentives would be implemented properly. The evidence from the women's interviews is that this did not happen. Attention to women's social interactions with caseworkers in the context of the welfare office shows that part of the reason voluntary incentives are less effective is that in the process of their translation through caseworkers to women they lose their power. These findings suggest that actors respond not just to rules as legislated but to rules as communicated and delivered by other actors in a social context. Voluntary incentives alone may appear less effective only because they are not considered credible and hence women discount them.[22] Coercive measures, on the other hand, are fully credible. Women have no doubt they will be carried out.

Women's distrust in the welfare office led them to have different responses to welfare benefits in the two time periods I studied. While the distrust in caseworkers and the welfare office remained across the two time periods, because of the changing policy rules the same distrust led to opposite behaviors. Before reform, when the policy focus was more on providing voluntary incentives, women were reluctant to risk labor market entry for fear that the promise of these benefits would be broken and they would lose all welfare benefits if they began to work, even in very low-wage jobs that did not provide enough to support their families. After reform, women continued to doubt the reliability of the voluntary incentives but now were anxious to get into the labor market quickly before the coercive time limits and other benefit restrictions hit them.

UNDERSTANDING DISTRUST IN THE WELFARE OFFICE

Taking a job poses risks for a welfare recipient. She risks not being able to earn enough to keep her family afloat. She risks having no medical insurance coverage for herself and her children. She risks not being able to afford child care. Finally, given the bureaucratic hurdles involved, she risks not being able to get back onto welfare if the job does not work out. In short, for a recipient to respond to a work incentive and to voluntarily leave the welfare rolls for the workplace represents a risk that she will be worse off once she does so.

Having trust in one's interaction partners gives one the confidence to take risks in the face of uncertainty. But as we have seen, few welfare recipients trust their caseworkers. They thus do not believe work supports such as Work Pays and continued medical coverage and child care subsidies will be delivered. Many women before reform thus deemed voluntarily moving from welfare to work too risky.

Women since reform also did not believe that responding to voluntary incentives—Work Pays or other work supports—would pay off. Trust was less necessary to get women to respond to the post-reform coercive measures, however. In fact, the very fact that the women distrusted caseworkers made them believe that the coercive measures—time limits and work requirements—would be applied. It was their distrust in caseworkers that made women believe these measures would be carried out. In a world where distrust is pervasive, it is true that sticks are more effective than carrots. But it is a mistake to conclude that coercive measures are required for results. Voluntary incentives would achieve greater success if the people at whom they were directed trusted that they would be honored.

Why did the women interviewed distrust their caseworkers? Most women learned their distrust through direct experience. They entered their interactions with the welfare department trusting that they would be treated respectfully and that certain benefits would be delivered dependably. When their expectations were not met, their attitude toward the department shifted and they began to doubt that caseworkers would be supportive or reliable. We cannot know whether their perceptions of caseworker untrustworthiness reflected actual untrustworthiness or simply miscommunication about what the rules were and hence what benefits were deserved. Either way, their expectations were not met and the lesson they learned was to distrust.

Some women heard stories from friends or family about unreliable or disrespectful caseworkers and thus entered into their interactions in welfare offices already skeptical about how they would be treated. Others provided less concrete stories about caseworkers in explanation of their distrust, reflecting a more general community wisdom that caseworkers could not be trusted. Their distrust was assumed preemptively, as if it might provide some kind of protection against the attacks on their egos or their economic well-being that they suspected were coming. We also might note, as Kala did, that to the degree women enter their interactions with caseworkers with a distrustful stance (Kala calls this an "attitude"), they may bring out hostility in caseworkers. A resulting mutual escalation of distrust may result.

But in all cases, what undergirds distrust is the enormous power caseworkers hold over clients and the structure of the welfare office itself. Caseworkers are the gatekeepers to desperately sought financial resources. In addition, because the goal of welfare policy is to move people off the rolls as quickly as possible, the welfare office is structured in a way that rewards caseworkers for doing so and not for treating people respectfully, making sure they understand policies, or reliably delivering benefits. There is also no penalty against caseworkers who express their frustration with the demands of their job and with clients (who may themselves be uncooperative at times) by treating those clients rudely.[23] Welfare recipients need cash assistance from caseworkers because they are at the very bottom of the income distribution. Most have incomes greatly below the poverty line. They are also at the bottom of the power hierarchy in welfare offices, since they need the resources that caseworkers are in charge of doling out. Their need for the assistance that caseworkers control is acute. Without it, many risk homelessness, food insecurity, loss of heat, and other hardships. It is thus welfare recipients' location at the bottom of two different structures—the macrostructure of the U.S. class system and the mesostructure of the welfare office—that leads them to feel vulnerable to caseworker power over them. Their disadvantaged position in both these structures exposes them to all sources of distrust. It causes them to have actual experiences that teach them to distrust caseworkers, to know others with such experiences, or to draw upon a general distrust of government authority as a way to preemptively protect themselves.

REDUCING DISTRUST IN THE WELFARE OFFICE

If indeed distrust stems in part from the structure of the welfare office, then shifts in that structure, particularly in how it shapes caseworker-client interaction, are the key to reducing distrust. Changing the incentive structure in which caseworkers operate is highly unlikely given the political popularity of moving welfare recipients off the rolls, but it may be the only way to increase low-income women's trust in the welfare office. An experimental program for low-income families in Milwaukee called New Hope, which offered sizable and voluntary work incentives to move families into the labor market, enjoyed remarkable success.[24] The incentive structure for New Hope program personnel was quite different from that for welfare caseworkers and stressed the importance of respectful and supportive interaction with clients. Clearly, the nature of the work incentives is important, but this different approach to program personnel-client interaction and the related focus on voluntary carrots rather than mandatory sticks probably also played a role in New Hope's success.

Distrust in caseworkers and the welfare offices they represent also stems in part from a lack of transparency. Welfare rules are complicated and hard to decipher. When women were denied benefits, it could have been because a byzantine set of rules rendered them ineligible legitimately. It also could have been because rules were not implemented as they were written. Building trust requires that both of these potential problems be addressed. Welfare rules need to be simpler and clearer so that when they are applied women understand why they were applied. These rules then must be implemented the way they are written so that women trust that the incentives of official policy will be delivered.

Many low-income mothers' lives are chaotic, stressful, and filled with tragedy. The near-total inflexibility of current welfare policy ignores this fact. Many of the women I interviewed agreed with the basic goals put in place by reform but questioned why it had to be so unforgiving if circumstances made fulfilling requirements on time too difficult or too costly for children. Making the system more flexible would go a long way to reducing distrust in what is perceived as a draconian system. Interestingly, the welfare office personnel with whom I had informational interviews also expressed the belief that the system was too inflexible given recipients' situations.

Trust would also be enhanced if incentives were bigger. Many incentives, such as the Work Pays program and the child care subsidy, are of small monetary value. If they were more sizable (and assuming they were credible to low-income women), they could help women move voluntarily into the labor market before coercive measures such as sanctions and work requirements would take over. Credible and valuable voluntary incentives would probably increase recipient trust.

I believe all of my above suggestions would increase recipient trust in caseworkers and in the welfare offices they represent. But I do not believe they would eliminate distrust in the welfare system. As long as we have a punitive and stigmatizing welfare state that does not provide an adequate level of support to families and as long as the dominant society blames low-income families for our social ills, low-income mothers will probably retain their distrust in dominant institutions. This distrust keeps them from taking the risk of responding to voluntary incentives (in this case to enter the labor market). When those incentives are real, distrust costs these women the chance to improve their lot. But if they are indeed just an illusion, distrust may protect the women from further economic hardship.

THREE "I Couldn't Put Up with It No More"

PERCEIVED MISTREATMENT AND DISTRUST AT WORK

> He said, "Either you stick those kids in a closet, or if you
> don't come back to work on Sunday night, then don't
> come at all." . . . If he's willing to say that, he's willing to
> say a lot more. And that was it. That was it for that job.
>
> —Elena Salinas

Juanita Soto, the thirty-eight-year-old Puerto Rican mother of three whom we met in the last chapter as I folded laundry with her in her kitchen, had once considered herself a success. All the talk about welfare mothers turning their lives around was really true in her case—and she had done it even before welfare reform. She signed herself up for classes at the Learning Place, a job-training center for low-income women with a two-year program that first addressed her experience with domestic violence and then taught her basic skills and eventually specific office skills. Finally, the icing on the cake: she landed a job as a receptionist in a health care clinic and left the welfare rolls. The pay was $8.00 per hour, almost twice the minimum wage at the time of $4.25, and she received medical benefits.[1] Not only had the job allowed her to use her new office skills, but since she also did all of the needed translation for

Spanish-speaking patients her dream of a job helping people had come true as well.

So why did the job last only two years? Did Juanita's child care arrangements fall through? Were the skill demands of her job beyond her level of training? Did she get sucked back into the type of chaotic personal life she had shared earlier with her former husband, who was a drug dealer? No, the job did not end for any of these individual-level reasons. Instead, it ended because of what was happening at Juanita's workplace. Juanita could no longer stand her boss's treatment of her, and on the basis of her experiences at work she lost all trust that she would ever be treated the way she felt she deserved.

During her two years of employment at the clinic, Juanita and her two young children enjoyed their new financial position.[2] Juanita could buy the children the clothes they needed, there were enough groceries to last each week, and the constant anxieties about paying bills subsided. Despite these financial benefits, Juanita quit. As she explained, "[My supervisor] kind of stressed me out really bad. It affected my asthma . . . so I just ended up leaving there." The decision had enormous financial consequences. Juanita had to return to welfare for a few months, and, she says, "I was constantly selling my food stamps or selling my furniture . . . which is half [of what it was] now. And with two kids, it's kind of hard. . . . Girl, it was the worst three months in my life."

At one point in time, Juanita could have been held up as a model success story for those supporting welfare-to-work policies, but a mere two years later she fell right back to where she had started. It is hard to imagine what would lead Juanita to leave a job that offered her security, but her description of her boss's behavior makes her decision clearer. Juanita felt that her supervisor singled her out, treating her with particular insensitivity.

> She like kind of insult me or embarrass me in front of people or talk loud to me or make me feel like I was invalid, you know. And I would just [be] like . . . "You have something to say, pull me to the side. Don't do this in front of patients, you know . . ." I'm with a patient trying to see them scheduled and she'll come and [speaking loudly], "You need to get your timesheet. You know your times has got to get in today." You know,

instead of saying, "Excuse me, make sure you get your timesheet in today . . ." You know, real bold.

Juanita also felt that her supervisor was unduly inflexible, particularly in response to the asthma attacks Juanita suffered. "There was twice I had an attack . . . and the doctors there examined me and they even gave me a shot and recommended for me to go home, and she said 'No. . . . Let her just lie there for an hour.' . . . I would come home upset, stressed out. I would even cry because . . . I didn't like the way I was being treated, but I didn't want to quit because I had to work for the kids."

Juanita's parents encouraged her to stick it out, but Juanita finally reached a breaking point and quit. "And my father kept saying and my mother, . . . 'Hang on, hang on, hang on.' . . . One day I just said, 'I can't take it, God forgive me, I'm not going to go back.' . . . I just told [my supervisor], 'I'm not coming back.' She said, 'That's the best thing you ever did.'"

In our interview, Juanita was hesitant at first to speculate about the reasons for her supervisor's behavior. At first she indicated that her supervisor might have felt "threatened" by her for some reason. But after some probing, Juanita explained that her coworkers attributed the supervisor's actions to racial and ethnic prejudice. Her coworkers were all African American, but they had no trouble telling Juanita that their African American supervisor did not like her because she was Latina.

> I was the only Puerto Rican. . . . One of the girls that used to work there, she came out and told me, "She has it in for you because she's prejudiced." . . . I overlook it because sometimes people just talk just to talk. But . . . another elderly lady said the same thing. "Baby, she has it in for you. She has it in for you because she doesn't like Hispanics; especially when there's a lot of Mexicans coming in [and] you got to translate. . . . Baby, you just gotta hold onto yourself because she's one bitch." You know, I could understand if I wasn't working right or I did something wrong or I wasn't catching on to the work or something, but to be treated like . . . I hate . . . people being prejudiced.

At first, Juanita resisted accepting her coworkers' explanation for her supervisor's behavior, but over time she came to agree that she was the victim of prejudice. She felt trapped. She needed the job and knew that there were very few jobs that she could get that would pay as well and let her do work that interested her. Worse yet, she knew her supervisor knew she needed the job. Juanita figured that's what made her supervisor think she could treat Juanita however she liked.

Eventually Juanita lodged a complaint with the Human Resources Department. She was told that there had been other complaints about her supervisor and was asked to write down what had happened for the supervisor's file. But three of the others who had complaints had left the job, and two more were very young (in their early twenties) and were, in Juanita's words, "too scared" to pursue it. As a result, no action was taken. Human Resources' failure to do anything beyond collect written complaints left Juanita convinced that she would never be treated fairly at work.

After deciding to leave, Juanita returned to public aid and had the three terrible months mentioned above. She soon found a job, however, at another health care center. At this job Juanita was just filing, which she saw as a step down from the receptionist and translation duties of her previous position. "So it's like I went down instead of up," she explained.

Even so, Juanita did not regret her decision to leave her receptionist job. She felt that the emotional stress created by her previous job was unhealthy both for herself and for her eight-year-old daughter and twelve-year-old son who lived with her. At the new job, her interactions with her supervisor had none of the tension of her past experience. She was free from the suspicions about discrimination that she harbored in her old job. "I like it. I like it a lot. . . . I look forward to getting up in the morning, going there, because it's like . . . I'm not being overlooked at or talked about or anything like that. And my boss . . . she's real nice, she's a very nice lady."

Still, the financial cost of changing jobs was substantial. The new job paid only $6.25 an hour compared to the $8.00 rate of the previous job, almost a 25 percent pay cut.[3] Even though she still received medical benefits, Juanita felt the difference.

It is hard. And I'm used to having groceries in the house. Now it's like . . . once again, once a month, have groceries and then there's like a limit

... what they could eat and then we'd have to save the rest for the next week. . . . I don't like that. I'm not used to living like that. And now it's like . . . one loaf of bread for this whole week. The next loaf for the next week. . . . They're used to just eating whatever they wanted that's there, you know. And now it's like . . . "You can't eat this because we have to save it for next week." I wasn't raised like that. And it bothers me.

Juanita's experience shows the role played by social interactions at work and the distrust they can produce. Conflict-laden interaction and distrust can lead women to leave jobs even if those jobs provide greatly needed financial advantages. We of course do not know what actually happens inside workplaces and what supervisors' perceptions of the events are. No doubt, supervisors face challenges managing workers, particularly those with little previous work experience. They too go through a process in which social interactions teach them to trust or distrust their employees. Workers who enter into these interactions distrusting their bosses may behave in ways that are a warning sign to those bosses that the workers will not be committed to the job. In Juanita's case, the fact that she was hesitant to believe her supervisor's prejudices and that her coworkers (rather than she) identified them lends support to her side of the story. Ultimately, however, just as in the case of the welfare office and caseworkers, it does not fully matter what the supervisor's side is. What matters is that Juanita perceived mistreatment, that this perception led to her distrust in her boss, and that the perceived mistreatment and distrust were related to her decision to quit.

Juanita was not in a strong position to make matters better at work. She needed the job more than the workplace needed her. Jobs paying that much over the minimum wage and offering more stimulation than flipping burgers or cleaning offices were not easy to come by. Given that, Juanita knew she had little if any power to demand better conditions, and the unresponsiveness of the human resources complaint process proved her right.

Juanita, and all of the women interviewed, had to operate in a labor market and in specific workplaces that were not hospitable to low-wage workers. As discussed in chapter 1, wages for low-skill workers have been falling because of both globalization and technological advances requiring workers to have technical skills; income inequality has been growing; and job security and unionization have declined.[4] These structural features of the labor market at large have eroded worker power in their specific workplaces. Workers like Juanita have very little recourse when they feel mistreated, and they know it. The larger context of the labor market sets the stage for workers like Juanita to distrust their supervisors and the work enterprises they represent. They also lead workers to consider lodging complaints futile.

A persistent and dominant goal of welfare policy is to move low-income women into jobs and off the welfare rolls. The women want this outcome too. Even more important for the women's long-term financial well-being than finding jobs is the longevity of those jobs. The interviews with the women in this study revealed the close relationship between job longevity and the level of trust in workplace social interactions.

In the workplace, both employers and workers face uncertainty and risks. Employers do not know if employees will be competent and honest. Workers do not know if employers will treat them well. In interactions where uncertainty and risk are present, trust encourages cooperation and, potentially, desirable outcomes. In the women's descriptions of their work experiences, it became clear that distrust on both sides was frequent. Employers often doubted the trustworthiness of the women, at times accusing them of stealing from the workplace or breaking other rules, which in turn led the women to lose trust that they would be treated fairly.

This mutual distrust often resulted in the women being fired or quitting. Quits often occurred without any attempted recourse. That is, women did not trust that a procedure that respected their rights would be followed. They might even assume that they did not have *any* rights in the workplace. They chose to instead leave the job. Some women did take steps to address mistreatment, such as not being allowed to leave when a shift was over or not being paid promised wages, but they eventually quit when no action was taken. Thus the lack of cooperation and trust between the women and their supervisors, and at times their coworkers, played an important role in the sustainability of the women's employment.

Juanita gave her job much more of a chance than other women gave theirs. She stayed for two years before giving up. As their stories will show, other women were quick to quit at the first sign that supervisors could not be trusted to treat them well. While their cases may give us reason to be skeptical about what actually happened, they nevertheless highlight the premium that many women put on being respected. Women who were quick to see disrespect, and to quit on that basis with no real information about an employer's mind-set or intentions, might be more generally primed by their disadvantaged position in the labor market and society at large to assume they would be disrespected and mistreated and to use distrust as a way to protect themselves.

As Elijah Anderson, Philippe Bourgois, and others have discussed, the importance of respectful treatment in low-income communities is high.[5] Perhaps one's self-respect is one of the few things one can "own" or control when resources are so scarce. Low-income people may also be keenly aware of a dominant society that holds them in little esteem, and this may make them particularly sensitive to signs of disrespect. Finally, getting respect on the street is probably an important survival skill.[6] For all of these reasons, low-wage workers may be especially quick to sense disrespectful treatment from a supervisor at work even if none is intended. Again, for my argument, the intentions of supervisors do not fully matter. What matters is that the social interaction leaves a worker with an impression, and that impression often leads the worker to leave her job. The structural changes in the labor market discussed in chapter 1 have left low-skill workers with little power. Low-skill workers know the employers have little reason to invest in them. They know that managers want a flexible workforce while workers want security. This lack of shared interests sets the stage for workers' distrust in their supervisors.

WELFARE REFORM AND THE WORKPLACE

Before the welfare reform act was passed in 1996, if women left jobs and had no source of income, they were usually eligible for cash assistance benefits that were not time limited.[7] In fact, prior to reform, holding a low-wage job was not always a financial advantage over receiving welfare and being unemployed.[8] Kathryn Edin and Laura Lein painstakingly show that the job-related costs of child care, transportation, and work clothing often made the budgets of low-wage workers as tight as, or even tighter than, those of women who relied on welfare alone.[9] If "work does not pay," as David Ellwood warned in his 1988 book *Poor Support*, few incentives to maintain employment remain.[10] Caseworkers did encourage clients to find work and leave the rolls, but employment was in most respects voluntary.

Increasing the Incentive to Work

Since reform, the financial incentives have been dramatically altered. Women can cycle between low-wage jobs and cash assistance only until they have exhausted their time limits.[11] Each time a woman returns to welfare, that time limit creeps closer. Caseworkers pressure clients to find jobs long before time limits approach and discourage would-be clients from taking welfare benefits except as a last resort. The application process for cash assistance has always been difficult, and proving eligibility was not assured even before reform. But since reform, when women leave jobs they do so with much less confidence that reliable cash assistance awaits them to fill the financial void left by lost wages. In addition to attempting to force a transition to work through work requirements and time limits on welfare receipt, reform increased funding for work supports such as job training and child care and transportation subsidies. While these policies did address some of the barriers women faced in seeking employment, the policies exclusively addressed factors outside the workplace itself. Welfare reform did not make changes to any of the structural aspects of the labor market or of specific workplaces. As we shall see, these structural aspects, which result in low-wage workers' subordination and lack of power, promote distrust.

Distrust and Job Turnover Levels Remain Unchanged

The increased financial incentives to work since reform might be expected to trump the challenges of difficult social interactions in the workplace. The experiences recounted by women interviewed since reform, however, do not support this expectation. Women interviewed after reform discussed mistreatment at work and reported distrusting relationships with employers just as those interviewed before reform did. More important, they too left jobs or lost jobs because of various forms of workplace conflict and the distrust that ensued. Conflicts arose typically over accusations of stealing, perceived sexual harassment and discrimination, and scheduling and work conditions.

Before reform, about a fifth of the twenty-six women (21 percent) reported quitting jobs in response to workplace conflict, and an additional 17 percent were fired after conflicts. Some women whose jobs ended because of workplace conflicts had extensive work histories, including long tenures in some positions, so they had demonstrated their capability of holding jobs. But the atmosphere inside the workplace often posed challenges to maintaining employment. The only reasons for leaving or losing a job that were reported more frequently were pregnancy and childbirth (46 percent of women) and the closure of workplaces (23 percent).[12]

After reform, almost a third of the sixty-nine women interviewed (31 percent) said they had quit work after conflicts with supervisors or coworkers, and another 15 percent had been fired because of workplace conflicts. Only pregnancy and childbirth was a more common reason for jobs ending (43 percent).[13] After reform, only 13 percent of women lost jobs on account of a workplace closing.

These similarities before and after reform may seem surprising since the incentive to retain employment after reform would be so much higher. However, welfare reform did nothing directly to change the nature of the interactions between low-wage workers and their employers and coworkers.[14] Given the continuation of the structural forces that shape these interactions, such as increased skill demands that lower the value and hence the voice of low-skill workers, the fact that workplace conflict and its resultant distrust still constituted a major cause of turnover for the women interviewed after reform is not surprising. In fact, it is to be expected.

Low-wage jobs usually require few of the hard skills developed through conventional education and training.[15] Workers sign on to the jobs without having high levels of such skills, and once they are in the jobs, employers spend almost no time or money training them. Hence employers are not invested in any one specific worker; they can easily find another to take her place. Employees are not naive. They know that while employers need workers, they do not need any particular worker. This basic fact gives employers a lot of power and low-wage workers almost none.

Other changes in the labor market over recent decades have even further reduced the power of low-wage workers. The great decline in unionization has eroded the ability of workers en masse to demand job security. Technological developments that brought a computerized revolution to the workplace have caused the demand for low-wage, low-skill workers to plummet. Companies' movement toward hiring a contingent, temporary, and flexible workforce rather than permanent workers renders low-wage workers even less secure.[16]

All of these structural aspects of today's low-wage labor market that make the worker so powerless come into play in how workers and supervisors interact. Many of the women I interviewed knew how easily they could be mistreated or let go by employers who had no investment in them, and sometimes the women acted, perhaps preemptively, by distrusting quickly and quitting at the first signs of trouble. As we saw in the case of the welfare office, some of this distrust was learned through actual experiences of being mistreated (or at least perceiving mistreatment) by supervisors, and some might have been brought into the workplace by women whose practice was to use distrust as a way to maintain dignity in a demeaning situation.

Structural aspects of the labor market sometimes work in concert with structural aspects of the new welfare policy. One difference since reform is that employers know that people need to keep their jobs in order to fulfill welfare requirements. Some women I interviewed felt that employers took advantage of them, assuming that they would have no choice but to put up with mistreatment.

ISSUES OF DISTRUST IN THE WORKPLACE

What emerges from the workplace stories told by women interviewed both before and after reform is that work skills, the ability to perform job

tasks, and problems external to the workplace, such as child care interruptions, do not seem to be the only explanations of job turnover. What
happens inside the workplace between workers and supervisors also
seems to play a role. The full validity of the women's stories is not clear,
nor does it matter. What matters is that supervisors act in ways, or are
perceived to act in ways, that produce the women's distrust, and that the
women then quit.

A comparison between two women, both interviewed after reform, at
opposite extremes of workplace performance makes this point abundantly clear. Loïc Wacquant, Sharon Hays, and others have warned
against idealizing the character of those in poverty.[17] Low-income people, like anyone else, they argue, are imperfect and varied. Some are
more virtuous than others, and most are more virtuous at some times in
their lives than at other times. This point is well taken and is supported
by the stories of the women in this book. When I describe Anabella
Mendoza, however, it is difficult to avoid painting a saintly picture.

Anabella arrived in Chicago in the early 1990s, alone and pregnant,
having entered the United States undocumented from South America.
Ever since, she had worked tirelessly to raise her now three children,
had become a leader in the immigrant rights movement, had been a presence (and even surrogate parent) for neighborhood children in need of
adult support, and had started an organization to teach children in her
community South American folk dance (both to keep the tradition alive
and to keep the kids off the streets). With a few short interruptions
during which she received welfare, she had also worked steadily in a
series of often backbreaking jobs—literally, as one at a golf club ended
when she fell on the job and needed back surgery—to support her family,
which included herself and her three children, ages fifteen, twelve,
and ten.

Having to leave the job at the golf club, which she had last held
about four years before I met her, was especially hard for Anabella. She
had been close to her supervisor, who had treated her like a surrogate
daughter. He had allowed her to bring her kids to work if she ever had to
work on a weekend or a holiday. She was obviously committed to the job
because it was a two-hour bus ride each way to and from the job and

sometimes she had to start at five a.m. She would have returned to the job, but it was just too difficult for her back. She remained close, however, with the supervisor and his family, who sometimes had her and her kids over for dinner.

Anabella maintained a cheerful demeanor and sense of humor even though at age thirty-six she had survived many difficulties, including cancer surgery. Her most recent job as an administrative assistant at a social services agency had ended (after two years and after I interviewed her several times) only because the funding for the position ran out. Her supervisor, whom I met on several occasions when I interviewed Anabella at her workplace, had nothing but praise for Anabella, whose talents the supervisor immediately recognized and groomed by giving her more and more responsibility over time. According to her supervisor, she was always on time, always did the work, and was always reliable. Of all the women I interviewed, at both time points, Anabella appeared one of the most capable, hardworking, and dedicated.

But despite Anabella's clear talents as a worker, she too was driven to quit a job because of an interaction she had with a supervisor. She was working as a cashier in a restaurant. One day she had a doctor's appointment for one of her children and asked for the morning off, which her boss granted. After the appointment, she dropped her child off at the babysitter's and called her boss on her way to work. Anabella's English was proficient but not fluent, and her boss only spoke a little Spanish, but sometimes he liked to speak Spanish with her. In a playful mood, Anabella spoke Spanish and joked about whether the boss needed her because otherwise she might not come in. "I said in Spanish, it was a joke, 'Oh, like do you still need me?' You know, 'I'm on my way.' And he got mad, saying, 'You know that you're supposed to be in. You have to come. It's not . . . if I need you or not.' . . . Sometimes I joke, but for me it was a little joke. Anyway, he got mad, and I was just calling saying, you know, 'I'm on my way.' I just said, 'Do you still need me?'"

When she arrived at work soon after, her boss was furious and began to berate her. To this day, Anabella does not really know why he was so upset. She suspects either that they miscommunicated in their Spanish conversation and he thought she had said something else or that deep down he was angry that she had taken the morning off for her child's medical appointment, even though he had given his permission. "I think he maybe didn't understand exactly. When I got back, he was very mad and he was screaming at me. And I was like, 'Okay, I'm sorry, I had a doctor appointment.' And [he said] 'But why you wouldn't make an appointment . . . when you're not working?' [I said] 'When it's about my kid, I'm sorry, if I have to go, I'm going.'"

Even though Anabella was a conscientious worker, as her long work history, her long tenure in other positions, and the glowing report given to me by her most recent supervisor all attested, she drew the same line that many of the women before reform did. If a supervisor did not speak civilly to her and did not respect important personal needs such as health or parental responsibilities, she was unwilling to remain in the job. Anabella quit on the spot. "So he start telling me that . . . it's not gonna be like that all the time. So I said, 'Okay.' I take off my little hat that I had and my apron [she pantomimes removing the hat and the apron that were part of her uniform] and I put them on the table and I left. I said, 'Thank you very much and see you.'"

Actually, Anabella elaborated later that she had first offered to stay for two days while the manager tried to find someone else, but when he said he did not want to find somebody, she left. Later, he called her, apologized, asked her to come back, and even offered a promotion, but she declined. "First I said, 'Okay, you have two days to try to find out somebody.' But he said, 'I don't wanna find somebody.' . . . So I left and he called me after saying that okay, I should come back, but I didn't want to. I was kind of upset and I said, 'No, I can find some other [job].' . . . He called me and he even offered me to be a manager, because he saw that I know everything from that store. I didn't want to go back."

She then found a job cleaning a private house and, soon after, joined a friend doing office cleaning. The work was definitely a step down from what she had been doing, but Anabella believed in honest work.

> I find a job where I used to clean a house twice a week, so that's what I was doing . . . . Like I said to my kids, "It doesn't matter what you do, you know. It's honest job, you don't have to be ashamed, you know. I

used to clean a house and then I had a friend that she used to clean an office and she told me that if I go and help her that she was gonna give me twenty dollars and I said, "Yeah, why not," and I used to go with her to help her.

The cleaning jobs offered fewer hours and provided less income than the cashier job. They also did not enhance Anabella's résumé as the manager position would have. It took Anabella a long time to find a better job that offered more money and responsibilities. But Anabella was resolute. She would not work for someone who did not respect her or her responsibilities as a mother. In sharp contrast, the job at the golf club, which she had held prior to the cashier job, had allowed her to bring her children to work when her child care arrangements fell through. She stayed at that job for three years and left only when she sustained her back injury. Anabella had a long history as a good worker, but the assault on her dignity by her supervisor at the restaurant cashier job was a core issue for her.

Latreece Allen, an African American mother of six (three preschool girls and three teenaged boys), was very different from Anabella Mendoza. She talked a mile a minute and often got ahead of herself, having to backtrack when it became clear the listener had not followed. She joked a lot with those around her and seemed pretty adept at getting out of responsibilities at work by just being Latreece—that is, by laughing off requests, saying she was getting right to something and then winking as if to indicate she would get to it only when she was ready, as I observed when visiting with her at work. She was engaging and personable, often laughing and smiling, but used a completely different, angry voice when imitating herself talking to other kids' parents, school principals, or whoever else she felt had unfairly accused her children. While Latreece at first seemed a little scattered and lacking in seriousness, almost like a teenager herself, she was probably pretty good at sticking up for her rights.

Latreece worked in building maintenance at a not-for-profit housing agency that managed several apartment buildings providing low-income housing. She answered to the building manager and conducted tasks such as cleaning common areas and hauling trash out of the buildings. Because she worked on her own in the buildings, she had more autonomy than workers in a fast-food restaurant or on an assembly line. By all accounts, her own included, Latreece found it hard to show up on time and to get her work done. On three separate days that I visited with Latreece at her workplace, she was late for work, once by more than an hour. It was especially hard for Latreece to get to work on time now that she had moved far away from her job doing janitorial work in a housing complex. While her new house was inconveniently located, it was large enough for her six children and was farther away from the temptations of the street facing her son.

Mornings were chaotic getting her three little girls dressed, fed, and off to whoever was watching them for the day. She was often also managing the latest problem with James, her second-oldest son, a young teen who frequently ran away and who Latreece feared was already in the grips of gang life. Latreece had spent many nights searching the streets for her son, banging on the doors of his friends' houses. Our first visit, to which she was late, occurred the morning after one such night, and Latreece was a mess. She kept clutching her heart, saying it was beating fast and she was stressed out. Another time she called me, exasperated that none of her calls to city agencies had produced any help. "Basically they got no help for him. I want to try to keep him from jail. But I guess I just have to let him go, whatever happens happens. If I have to bury him, I bury him." Latreece was a devoted and fiercely protective mother, but she thought she had lost James. It is no wonder she found it hard to make her job her first priority.

If anyone would have trouble holding a low-wage job, it would seem to be Latreece. Routine tardiness and disregarding supervisors' requests seem fairly guaranteed ways to lose jobs in the low-wage sector, where punctuality and obedience to authority are often mandatory. Yet at the time of our interview Latreece had held her current job for five years, ever since welfare reform policies had forced her into the labor market. Five years was an unusually long job tenure among women at either time period. Many jobs lasted for only a few months. Many others lasted for a year or two at most. Very few women held jobs for longer than two years. Latreece attributed her success to her understanding and flexible supervisor. "Oh yeah, she's really supportive. My boss know the thing isn't, see we, I'm so open to her, I don't lie to her if I'm late. Whatever the needs is, when I need it, I tell her the truth. I don't try to scheme outta or get paid or none of that. I tell her exactly what the issues is and how I'm gonna resolve it and what I need from her, and we work it out from there."

I asked Latreece how her boss handled her pay when she was late, since I had observed (and Latreece had discussed) her frequent tardiness.

> She let me, not all the time though. She been on me lately. I'm late, she just take it [meaning her pay for the time she missed] away. But if sometimes, 'cause my job could last over, past five o'clock, it not supposed to, but if I'm in the middle of something . . . why not go and finish it. So, we'll finish it up. So sometimes I be forty-five minutes over, . . . maybe a hour in some cases, so she blend that in. But it's not always the thing to do. . . . If I just said I woke up late and ran late, that's not a good excuse. But if, sometimes I get the kids ready in the morning and I move[d] farther away and I be running late, and [in] that case, then she might give me a little [break].

Latreece trusted her supervisor to be fair, and her supervisor appeared to trust Latreece to be honest. As a result, Latreece's infractions led neither to her being fired nor to the acrimony that led other women to quit.

The comparison between Anabella Mendoza and Latreece Allen is telling. Anabella was a model worker—reliable, serious, hardworking, and a leader able and willing to take on more and more responsibility. Her work performance was supported by a stable home life, with three children who stayed off the streets and did well in school. Latreece was an unreliable worker. She was routinely late and did not seem terribly committed to getting job tasks done on time, as her winks to me after telling her supervisor she would get right on a task attested. Her six children were a lot to manage, especially since three of them were under the age of six and one was a deeply troubled teen.

Yet it was Anabella's job at the restaurant that did not last, not Latreece's janitorial job. It is impossible to argue that Anabella's shorter tenure was due to inferior performance. Instead, it was due to the different relationship she had with her supervisor. Latreece probably would not have lasted in Anabella's restaurant job either, and Anabella had flourished in other jobs with other supervisors. These two women's cases—and many other similar stories in my data—provide one clear indication that conditions within the workplace play an important role, separate from workers' individual traits, in shaping employment outcomes.

Many other women, at both time periods, shared stories about workplace conflicts and their related distrust of employers that were similar to the one Anabella told. The conflicts in the workplace reported by the entire sample of women mostly fell into three categories: employers' suspicions about stealing or employees' suspicions about nonpayment of money owed; overt or suspected discrimination, whether racial or sexual; and disagreements over work schedules and work conditions.

Suspicions about Stealing and Nonpayment of Money Owed

Distrust over money flowed in both directions between women and their employers. Employers feared that their employees would steal from them, while workers did not believe they could rely on bosses to pay them what they were owed. A number of women told stories in which their supervisors suspected them of stealing. These accusations led the women to distrust that supervisors who were so quick to suspect them would ever treat them fairly.

Tahiera Jackson, an African American mother who was twenty-eight and had one six-year-old daughter when we met during the pre-reform interviews, explained that she had left her most recent job because her bosses did not trust her and thus she did not trust them to treat her fairly. She had worked at a neighborhood family-owned convenience store until she was accused of stealing money from the cash register. She explained, "I quit there, because the cash register kept coming up short, because everybody go in the same cash register, and they were saying I was taking money. And I didn't take no money from them. . . . I told them I didn't take their money. I have money on my own. I don't need to steal no money from y'all."

When I asked what had happened next, Tahiera explained that nothing had happened on the owners' end. They listened to what she said and did not fire her. However, Tahiera was offended by the accusation and took it as a sign of racism. The store was owned by an Arab American family, and, pointing to their treatment of both herself and a friend who had worked in the store previously, Tahiera believed they were prejudiced against African Americans. Certain that racial prejudice would lead her to be accused again, Tahiera quit. When I asked if she thought about it a lot, she said, "No, I just quit. I just walked out of the store. . . . I just couldn't go back after that." After a few days, the owners discovered that another worker had been the one stealing. They apologized to Tahiera and asked her to come back, but her mind was made up. She did not trust that it would not happen again. "They found out who was taking it and asked me to come back, but I didn't want to. . . . Yup [they apologized], but I didn't want to come back now, because it might happen again. Because I was the only black person working in it. . . . They do a lot of people like that, that come in and work for them. My friend used to work there too. They did her like that too."

It is not clear from Tahiera's side of the story whether the owners simply interviewed all of the employees as a matter of routine when the register was coming up short or whether they singled out Tahiera and actively accused her. She says in the first of her quotes above that "they were saying I was taking money," which certainly sounds as if they were directly accusing her, and only her. But later, when I asked what had happened after she denied it, she said, "Nothing, they just let me go. [By which she meant they let her go from the conversation, not that they fired her]. So I quit." This second quote makes it sound more as if the owners asked her questions about the incident and accepted her denial, at least at that point. If this latter scenario is what occurred, then we might consider Tahiera to have read into her employers' actions motives that were not there from the employers' perspective.

What is clear is that Tahiera took the conversation with the owners about the incident as an accusation and, further, that she attributed the accusation to her being the only African American employee. It is possible that other previous interactions with the owners had given Tahiera more evidence of racism, but she did not share these. The interview indicates instead that her reading of the incident was based on her knowledge of her friend's similar interactions with the owners. We might also imagine that Tahiera was aware more generally of the racial attitudes employers hold about workers.[18] Tahiera's story thus may be an example of distrust being learned not only from direct experience but also from the experiences of others and from general knowledge of employer beliefs about low-income minority workers. Her response may also be in keeping with the importance of the maintenance of self-respect, as discussed above. A reader might wonder whether Tahiera was too quick to come to her conclusion and whether she gave up a job unnecessarily. Tahiera, however, asserted she had no choice. She felt she had seen this movie before and she knew what was next in the script. She figured if she was not fired this time, she probably would be next time. It was better to get out before that happened.

As in Juanita Soto's case told at the beginning of this chapter and in Tahiera's case, the suspicion that employers hold racial and ethnic biases was a prime source of distrust for employees who were trying to assess how much they could count on fair treatment and stability in a job. Some entered workplaces trusting, as Juanita did, only to develop distrust over time through experience and coworker confirmation. Others, such as Tahiera, might begin with doubts about employers' motivations gleaned from friends' experiences and probably also from a more general sense that it was hard for some groups, African Americans in Tahiera's case, to get a fair shake in the workplace. One's own experiences on the job then might confirm these initial suspicions.

Tahiera's story shares elements with the story I told in the Introduction about Bethany Grant quitting her job as a cashier in a downtown office building's convenience store. Bethany, like Tahiera, was accused of stealing on the job and was later vindicated. While she did not raise racial discrimination as a factor in her accusation (perhaps because her supervisor was also African American), she was similarly offended and concluded that she could no longer count on being fairly treated at work. She too quit, returning to welfare before cycling into another job.

Bethany took longer than Tahiera to make up her mind about quitting, though she left more quickly than Juanita did. For her, quitting was less about a single incident, since her feelings of mistreatment were based on an accumulation of her supervisor's actions, starting with the supervisor not doing her own job and asking Bethany to run personal errands for her and culminating in the accusation of stealing. But her decision, very much like Tahiera's, was related to a refusal to be disrespected and a sense that she had no recourse other than to quit. Perhaps Bethany and Tahiera were wrong in that assumption, but the assumption is understandable given their knowledge that low-wage workers had such little power in the labor market they faced. When Bethany said, "I'll leave the job before I sit up here and be ridiculed like that," she was saying that although the job paid a steady wage, provided learning opportunities, and was interesting to her, her requirement of respectful treatment was non-negotiable for her.

Frida Alvera, a thirty-six-year-old Puerto Rican mother of three children ages fifteen, fourteen, and eleven, was similarly disturbed by disrespectful treatment by her supervisor when she was accused of taking food from her workplace. She had worked fairly steadily throughout her adult life, though she had combined work with welfare for much of the time.[19] Unlike some women who held jobs for only a few months, Frida stayed in a series of jobs for several years each. She left two jobs more quickly, however, after clashing with supervisors.

The first of these two jobs, which had lasted only about six months, was in the cafeteria of a Catholic school. The job fit her needs well because it was just for a few hours in the early afternoon, so it did not interfere with her ability to get her kids off to school in the morning or to be home when they returned. But, like Juanita, she eventually left it because of her supervisor's tendency to correct her publicly: "I had it with her. She would embarrass you in front of—she doesn't care if all the boys are there, or the priest is, or whatever. You know, she has something to tell you, she'll just come out and tell you, right there. She was horrible, . . . but I put up with it for at least six months or so and then I didn't decide to go back."

I asked Frida if she could give me an example of her boss embarrassing her, and she told the following story, reiterating that the problem was not that her boss had corrected her behavior but that her boss had not done it appropriately, meaning in a way that respected her privacy.

One time I took an orange. I was, really like an upset stomach. And right there, she had a heart attack. You know, "I'm telling you many times not to take food," and the cafeteria wasn't open yet. It was like a half hour before it opened. "I'm telling you"—and she's throwing stuff on the table, and pounding. Yeah, I was going to walk out that day, but I said, "Relax, relax, here's your orange, no big deal, here." And I left and did my job. And she apologized to me . . . before the day ended. . . . God, if you screwed up in your job, then take you to her office, you know? Talk to you then. It's nobody's business. You know? So, I didn't go back there.

Frida claimed that her supervisor's behavior was the only reason she left. Even though the job paid minimum wage, she felt that she was learning skills that would help her in the long run. Despite the steady work, the chance to learn skills, and the fact that the hours fit her schedule so well, Frida was unwilling to put up with the humiliation of her boss's public scoldings.

As with Tahiera and the others, we do not know Frida's supervisor's side of this story. If Frida routinely ate food from the cafeteria when she was not supposed to, her boss's frustration is understandable. But the fact that her boss apologized for the way she had scolded Frida indicates that perhaps the boss's initial reaction was indeed inappropriate. Frida did not seem to think taking the orange created any real problem. If she was wrong and it was problematic—because it ruined the inventory count or contributed to earnings losses or some other reason—then at the very least we can say that her supervisor did not communicate to her why the seemingly innocent act of eating an orange actually had important consequences.

Frida contrasted her experience at the cafeteria with a job she had held at an arcade where she considered her boss to be wonderful: "He was terrific. You wouldn't want to quit on him because he's such a good boss, you know? . . . He understood. He listened, he understood. And if you needed more hours, he would give you more hours."

After about a year in the job, however, the boss's daughter, who did not inherit his supervisory temperament, took over the business. Shortly afterward, Frida quit. "I wouldn't take no crap. So that was the end of that." Again, what appeared most important to Frida was being treated respectfully by her supervisor, and again, her belief that she had no other recourse than to quit was a sign of the powerlessness of low-wage workers created by the structure of the labor market. Since Frida had quit jobs twice over this issue, it is possible that she herself was entering jobs predisposed to be distrustful—that she was quick to categorize supervisors as disrespectful and hence untrustworthy. On the other hand, we also have evidence that any such possible predisposition did not always trump what happened in interactions with bosses themselves, since she had had a trusting and respectful relationship with at least one boss.

Esperanza Sanchez, interviewed after reform, worked for a year as a cashier in a family-run grocery store. She enjoyed the work, the regular customers, and being part of the family enterprise. Her feelings shifted, however, with the changing behavior of the elderly owner, who became increasingly suspicious and ornery. She figured it was because of his advancing age, but she also traced his behavior to an unfortunate event. A longtime trusted employee (not Esperanza) was caught on videotape stealing from the store. While the owner never specifically accused Esperanza of stealing, he began to act as if he did not trust her. For example, every time she needed to void a sale, he had to be present because he did not trust that she was not voiding sales that were actually legitimate. Eventually, she could take his behavior no longer. Even though the elderly owner's son also worked at the store and was a more reasonable and supportive boss, the father's behavior was just too much for Esperanza.

> He was an old man. He didn't care. He would just scream at you. . . . I said, "No. I can't take this." I remember on two cases, I would start crying. . . . He had a bad experience with a lady that he really trusted for so many years. They decided to check a video and caught her stealing, so I can understand him. But not everybody's the same, and I told his son, "I can't take this. I'm sorry. . . . I'm not dying of hunger. I have a home. I have skills. I'm not gonna take this." And that's when I just didn't come back.

The son tried to keep Esperanza, but she would not stay. She encouraged him to speak to his father so he would not keep losing employees. As in most of the women's stories, after she quit, the employer (in this case, the son) asked her to come back. But Esperanza drew the line in the same place that Tahiera, Anabella, and others did. If she did not trust that she would be treated fairly and with respect, she would not put up with the situation. "The son ... was devastated. I said, 'I'm sorry. You're gonna have to talk to your father.' Because it wasn't me only [that was leaving on account of the father's behavior]. 'You were getting left, because of his attitude.' . . . And I told him, 'I really want to work here, because I like it. I like the hours. I like the people. The people really know me.' [Afterwards], the son did call me twice and I said 'Nope.'"

Esperanza's statement makes clear that the only problem with the job was the old man's treatment of her. Leaving the job was a loss for her. It is not easy to find a low-skill job one likes that has hours that work well with parenting responsibilities. Although this job met all of those criteria, Esperanza left it, again not because of her traits or her personal life, but because the boss's distrust in his employees led her to distrust him.

Susan Schiller, a post-reform interviewee whom we met in the Introduction, would never describe her fast-paced job selling concessions at a large arena as having a friendly family atmosphere. Susan's story about this job is different from those of the other women up to this point in the chapter because it is not one of a woman quitting after developing distrust in her supervisor. It is instead a story of a woman getting fired. It is useful, however, because it illustrates well the complex web of distrust across a network of players that can develop in a workplace. As we learned in the Introduction, Susan's boss distrusted Susan's coworkers and Susan, and Susan distrusted her boss and her coworkers. While we have no evidence of it, perhaps Susan's coworkers distrusted her as well. It seems clear that distrust played a role in Susan's job loss even if it was her boss's and not her choice to terminate employment. Susan found the explanation that she was being fired because she failed to ring up a hot dog preposterous. "This is the craziest thing: they fired me because they said that I did not punch in a hot dog on the register. . . . They said that I gave it to a customer and did not push it in the register. . . . I was like what are you talking about? $1.75? You know what I'm saying?"

Susan instead suspected she was let go for a combination of two other reasons. First, she thought her boss wanted to replace her with a temporary worker who would be paid minimum wage instead of the $11.10 per hour Susan was making.[20] "A lot of that had to do with, see what [the arena] does is they hire the old people back, okay, but then like midway through the year they'll go through a temporary agency to where they can get two people for the same price that they're paying you, and at that time I was making $11.10 an hour, so they got two people at minimum wage."

Here we again see the role played by larger structural aspects of the labor market. The increasing reliance on inexpensive temporary workers threatens the security of permanent employees and weakens their bargaining strength. Susan knew this to be so, and it highlighted for her a disjuncture between her and her supervisor's interests. It was in her interests to keep her job, while it was in her supervisor's interests to replace her with a worker who could be paid half her wage.

Second, as discussed in the Introduction, Susan suspected her supervisor wanted to get rid of her because she had refused to spy on a coworker suspected of stealing and had not been very diplomatic in her refusal. Again, workplace practices led to Susan's suspicions. If her supervisor wanted her to spy on a coworker, there was no guarantee that someone would not spy on her.

Susan's story is particularly interesting because of the many levels of distrust it reveals. Susan's boss did not trust Susan's coworker whom she suspected of stealing, and eventually she distrusted Susan as well. Susan did not trust her boss, nor did she trust her coworker. Part of her refusal to spy related to her concern that her potentially unsavory coworker (since the employers did not screen workers) might seek retribution against Susan.

It is hard to know exactly what happened at Susan's workplace. It does seem strange that she would steal a $1.75 hot dog and risk a relatively high-paying job, especially when she knew that the company spied on employees, but it is certainly possible. Perhaps she thought it was no big deal, just as Frida thought it was no big deal to eat the orange. Or perhaps she just did it out of spite one day when she was annoyed at her boss. Finally, maybe, in a very fast-paced job, it was simply an accident and Susan herself did not realize she had made the mistake.

It seems equally plausible that Susan did not actually fail to ring up the hot dog and that her refusal to cooperate in her supervisor's surveillance plans led to her supervisor's disapproval of her. The fact that she could be replaced with a less expensive temp worker made it easy to let her go. In addition, Susan herself indicated that she might not have been particularly diplomatic when refusing to get involved in spying on coworkers. "You can see I'm very talkative and I just don't care," was the way Susan described to me how she had spoken to her boss in response to the request to spy. One could hardly blame her boss for firing her if indeed Susan did not care.

Her firing could also have stemmed from a combination of all of these factors. Susan could have failed to ring up the hot dog (either intentionally or not), and her supervisor could have used it as a convenient way to get rid of an expensive and strong-willed employee. Here Susan's individual trait of being strong-willed certainly might have played a role. But her case also shows that workplace processes, especially those in workplaces that hire low-skill workers—the screening or not screening of employees, employers' strategies to manage stealing on the job, the hiring of both inexpensive temp workers and relatively expensive nontemp workers—contribute to an atmosphere of distrust and that this atmosphere is related to employee turnover.

It is much clearer what happened in Rasheba Stokes's job. Rasheba, also interviewed after reform, had stolen from the large chain store where she worked, as she readily admitted. Her employer's suspicions about employee theft were clearly legitimate. It was Christmastime, and Rasheba was relatively new to the job. When Rasheba did her own shopping at the store, a coworker passed some of her items through the line without ringing them up. Rasheba was surprised, but she went along with it, seeing it as a "blessing" when she was financially strapped. She was caught and fired—along with six other employees. As a result, she had a felony on her record—her first criminal offense—making it difficult to find another job. She had been receiving TANF ever since. Rasheba suspected that her coworker had told management about the practice, which it turned out had been going on among workers for quite a while.

They charge[d] everybody who was doing it 'cause what happened was one of the coworkers got caught doing it for me, and when she got caught she told on everybody that she done it for. . . . I wasn't even there for two months. . . . And it was during Christmas and I thought that was a blessing I was given. But, like I say, it was just a bad judgment on my part 'cause we got paid that day. I was gonna pay for my stuff, but she let it go through and didn't charge it, and I didn't say anything.

While most of the women interviewed who told stories of bosses who had distrusted them denied any wrongdoing, Rasheba's story indicates that employer distrust is warranted in certain cases. In others, however, its expression appears to lead to unnecessary turnover, as in the case of Esperanza Sanchez, who quit her grocery job because of her elderly boss's suspicions of her.

Even though Rasheba was not innocent, the point remains that her crime was not committed alone—it was not even conceived of alone. Instead, she joined a practice that had been established in her workplace before her arrival and that probably continued (at least in some form) after she left. She lost her job because of her interactions with her coworkers, although a different person might have resisted participating in her coworkers' crime.

Distrust about money also went in the other direction for some women, as some employees also distrusted employers to pay them what was owed. At her most recent job, working as a certified nursing assistant (CNA) in a doctor's office, Tasha Blackwell was repeatedly promised payment and training opportunities that the doctor did not deliver. As she explained,

When I first started, we made the agreement, . . . "I'll give you $8 an hour, to start you off for three months and then I'll give you a dollar [an hour raise]." I said, "Okay, fine." Three months came and went. My first check came through at the end of the month, I did get $9 now. The day after that, he started telling me, "We gotta cut back on a lotta stuff," because he's trying to buy this other clinic . . . "but you're gonna stick with me, right?" I'm like, "If you give me reason to stick with you, yeah, I'll stick with you." He said, "Well, this is how it go. This is our plan." I mean, he sat me down and we mapped it out. He said, "After your six months here . . . we gonna start looking for schools and put you in school and I'm gonna help pay for you to go to school, so you can be a RN, so you can make you some money." I'm still waiting to go to school. . . . [And] he was only paying me, after he got the other clinic, $7 an hour. But I stayed with him. That's how determined I was to keep my job.[21]

I asked Tasha if her employer had talked to her about the fact that he was going to be paying her less. She replied, "Yeah! He said, 'because of expenses,' but that's not my deal. 'I'm an expense to you, too!' I can't . . . tell the office where I live at that I can't pay my rent this month because I got other expenses. They gonna tell me to pack my bags and get out."

Eventually, Tasha quit. She went back on assistance after years of being off welfare and employed. She found welfare receipt demeaning, but somehow she found it even more demeaning to be misled by her supervisor.

Distrust over money led to work disruptions for several women. Tahiera was so offended by her accusation of stealing from the liquor store cash register that she quit immediately. For Bethany, the accusation of stealing from the convenience store was the last straw in a series of events in which she felt mistreated. For Frida, it was the public scolding that accompanied the accusation of taking an orange that led her to quit. For Esperanza, the grocery store clerk with the elderly boss, employer distrust in employees suspected of stealing created a hostile atmosphere that drove her to quit. Rasheba's participation in untrustworthy practices with her coworkers led to her being fired. Susan too was deemed untrustworthy and fired, although she maintained her innocence and shared her own distrust of her employer's motives. Tasha's loss of trust in her employer's word about promised pay and benefits led her to quit.

Suspected Harassment and Discrimination Based on Race or Sex

Women in both time periods discussed their suspicions of harassment and discrimination based on race, ethnicity, or sex as the root of their distrust in employers. We have already discussed Tahiera Jackson's suspicion that her employers were motivated by racism when they accused her of stealing on the job. Similarly, Juanita Soto slowly came to believe that racism played a role in her supervisor's harsh treatment of her.

Estrella Cervantes, interviewed before reform, pointed to sexual harassment as the reason she had left her job. Only a handful of women had held a job longer than Estrella. She had happily worked in the film-processing department of a large chain drugstore for nine years, a highly unusual length of time for the women I interviewed. Obviously, it was a job that worked for her, and the company must have been happy enough with her performance to keep her all that time. She left, however, when a new supervisor was hired and, according to Estrella, began sexually harassing the female employees and threatening workers. She explained, "He was getting out of hand. . . . Trying to get involved with us. Involved." She stretched out the word *involved*, and as she did so she caught my eye with hers and, widening her eyes, made it clear she meant "involved sexually." She continued, "And I had to go through all that. But I didn't get involved with him or anything like that. But I had to put up with all his habits. Like, he would tell me, 'Well, you keep up like that, I'm going to fire you.' . . . And there was no union there. And I liked my job. And I wanted to keep—and I stayed there as long as I could, but I couldn't put up with it no more. I said, 'Uh huh, it's time for me to quit.'" Here Estrella herself noted that the lack of union representation meant workers had less ability to protest her boss's behavior than they might in a union shop.

Leaving her job was quite a shock for Estrella, as it resulted in her first time on public aid. She missed her coworkers, her paycheck, and the self-esteem she felt work provided. She even considered returning to the job. "Sometimes I feel like getting off of this and going back over there. But to go through all that hassle? I don't want to go through that. You know?" Again, we do not know exactly what Estrella's boss did. What we do know is that Estrella successfully held onto her job for nine years before his arrival. Thus it is hard to imagine that her quitting was not directly related to the arrival of the new supervisor and her deep distrust in him.

On the other hand, given that she had held the job all that time, it seems odd that she left without pursuing any other lines of recourse. We might suspect that there was something else going on either at the job or in her life that would explain why she left. But sexual harassment cases are notoriously hard to prove, and there is evidence that harassment is common: for example, a study of 522 workers in Minnesota reported that in 2004 (the same year as many of my post-reform interviews) 36 percent of the workers indicated that others in their workplaces had committed at least one behavior that met the legal definition of sexual harassment.[22]

Mayra Cuella, interviewed after reform, similarly complained of sexual harassment. Mayra lasted in a job in a flower shop for only two weeks. She quit because the boss's attention made her uncomfortable: "He was kind of fresh. . . . Yeah, that's why I stopped too. It was like, I don't know, just nasty. . . . Yeah, like . . . every time I bend, he started looking at my butt. . . . He was nasty! He was a Cuban guy. [Mayra is Puerto Rican]. And I didn't like it."

When I asked Mayra if she had ever said anything to him about how he made her uncomfortable, she said, "No, I just look at him. . . . And then he tells me, 'Go downstairs in the basement and go look for more flowers.' And I'm thinking, 'Not even! Maybe he's saying that [to] catch me in the basement.' That's what I was thinking! So I said no, I better quit."

Ronnie Simpson, another post-reform interviewee, did not trust her supervisor with female employees either. She worked in a fast-food restaurant for six or seven months before she was let go because, she suspected, she would not go out with her manager.

> I think it 'cause the manager of the . . . restaurant, he was a big flirter. He flirted with every girl that came in there, and I think he had sex with quite a few. . . . [He said] "You wanna go out to eat somewhere after you get through working here?" . . . I said, "No, I'm going home to my kids. I ain't got time." "Are you sure?" And so the next day, Ronnie's fired! [Ronnie is referring to herself here.] That's all right, Ronnie quit! And then a week . . . after that happened, the manager also got fired. They must've, they caught him in the act.

Three other post-reform interviewees who had all worked in traditionally male jobs believed that they were the victims of sex discrimination.[23] Each felt that the workplace environment, and in particular the supervisor, did not accept the presence of female workers. One felt forced to resign, one was fired, and one quit.

Marisela Suarez was a shipping and receiving clerk, with seven men under her supervision, at a large warehouse. A new manager was surprised to find a woman in the job. "Yeah, he was a college guy and . . . when they introduced him to all of us . . . I say, 'Hi, how are you?' He say, 'You're a woman.' I say, 'Yes.' He look at me like [Marisela makes a disparaging face]."

Marisela was convinced that the new supervisor started to look for reasons to fire her. She claimed he had blamed her for things that happened when she was not even at work or for things her workers had done after hours when she was no longer responsible for them. As she said, "So, he started looking for everything—for stuff that happened a year ago—just to let me go. Like little stuff they could put on me." Each time he noted one of these infractions, her boss suggested that she resign. Finally, she gave in. "So I got fed up and I finally wrote the resignation papers and I left. I say, 'Okay, you want me to resign, I will.' I couldn't take it, I couldn't work with him no more. He was gonna nail me to the point that he was gonna make me do something to use it against me. . . . I said, 'I'm leaving.'"

Beverly Manning had been fired from her job for reasons she still did not understand. She thought she had hit the jackpot when she first got the unionized job as a forklift driver that paid $11 an hour with benefits.[24] It was the best money she had ever made, but it came with a high price. She was the only female worker, and her male coworkers were not happy about her arrival. "Everything that would go wrong, they would blame it on me. You know what I'm saying? When somebody else done it! One of 'em cuss me out, you know, call me all kind of bitches and motherfuckers. You know, verbal abuse. You know, I coulda had a big lawsuit on them, but I decided, 'no.' And you know what? It bothers me when I think about that, it really do." Beverly regretted that she had not pursued legal action, but at the time she felt too demoralized from the experience to seek it.

Finally, Rosibel Ernesto quit her job. She worked at a large home renovation store, but felt she had been encouraged to quit because her boss did not like having a female employee. Rosibel felt she knew more about home renovation than her male coworkers did. Despite this, she was transferred to another store while her male colleagues were allowed to stay in the store where she preferred to work. "They were idiots. . . . I'm being honest. They were idiots, and I knew more about carpentry and construction and plumbing than they did, but they got to stay there and I didn't, and that was upsetting."

She finally did quit when she was transferred to a store far away, where she would not be able to get home on time to her children, while her male coworkers were allowed to stay. I asked Rosibel whether she ever thought of formally filing a complaint. She said, "No, 'cause it's a waste of time." When I asked her why it was a waste of time, she replied,

> You'll be singled out later as a troublemaker, and why bother having that label on top of [everything] . . . ? If you try to find work someplace else that stays on your record. . . . It's not worth it if you can't sue with big expensive lawyers. You never gonna win cases like that. So, it's just a waste of time, and it's a bad label on you as a worker 'cause that does stay on your record. Blue-collar workers . . . you're just another pawn if you're just a laborer in a job like that. You're just a laborer. You're a dime a dozen. They can find anybody to take your spot, so why waste your time?

Rosibel's distrust of not only her coworkers and supervisors but also of any systems to rectify discrimination was common among the women of the study. None of the women who felt they had been sexually harassed or discriminated against filed complaints or sought outside legal advice. But the choice not to pursue any kind of amelioration was not limited to women who felt unfairly treated because of their sex (or race). Many women with a variety of experiences quit without complaint in the face of what they saw as unfair treatment or accepted being fired seemingly without good cause. They had no faith that they would prevail if they were to complain, or they felt the costs of the process would outweigh any potential gain.

As Rosibel made clear, her assessment that complaining was futile was closely tied to her understanding of the structural aspects of the labor market I have discussed. Because she knew "blue-collar" workers were easily replaced, she did not believe she had any power to improve working conditions. In addition, she did not want a "bad label" on her "record" that would hurt her ability to compete with other workers for scarce employment opportunities. Rosibel's comments provide a way to understand the otherwise mystifying actions of all the women in this chapter who quit jobs they needed without attempting to address their perceived mistreatment. On some level, all of these women understood how the labor market was structured and what implications that had for their workplaces. They knew low-wage workers were expendable, and thus they suspected that they had no power to demand the treatment they believed they deserved.

Disagreements over Work Schedules and Conditions

Work schedules are an important source of employment instability, especially in low-wage, hourly jobs where managers increasingly use "just-in-time" scheduling practices that result in scarce and variable hours for workers.[25] Several women interviewed after reform reported leaving jobs over disagreements with their supervisors about how their work was to be structured. No woman interviewed before reform told a story of mistreatment based on these factors. Perhaps this is just coincidence, but as Germaine Charles suggests, perhaps the work requirements of welfare reform play some role in the difference.

Germaine was routinely forced to stay late at her job at a fast-food restaurant without being asked ahead of time, which made it very difficult for her to manage her child care needs.

> They didn't ask you half the time, you was just there, and you had to go ask them, "Okay, I'm supposed to get off at four o'clock, it's five o'clock, why am I still here?" [Sternly, imitating her supervisor:] "I need you to stay." "Well, ask me, you know, beside this job I got other things to do too." And then they get mad when you ask could you leave. If you need me to stay, ask me. Don't just leave me up there like, "Okay, she gonna stay." If I'm scheduled to get off at four o'clock that's the time I expect to be walking out the door, at least by four fifteen. Five o'clock or five fifteen, I'm still standing here and nobody tell me why I'm still standing here. And they did that, they did that real bad.

Germaine's supervisors knew she was receiving welfare because she got the job through a job-training center for welfare recipients that matched workers with the fast-food chain. She suspected that they took advantage of her since they knew she had to keep the job in order to stay compliant with her work requirements. She explained, "I think just like making you stay there, like you ain't gonna quit 'cause you know you need this job. You know you ain't gonna quit. You need this job or Public Aid gonna sanction you if you quit."

Jane Pearce had quit one of her recent jobs working a 4 a.m. to noon shift at an airport store after having a similar problem to Germaine's. She explained, "I quit a job because I felt like they were trying to take advantage of me. . . . If I was due to get off work at twelve, I still wouldn't get out of there until like one, closer to two. That's because . . . I have to wait for my relief to come. So that person would always be late and I got tired of it."

Jane had discussed the problem with her supervisor, but the supervisor did not offer to do anything about it until it was too late. When she told her boss that she was quitting, her boss said, "You don't have to quit, I can move you from the unit." But Jane had made up her mind. "I was like, I'm just tired of it, so I quit." For Jane, it was too late. "I was like, '. . . I quit.' And I used to love working at the airport because I would be at home at least by one o'clock, one thirty on the times that I didn't get messed around, enjoying the rest of my day."

It is perplexing that Jane left a job with good hours (at least according to Jane; some might not feel starting work at 4 a.m. would constitute good hours), especially when her boss offered to try to rectify the problem. But, as was the case with other women in this chapter, she had reached a breaking point when she decided she had had enough. She did not trust that things would really get better, since the problem had been previously ignored. Elena Salinas also quit her job at a restaurant after an argument with her supervisor over work hours. He had asked her to work on a Sunday night, but her mother, who usually babysat for her kids while she worked, was in Mexico for two weeks. She told her supervisor that she had child care only during the day for those two weeks but that she would be happy to work at night after that. As Elena explained, her boss then got very upset.

He said, "I don't know what you plan to do, but either you stick those kids in a closet, [or] if you don't come back to work on Sunday night, then don't come at all." I said, "Fine." I took the shirt off, I threw it and I said, "I'm not coming. I'm not gonna do it." So he said, "Well you gonna leave me like this?" [I said] "I'm not gonna leave my kids in the closet either." . . . If he's willing to say that, he's willing to say a lot more. And that was it. That was it for that job.

Adriana Marquez, a mother of a young son, was sent to a new job by her job-training program between the first and second times that we spoke. In our second conversation, she was dismayed about her treatment at work. She worked for an industrial cleaning service that did after-hours cleaning in a large chain store. She worked thirteen-hour shifts and had no advance notice of when her days off would be. She was also assigned to different locations to work with little or no notice. She had an older car, which made the transportation a challenge. At the time of our second visit, she was working the night shift so she could watch her son during the day. However, her supervisor sometimes would ask her to come in during the day as well. Adriana was also disturbed that "they just lock us into the store overnight and they only let you out for a family emergency." Adriana was experiencing the same kind of workplace conditions as the Walmart and Sam's Club employees discussed in chapter 1.

She attributed the poor treatment to the fact that the company hired many undocumented immigrants who had no recourse for demanding fair treatment. She was tempted to report the company for this practice, but she resisted the impulse because she had befriended a coworker who was undocumented and needed the job. In addition to these poor conditions, Adriana also found her supervisor "very unprofessional." For example, she said that she had tried calling him on the radio to ask a question but that he did not answer. When she later saw him and asked why he was not answering, he replied that he was having sex. "I told him he should not be talking to us like that," she explained, but he continued to behave similarly. She wanted to report him to his supervisor, but she did not know who that would be. By our third visit, Adriana had quit the job. She had been there just under two months, but she felt she could no longer stand the environment or her supervisor's behavior.

Macro-level labor market factors, including the drive to hire workers as cheaply as possible and hence the use of undocumented immigrants too fearful to protest mistreatment, translate into the local workplace conditions Adriana encountered that fed her distrust.

Germaine, Jane, Elena, and Adriana's complaints about the structure of their work hours and practices and supervisors' inadequate response to their complaints were echoed by additional women after reform. While some of these concerns related to structural conditions of the workplace that did not initially derive from social interactions with supervisors, most women describe these conditions as being expressed through interpersonal contact with supervisors. Thus women blamed their experience of workplace conditions on the actions of specific supervisors whom they deemed incompetent, insensitive, and even deceitful. Once women lost trust in a particular person to deliver workplace practices fairly, leaving the job often followed.

UNDERSTANDING DISTRUST IN THE WORKPLACE

What produces worker distrust? Most women pointed to specific incidents that occurred at work as the source of their distrust in the workplace. These reports suggest that experiences at work teach women to have low expectations of positive work outcomes and hence to distrust their bosses and coworkers.

Of course, the interpretation of these incidents is in the eye of the beholder. Most readers of the women's reports will probably agree that employers who do not pay their workers their promised wage or who make unwanted sexual advances are untrustworthy. Some readers may be less sure, however, if every insult the women reported truly indicates untrustworthiness. Some women may appear quick to see potentially innocent behavior as a sign of disrespect or malfeasance. This quickness may relate to a desire to protect oneself from the indignities of low-wage work by responding to signs of potential mistreatment even before there is evidence that they are really there. Women who bring this preemptive distrust into their interactions with employers may create a self-fulfilling prophecy in the sense that their distrust of employers may initiate employer distrust of them, since their distrustful stance may appear suspicious or hostile.

Even so, I argue that both distrust based on concrete evidence of untrustworthiness in interactions and distrust based on a more preemptive strategy brought into interactions as a protective tool are related to structural factors. As discussed above, low-wage workers are powerless in a labor market in which they are easily replaceable. This macrostructural fact means their wages are low and their jobs are unstable. Powerlessness that stems from these macrostructural features of the labor market translates into powerlessness within the mesostructure of the workplace itself, where low-wage workers typically have little say over how work tasks are organized and face close supervision with little autonomy.

Low-wage workers who experience such powerlessness are unlikely to feel on an equal footing with their supervisors. We know from the experimental literature on trust that equality between partners in an exchange promotes trust (and hence that the opposite probably promotes distrust).[26] Ethnographic evidence further shows a relationship between inequality and perception of disrespectful treatment. In his ethnography *In Search of Respect: Selling Crack in El Barrio*, Philippe Bourgois demonstrates how workers' experience of inequality exacerbates low-level workers' sense of disrespectful treatment and promotes turnover.[27] He argues that the connection between inequality, the desire for respect, and high turnover is strengthened further when supervisors and employers are of different races and ethnicities.[28] Many of the subjects in his work entered the drug trade in part as an escape from the disrespectful treatment they felt they received in mainstream workplaces.[29] The women I interviewed shared some things with Bourgois's study participants. They too sensed their unequal structural position and its powerlessness, and they too demanded the only thing they felt they could control: respectful treatment.[30]

Workplace conflict, especially in relation to the lack or loss of trust between workers and employers, was associated with job turnover and the instability of welfare exits for the women I interviewed both before and after reform.[31] While this claim is in keeping with scholarship on trust and cooperation and is also supported by the literature on organizational commitment, it is largely absent from policy discussions of welfare-to-work transitions.[32] In such discussions, the determinants of labor market success are perceived almost exclusively as residing within the individual.[33] Welfare recipients' limited success in the labor market is seen as due to their low levels of education, their lack of skills both hard and soft, their nonmarital fertility and subsequent child care problems, their substance use, their physical and mental health, their partying, their attitude problems, and other such factors either real or imagined. Each of these individual factors may indeed play a role for some women, but clearly they do not tell the whole story.

BUILDING TRUST IN THE WORKPLACE

Policy makers' individual-level diagnosis of low-income women's high rate of job turnover results in individual-level solutions: job-training programs, child care subsidies, substance use treatment, welfare program sanctions to teach "responsibility," and similar approaches. While individual-level problems clearly exist and individual-level policy responses are often appropriate—few people think offering treatment to substance abusers is a bad idea, for instance—they do not treat the social context of the workplace.

Even the current approach of providing limited job-training and placement services through the welfare system fails to do what it could to recognize the role of workplace interaction in job maintenance. Job training and placement programs are under contractual pressure to place clients in jobs as quickly as possible. While many are rewarded when clients remain in positions for some period of time (often ninety days), most pay more attention to initial placement than job stability. If caseworkers and job-training centers were rewarded more highly for making sustainable employment transitions, they would need to become involved in addressing the conflicts that arise in the workplace that lead to worker distrust and quick turnover.

Some job-training programs for welfare recipients teach what is expected by employers in workplaces. They stress the importance of showing up on time and displaying a positive, professional demeanor. Yet little effort is spent teaching specific tools for addressing workplace conflict and protecting one's rights at work. Women both before and after reform walked away from jobs at the initial onset of any kind of conflict. They lacked either information about or faith in the availability of channels for addressing their complaints.

Training programs that taught not only the worker's responsibilities to the workplace but also the workplace's responsibilities to the worker might reduce the incidence of this form of turnover. Programs that made job stability a priority (encouraged by the proper incentive structures and supports) would screen employers for workplace environment and would provide conflict resolution support for their placements.[34] While a handful of programs take these steps, most do not. Welfare policy is short-sighted in its approach to job placements, often preferring quick and easily found but potentially unstable placements to potentially more long-term placements that require more resources to groom and support. As one study found, job-training programs do not always recognize the realities of the low-wage labor market and place clients in positions that will not even offer enough weekly hours to meet welfare work participation requirements.[35]

Policies that address the employment challenges posed by workplace social interaction have received little attention but are an important element for increasing low-income women's success in the labor market. They will not enhance human capital or raise wages and labor demand, but coupled with programs that address these concerns they could play an important role in supporting low-wage workers.

Ultimately, however, worker distrust is unlikely to change without structural changes in workplaces. Organizations in which owners and high-level employees' compensation is many times that of entry-level workers, in which low-level workers are disposable and easily replaced, in which there is no guarantee of stable work hours (and thus pay), in which benefit packages are continually dwindling, and in which working conditions continually regress are breeding grounds for distrust, for presumed supervisor malfeasance on the part of workers, and for hostile interactions between workers and their supervisors.[36] These forces are even present, or perhaps are especially present, when supervisors are just a few steps up the hierarchy from entry-level workers and operate out of their own sense of distrust. Thus, while welfare-to-work programs might do a better job than they do of addressing factors outside the workplace, only more fundamental (and unlikely) workplace restructuring can fully alter the interaction patterns that promote distrust and turnover.

Some employers might recognize that there are performance costs of worker distrust. The literature on "procedural justice" provides evidence that workers who feel they are victims of "psychological contract breach," which occurs when employers do not live up to workers' understandings of what employers owe to them, not only lose trust in their employers but also perform less well on the job.[37] Managers who invest heavily in a flexible workforce pay costs in terms of employee turnover.[38] Employers who recognize these performance costs and take interest in building their workers' trust in them could also invest in training so that workers would be less replaceable and could take respectful treatment of workers seriously through diversity and sexual harassment training of managers. Ultimately, however, easily replaceable low-wage workers and the lack of union or other protections against mistreatment are structural conditions that make it unnecessary for employers to reciprocate women's cooperation and thus to exhibit the trustworthiness that would promote future trust.

FOUR

"I Don't Trust People to
Watch My Kids"

MOTHERS' DISTRUST IN CHILD CARE PROVIDERS

David got bit three times in the face and that was enough
for me. I said, "Take your welfare grant, do what you
wanna do with it." I had enough. . . . Until he goes to
school, I'm not working and I'm not taking TANF because
I'll have to work. . . . I'll make do.

—Kate Lawrence

Marguerite Guerrera had never imagined herself on welfare. And
for good reason, since she had an unusually strong employment history
and was married to a man who did too. For sixteen years she lived a
financially stable and even, in her estimation, comfortable life. During
those sixteen years, she worked in the same factory job on an assembly
line making containers; it paid above minimum wage, was unionized,
and gave her a healthy benefits package. Her husband, Miguel, worked
in the same plant, and between their two incomes they felt they had
made it. Even after having her two children, Marguerite was able to
maintain employment because her mother-in-law lived with her and
watched the children. In the early 1990s, when her children were still
young, however, her mother-in-law decided to return to Mexico, her
home country. Marguerite was distraught, unable to imagine anyone else

with her children. As much as she hated to leave a job she had been in so long, Miguel convinced Marguerite that she should stay home and that his income alone could support the family.

Miguel might have been right, but within the year he left Marguerite and the children, taking all of his financial resources with him. Stunned and reeling, Marguerite signed up for welfare, that step she never thought she would have to take. When asked if she then thought about finding child care so she could return to work, Marguerite said in a resigned voice, "You can't trust nobody. With everything you hear about sexual abuse and all that, no, I don't think so. I couldn't afford it, anyway. Not on my own."

Marguerite's resignation speaks of the experience common among most low-income mothers I interviewed regarding child care: that the biggest child care challenge is finding providers they can trust. Yet as policy began to demand entry into the labor market, mothers had few choices but to find child care of some kind to cover their children.

Few actions are more risky than placing one's children in another's care. Children are highly vulnerable and have few resources with which to defend themselves. To manage the risk of danger to their children, mothers have two options: they can either stay home with their children themselves or find child care providers they trust. Yet welfare reform made few structural changes in the child care system that would enhance the quality of available child care services. As a result, distrust in child care providers remained among the women I interviewed after reform.

WELFARE REFORM AND CHILD CARE

Welfare reform's main approach to child care has been to regard the absence of it as a barrier to employment. In his book *Poor Support*, which partly inspired Clinton-era welfare reform, David Ellwood argued that time-limited welfare would be an acceptable policy once adequate work support benefits were put in place.[1] One of the most pressing kinds of supports needed, in Ellwood's eyes, was child care. Clinton brought

Ellwood to Washington, D.C., as one of the architects of his administration's welfare plan. Indeed, funding for subsidies for low-income families to purchase child care was greatly increased.[2]

Enhancing Child Care as a Work Support

In roughly the decade after welfare reform passed, federal child care funding for low-income families more than doubled.[3] This funding was used almost exclusively to support child care subsidies for families to pay for existing sources of child care. Only 4 percent of funds were used to enhance the quality of child care available.[4] This federal funding is distributed by the states. In Illinois, parents who are income eligible and employed or are attending a job-training program may apply for a subsidy to pay a specific child care provider. Providers may be formal child care centers, "day care homes" run in private residences, or informal care providers such as relatives or friends of the parent. If both the application and the provider are approved, the subsidy goes directly from the state to the provider. While the subsidy existed even before reform, the increase in federal funding for the program means many more families can be served. The rate paid to providers has also increased over time, but it remains low. Child care subsidy payments in Chicago to nonlicensed caretakers (either informal sitters in the child's home or day care providers who take children into their own homes) were $8.49 for a full day of care in 1994 and 1995 when I conducted interviews before reform (or $13.12 when converting from 1994 dollars to 2012 dollars and $12.76 when converting from 1995 dollars to 2012 dollars) and $9.49 in 2004 and 2005 when I interviewed women after reform (or $11.51 when converting from 2004 dollars to 2012 dollars and $11.13 when converting from 2005 dollars to 2012 dollars).[5] Thus, once adjusted for inflation, the value of the subsidy actually went down between my two interview periods. Reimbursement rates for licensed centers have been higher ($24.34 for a full day of care during my post-reform interviews, which is $29.52 in 2012 dollars when converted from 2004 dollars, and $28.55 when converted from 2005 dollars), and all rates have gone up since the end of my interviews.[6] But rates remain below market rate. In setting subsidy rates, the state of Illinois aims to reach a goal of 75 percent of market rate but often falls short (below 50 percent of market rate for some services in some counties).[7] Despite the low rate of reimbursement, many of the women interviewed after reform were able to find providers willing to accept these low payment rates. Furthermore, the post-reform increases in funding for child care mean that more families are able to receive subsidies.

Different Words, Same Concerns

Given the vast increases in funding to the states for child care services, one might assume that since reform the child care problems low-income parents experienced before reform have disappeared or at least been greatly diminished. The reports of the women interviewed after reform, however, suggest that this assumption is only partially correct. Indeed, the post-reform mothers did not raise finding child care coverage for their children as a problem, but when asked about their experiences they described the same problems trusting the providers they found as women before reform did. Since women after reform were required to work or face loss of benefits, many felt forced to use care whose quality they came to distrust, often after painful experiences in which their children were hurt or mistreated. Many women pulled their children out of care arrangements they came to distrust, but often not until children had paid a price as a result of reform policies.

Among the women interviewed before reform, child care was often the very first issue they mentioned when the subject of employment was raised. They were beginning to hear that work requirements might be coming down the road. They did not object to the idea of working per se. Almost all of them expressed a strong desire to enter the workforce and rid themselves of what they described as a punitive and stigmatizing welfare system, but many discussed child care as a major barrier to employment and a reason they should stay home. One-quarter of the women said that they had no idea how they could possibly find, arrange, and afford child care of any kind for their children. Many spoke in disbelief that they should be forced into employment when the child care problem appeared so insurmountable. Only one woman, who could rely on her unemployed sister who lived with her, said that child care was not a problem at all for her.[8]

When I asked Catalina Mendes, interviewed before reform, what her employment plans were, the first thing she said was that finding the necessary child care would be impossible. "I can't work because I don't have any family, any friend. So I have my two sister-in-law, but one work and one study. So I don't have anything. I don't trust anything with my kid because something happen in the news. I can't trust any person." As Catalina spoke, she shook her head from side to side, and her searching eyes and furrowed brow indicated her utter bafflement at the proposal that a single mother of young children would enter the labor force given the difficulties in finding trustworthy caregivers.

Tahiera Jackson, whom we met in chapter 3, had a six-year-old daughter. Tahiera had left her last job because her child care arrangements fell through. She explained, "I had to quit, because I didn't have a babysitter then. . . . My brother used to babysit for me, when he didn't have to go to work. Sometimes he'd have to work, and he'd have to wait till I come home so he could leave and go to work, so he used to be late [to work] all the time. So I had to quit."

Later in the interview when Tahiera was asked if she was thinking of trying to find a job, child care for her daughter was the first reason she raised for why she could not. "I was still thinking about going to work. But I had to find a babysitter. And it was hard finding a babysitter, because I don't trust everybody with [my daughter]. And she don't like everybody. . . . I just stayed at home."

Luisa Estevez, whom we met in chapter 2, was the mother of a twelve-year-old son and was no longer receiving welfare at the time of our interview, having found a salaried job with good benefits a year before. But when asked about working when her son was young, she replied, "I raised my son, I'm a single parent so I raised him at home. . . . I didn't have a babysitter because the majority of my friends have three or four children and you don't really want to babysit an extra child, so I stayed home and I tried to do the best I can." Even though her son was now older and could take care of himself, she felt comfortable about working only because she had started living with a friend who could keep an eye on him.

Rafaela Fuentes tried to find child care for her four-year-old son and six-year-old daughter but had not been successful. "I failed, I failed because what I did was walk around and ask around my neighborhood . . . where it was more convenient for me." Since she was not able to find anyone in her neighborhood to watch her children, she was trying to get her son into a special program in the public schools, but he was lingering on a waiting list. Her daughter, who at four was not yet school age, was too young for the program, and she did not know how she could cover her care.

Rafaela had good company in other pre-reform women. When asked what made it hard for her to take a job, Ellen Graham said, "Just finding child care for [my daughter]." Similarly, Selena Martin's response to the same question was "To me, it's always been the babysitter." In the eyes of the women interviewed before welfare reform, finding child care was a primary barrier to employment.

At first the tone and content of conversations with women after reform about joining the labor force were quite different from the women interviewed in the earlier period. Unlike the pre-reform women, the post-reform women almost universally did not raise the issue of child care in conversations about the challenges of going to work. Many said that they had child care covered. Even many of those who were not working at the time of the interview said they would have access to child care if they found jobs. A few women did consider child care a major barrier to work, especially if their children faced health or behavioral issues. Yet over half of the women indicated that finding child care was not a problem at all.

When asked whether the welfare office had provided child care help when they sent her to a job-training program, Jane Pearce, interviewed after reform, indicated that she had had child care arranged already. "Well yeah, I had child care anyway. . . . Child care is not a problem for me."

Shandra Muse, a post-reform mother who had been employed and was now attending a mandatory job-training program, similarly was confident that she could rely on others for child care.

Interviewer: And what did you do about child care when you were [at your former job]?
Shandra: Oh, I had, child care was well taken care of. His uncle took care of him. . . . So it was no problem.

I: Oh, great. And who takes care of your child now?
S: Um, he takes care of him, and I'm there with him, and he has other uncles, aunts, he got a big family.

Many women after reform used family members, including ones that they might not have naturally thought of as potential child care providers had welfare reform not forced them to find care. Elena Salinas, who had five children ranging from four to eleven years old, used her eighteen-year-old brother as her child care provider. She did not have a child care subsidy, but she paid him what she could, when she could, and he understood why the payments were small and erratic. "My youngest brother . . . had quit school, so [my parents] had told him, 'One or the other: you get a job or you go back to school.' He decided to get a job, and I had the bright idea, 'Okay, well, babysitting is a job.' So he decided to go ahead and go for it. My kids already listen to him and they get along with him. They've grown up with him. . . . So it was no problem."

Latreece Allen, whose strong relationship with her supervisor we heard about in chapter 3, similarly could rely on her partner and family members to watch her youngest children. She had what she called "two sets of kids"—three teen boys who shared a father and three young girls whose father was Latreece's partner Darnell. While Latreece worked at her janitorial job, her children were watched by a variety of family members and by Darnell, who was often unemployed. She described how her child care arrangements worked, "'Okay, you got 'em?' 'I got 'em.' Fine. And [Darnell's] mama will watch 'em. . . . So, he gets 'em on the weekend and keep 'em up there and mama will watch 'em. So, I don't got no worries. So, I know everything all right over there. Same thing with me ... we ain't got no worries."

It is easier to cover child care for school-aged children, who may just need supervision for a few hours in the afternoon, than it is for preschool children. But school as a source of child care dries up every summer. Some women, however, had no problem covering child care even in the summer months. Lashawna Owens, who worked full time from 7:30 a.m. to 3:30 p.m., had a large extended family who were able to cover all of the care needs for her eight-year-old son, even when school was out of session.

Interviewer: And in the summer, when your son is not in school, your mother or his dad has him during the day?
Lashawna: He'll be outside. He go to whoever house he want to go.

I: Uh-huh. So he goes to ... So he has friends in the neighborhood?
L: No, whatever ... he got a friend that next door, but I'm saying if he want to spend the night, he spend the night out. He got friends, you know, family, you know.

I: Uh-huh. So ... that doesn't pose a big problem when school's out. It's okay.
L: Nah-uh. Ain't no problem.

Very likely, this difference between the pre- and post-reform respondents was partly due to reform's coercive measures driving women into the workforce. The post-reform respondents knew that they were under great pressure to participate in job search activities and employment. Rather than discussing child care as an explanation for why they were not working (or had not worked in the past), post-reform women discussed child care as an issue that they had to deal with in order to fulfill the work requirements of welfare.

The difference was also very likely a result of the increased availability of child care subsidies. Over one-third of the sixty-nine women interviewed after reform received subsidies, and another 10 percent were in the application process at the time of the interview, while only 13 percent of the twenty-six women interviewed before reform received a subsidy. The size of the subsidy was small and clearly below market rate. Still, many post-reform women were able to find someone willing to take the low rate, as the following exchange with Dawn Winters suggests.

Interviewer: So what is happening with your kids while you're here [at job training]?
Dawn: They're at home with the babysitter.

I: So you have a babysitter who comes to your house? [She nods.] And that is paid for by [a child care subsidy].
D: Uh huh.

I: And . . . how much do they pay?
D: They pay nine dollars and forty-nine cents a day for full time, which means five hours or more.[9]

I: And is it hard to find a babysitter for that amount of money?
D: No, not really.

I: How did you find your babysitter?
D: A close friend of the family.

The ease with which many post-reform women found some form of child care, however, did not mean that these women were free of child care problems per se. Most notably, post-reform women seemed to struggle as intensely with the issue of trusting child care providers as pre-reform women did. Even though they initially said they had "no problem" finding care, once I asked about their children's care arrangements, they described the very same problems finding care they deemed trustworthy as the pre-reform women did.

The pre-reform women talked frequently about the inability to trust child care providers. As Catalina said above, she could not work because none of her family members were available to provide care. Given this, she declared, "I can't trust any person." Danielle Adams, a pre-reform mother whom we met in chapter 2 when we learned about her job as a seasonal sanitation worker for the city, articulated the same concerns. "Your kids, you gotta watch your kids. Sometimes your kids more important than your job, you gotta watch them. Because if something happens, you'll regret it the rest of your life."

Danielle was the one pre-reform mother who actually said that child care was no problem for her since her unemployed sister lived with her and watched her children. In addition, her mother lived down the street and could be called on to fill in when needed. Danielle told me, "Family's about the only ones I would trust. Anybody else, with my babies?" She then shook her head vigorously as if to say, "No way." If pre-reform mothers did not have access to child care they could trust, they stayed home.

Though far fewer post-reform than pre-reform mothers raised child care as a problem when discussing barriers to work, they were just as likely as the earlier cohort to discuss problems trusting available sources of child care when they were asked about their child care situations. Alpha Walker, a mother of seven children, represented the views of many post-reform mothers when she said, "I don't like leaving my kids with anybody. It's so much going on and I have a real, I don't trust nobody." When I pressed about the nature of her concerns, she explained, "'Cause I seen it happen, the way some people treat other people's kids. I mean, I feel like a mother and a father is the best thing for kids. Ain't nobody gonna treat your kids like you treat them, even if they get paid that paycheck. . . . Basically most of them, I not gonna say all of them, basically all they want is a paycheck. They probably ain't watching them kids, letting them little kids do whatever they want to do. You know they [could] set the house on fire!"

Rosibel Ernesto, interviewed after reform, wished her sister would watch her children, but unless she could pay her a substantial amount, she did not think her sister would be willing. She actually did not think that her sister would provide the best-quality care, but at least she trusted her sister to keep her children safe. "She's hard with my kids, especially my son, but still it come down to the fact [that] I know how she is. I don't like anybody taking care of my kids. But still, at least, I know there's less a chance of anything happening when they're with her than there is with a neighbor. I don't know who goes in and out of their [the neighbor's] house and what kind of people they are. I'm being honest, because people are one way when you see them, but they're completely different [when you are not there]." In fact, many of the post-reform women discussed experiences in which, because of the increased pressure of requirements to work, they felt forced to use child care services that they either suspected or eventually discovered were not worthy of their trust and confidence.

Kate Lawrence described how her caseworkers pressured her to use a day care center even though she did not trust center-based care. In fact, Kate was one of the minority of post-reform mothers who did speak of child care as a "problem" when asked about ease or difficulty of going to work. "Well, they indicated to me there was no reason why you couldn't work because of child care. They provide the child care, so you might as well go ahead and adapt. They don't even want to discuss the fact that, you know, some people have specifics where they don't want their children in a child care [center]." Eventually, Kate did sign up her toddler son at a center. "I heard about it through TANF, 'cause they give you a listing and it's something that, you know, even though you may not feel comfortable doing, and it's a task because your child is customary to being around another individual. But then overnight, [the welfare office is] not concerned about it, the main thing is getting a job." Kate said her son David was bitten by another toddler on three separate occasions while he was at the center. After the third incident, Kate's level of trust in the center was so low she immediately removed David. She then decided to give up her welfare grant so that she could stay home with her son. "David got bit three times in the face and that was enough for me. I said, 'Take your grant, do what you wanna do with it.' I had enough. . . . Until he goes to school I'm not working and I'm not taking TANF because I'll have to work. . . . I'll make do."

Surviving with neither welfare benefits nor earnings was a real struggle. Kate could do it only because she lived in public housing, so she paid zero rent when she had no income. She still got food stamps, and she became an expert on all of the area food pantries and other organizations that offered goods, such as clothing and children's toys, to low-income families. She got some help from various family members, including her mother and cousins, and occasionally from a boyfriend. It was difficult, but Kate was determined to make it last until David was school-age.

Dawn Winters had a similar experience with a home day care, meaning a provider who takes several children into her own home to provide care.[10] She recalled,

> I tried . . . a home day care that another friend of mine had used. The young lady was giving my son Tylenol and what have you for him to sleep, and when I found out I didn't cause a big ruckus or anything. It was one [day] I went and I picked him up early and I noticed that he's in a room as big as this table with the door closed with other children and they're sleeping. . . . And I'm saying to myself, it's only eleven o'clock and they're sleeping. . . . I would pick him up and he was disoriented, my son knows me, why is it that when I pick him up he's out of it? It didn't look right, so I instantly pulled him out and I'd rather have him at home with me.

Anabella Mendoza, whom we met in chapter 3, was horrified to pick her three children up early one day from the family home day care she had recently found in her neighborhood. Inside the house, she found her children crying in the living room and hungry while the family ignored them and ate in the kitchen.

Anabella: Yeah, they told me, "Oh she's a very good lady," and this and that, so I left my kids. I think it was already like about a week, and my little boy was, he was just, you know crying. He didn't want to go. . . . I didn't know that they were treating them bad, very bad.

Interviewer: How did you discover it?
A: Because I left early from work and I went there. . . . My daughter was in the living room and the other one was like on the bed, sitting. And the other family they were eating and like inside the kitchen. You know the other ones are crying, and so the door was opened and I went in and they just jumped on me.

Anabella took her children home and never took them back. She found a neighbor to watch her children and was able to maintain employment.

Akira Smallwood's distrust of the center where she had placed her children was based less on a specific incident and more on a suspicion about the motives of the staff. She felt their main interests were profit and not her children's well-being. She hoped to remove her children from this center as soon as they got off a waiting list for a center at the community college where she was taking classes. "They pretty much have the money attitude. That it's really all about the money. It's not about nursery or caring for the children. It's about the money. I don't like that, so that's the main reason why they're coming out. . . . Children know when they're in a place if they're not wanted, or they're not treated right and my children truly hate to go there. But it's like truly the last result [sic] for me. It's like five minutes away from the house, and it's like the last result. The last result is pretty much day care."

Many women felt that they had to quickly find somewhere, anywhere, to place their children to participate in the training, work, and other activities that welfare receipt required. Often, such activities were required almost immediately after a woman applied for benefits and before she was approved to receive them. This meant that post-reform women frequently scrambled to find some kind of arrangement for their children during the needed hours.

When Gabriela Garcia was told she had to do volunteer work from 9 a.m. until 2 p.m. every day for forty-five days before being approved for TANF, she arranged for her neighbor to provide child care for her children. She did not feel confident, though, that her children were getting the best care. "She has cockroaches and they are, you know, my kids are spoiled. My kids are verbal. Whenever there is a problem, you know, we talk about it or whatever. And this lady is like, 'You sit there and watch TV.' And they're like, 'Watch TV? We don't want to be sitting here.' So they come and complain. There is nothing to do there, the whole family is very large people—about three hundred, four hundred pounds, they sit around, they have cockroaches. For right now, this is the best we can do."

Daeshawna Spurlock had much more dramatic reasons to learn to distrust the quality of care her children were receiving while she worked. After starting her job running an after-school program for children at a community center in her neighborhood, she asked a former coworker to move in with her to take care of her young children. After a while, Daeshawna learned that the friend was being investigated for neglect of her own children by the Department of Children and Family Services. "That should have been a sign that she wouldn't be able to take care of my kids either," Daeshawna said in retrospect. As time went on, Daeshawna became increasingly concerned that her children were not safe.

> I . . . come home, my baby got a burn on his arm, or . . . a knot on his head. . . . I come to her like, "How'd he get that burn on him?" "I don't know." "You watching him, . . . what you mean you don't know?" Okay, I let that go. Come home, my other baby, got a knot on his head. "How'd he get that?" "He was jumping in bed. . . . Girl, you complain too much. . . ." "I complain too much? These are my kids! How would you like it if I was watching your child and you come home and every day something wrong with your child? That mean I'm not watching your child." I had to let her go.

Few women in the post-reform sample raised child care as a barrier to employment or even said that child care was "a problem" for them. However, when specifically asked about their experience with the care providers they used, many post-reform mothers revealed that they did not trust—or, through experience, had lost their trust in—their providers. The disjuncture between their initial comments on child care not being a problem and their later discussions of their inability to trust and rely upon the providers they used was at first puzzling. It suggests, however, that these low-income mothers found *some* kind of care to cover their child care needs while they were at work or in other mandated activities when forced to do so by welfare policy requirements. Hence, they did not talk about child care as a "problem" in the same way as women before reform, who had more freedom to decline the use of unsatisfactory child care providers.[11] Almost none of the post-reform women actually had a problem finding child care, and thus almost none were prevented from working or engaging in other welfare-mandated activities by a lack of care. On the other hand, their narratives indicated that finding child care they deemed *trustworthy* indeed remained a problem. For women like Kate Lawrence, who told the story of her son being bitten while in a child care center, distrust in child care providers eventually led to leaving a job or, in Kate's case, leaving the labor market altogether.

DISTRUST IN CHILD CARE: WHOM DO MOTHERS TRUST?

For mothers looking for child care, then, the main challenge was to find not only caregivers who could cover the hours they needed but caregivers whom the mothers could trust. The majority of mothers felt that the most trustworthy providers were relatives. Mothers believed they knew enough about relatives' habits to know how the relatives would treat their children. They also believed that since relatives had been raised in the same extended family as they were themselves, relatives would share their parenting style. In some cases, they felt that because they had given relatives various services and resources in the past, relatives would be obliged to fulfill their care needs. But perhaps most importantly, mothers believed that because of the kinship tie between relatives and children, relatives would share the same interests as the mothers themselves in keeping children well protected.

Renee Steele expressed the same preference for relatives' care that many mothers shared. "I don't like different people watching my kids 'cause it's so much stuff be happening to people kids these days. Plus, I got little kids, and I don't like different people watching my kids. I don't care if they is gonna get paid. I don't trust people to watch my kids. I rather have my mother watch my kids than somebody else."

While most women preferred family members because they trusted them more, some spoke more directly of a general community belief, particularly in the African American community, in the inappropriateness of nonfamily members, or "outsiders," caring for children. As Shandra Muse stated, "One of the basic reason is being trustworthy. We, well us as a society and I think I can basically speak to it 'cause I've heard a few other black women state that they rather that they family member or someone in the family take care of their child than a outsider because so many things have happened, you know, in the child care."

Jamila Meeks similarly discussed a belief, ingrained in her from childhood, that only family members should provide care for children.

> Even though I had insiders like my sister, my nephew and my niece, . . . I still needed another backup, just in case, because it may be that all of them at one time be having something to do. . . . I hadn't considered actuality of like a child care [center] because that was a "no-no" from being the way I was raised. It was like, your family takes care of your children. And so for child care, that was like, totally, for me, I couldn't even see myself, and then my sister was like, "Well no, I'll take care of him."

Whether it was due to normative views that it was inappropriate for non-kin to serve as child care providers or whether it related exclusively to the issue of trust, most mothers preferred to use relatives or close friends rather than day care homes or formal centers for their care needs. However, not all mothers did. Some mothers did not trust family members to provide quality care, and others had learned through experience that trust in certain family members was misplaced.

Ronnie Simpson, whose two children were cared for by an aunt while she worked, was dismayed to learn that her cousin (one of her aunt's adult children) had hit her child with a belt while her aunt was out of the house. She complained to her aunt, who scolded the cousin, but Ronnie no longer trusted this arrangement. When I visited Ronnie a few months later, she told me she had taken her children from her aunt's house and that they were now being cared for by her fiancé, who was unemployed. Both Ronnie and her fiancé wanted him to find a job since they needed additional income, but she did not know what she would do for child care if he became employed and could no longer watch the children. Her child care situation was further complicated by the fact that she had become pregnant with twins. Given her precarious child care situation and her pregnancy, the longevity of her job seemed at risk.

Justine Parker knew that she did not trust many of her family members because she had grown up in a violent household and had experienced domestic violence with her own partner as well. She did feel, however, that she could trust a male friend (who was not a boyfriend) to watch her children. However, the Department of Children and Family Services investigated her children's safety after this friend brought naked photographs of her ten-year-old son for developing to a drugstore (which alerted authorities). After that, Justine felt that she literally could trust no one but herself with her children and was fearful that if she was not continually vigilant the children would be taken from her by the state.

As a child, Chantal Greene became a ward of the state because of her mother's substance abuse problem. Now, Chantal needed child care for her own children, but her mother was not a source she would trust. "I don't really want her to be around my kids, so I see her every once in a while, and then my kids see her like every once in a while, but no, I don't want her to be around my kids. . . . I don't let her take my kids nowhere. It's just 'cause how she is, no, she use drugs, and who knows if she using drugs one day and got my kids, might leave my kids somewhere. Nah uh. She can see 'em over at my house, but she can't take 'em nowhere."

Not only did Anita Anzaldúa have few family members or friends to help her with her children, but she was often burdened by having to provide care for others' children. In particular, her sister, whom she described as completely untrustworthy, regularly (and often successfully) tried to leave her children with Anita without asking or giving advance notice. These involuntary child care duties often made it hard for Anita to go to work. Anita described one time when she was able to thwart her sister's efforts.

> She just put them down and, you know, she tiptoed to the door and tried, and I said, "Where you going?" "Oh, I'm going downstairs to your car for a minute." I said, "To my car? Why are you going to my car? Where's my keys?" She had my keys and everything. "Oh, I'm just going to get um some toys or something outta the car." I said, "You're crazy." I said, "You know what? Take your two babies with you." She didn't want to until my [other] sister screamed, "Take those two babies

with you! You don't have no say around here." You know, she would always leave those kids. She would always pay somebody . . . to stay with those kids. And me? I wouldn't leave my kids to nobody, not my mom, not nobody.

Some mothers who did not have family available or who did not trust their family members to provide quality care considered formal day care centers a good choice—and often considered them more trustworthy than informal day care in which a provider would take children into her own home and was often unlicensed.

As Beverly Manning explained,

Well, they've been to a lot of day care. But I prefer like the facilities, not the home day care. Because the homes, in someone's home they have, you know, problems like anybody else, and it's at their house, and you really don't know what's really going on at their house when you're at work. And I was watching *Maury* [the television program] the other day and I had seen how this one babysitter, . . . she was beating the kids up, smacking 'em around and stuff, and I really don't like that. . . . I know with the public facility it's a little more professional 'cause it's at a actual facility . . . so I prefer to have them in [one]. I have a lot of family, my grandmother had sixteen children, and if she's not with family, then I prefer to put her in a licensed day care.

One day Tanya Barker's daughter had a bruise when Tanya picked her up from her in-home day care. Tanya asked the provider what had happened and got only a vague response. She immediately removed her daughter from the placement and found a formal center where there would be more oversight of caregivers and procedures to document any incidents in which children were hurt. "Yeah, I didn't even take her clothes. I called and reported her too. So if they let her watch any more kids over there, I don't know what's wrong with them. 'Cause I reported her 'cause I don't feel that's right. You don't be abusing nobody's child. When I took them to day care [the formal center] down there, she fell and hurt herself and they wrote up a incident report and gave me a incident report and told me why, okay. I feel a little bit comfortable, at least you put it on paper."

UNDERSTANDING MOTHERS' DISTRUST
IN CHILD CARE PROVIDERS

The mothers interviewed based their distrust on a combination of direct experiences with specific interaction partners, more distant information about the general category of interaction partners, and a practice of preemptive skepticism as a protective device. Some of the mothers were not initially distrusting. In fact, their lack of suspicion led to their use of providers who were not trustworthy, and these experiences led to eventual distrust. Ronnie's faith in her aunt and cousins and Daeshawna's confidence in her former coworker are clear cases of misplaced trust. The resulting physical harm to their children taught them not only that those particular child care providers could not be trusted but that they should be wary of all potential providers. These women did not enter into their interactions with providers armed with any kind of preemptive distrust. Quite the contrary, they entered without any such protection, only to learn their distrust through direct experience.

Some of the handful of women who sent their children to formal child care centers also learned to distrust through experience. Kate was open to using a formal center until her son David was bitten several times by another toddler and she began to distrust the level of supervision the children received. However, for many women, wariness of formal centers was not based on any direct experience of their own or even of their friends and family. Instead of basing distrust on direct experience, some women voiced a generalized distrust of formal organizations over which they felt they had little control. Akira, for instance, distrusted the day care center where her son went, not because she had any evidence he had been mistreated, but only because she suspected that for center staff "it's really all about the money." She felt staff were motivated by making money rather than caring for children, who would know "if they're not wanted."

Clearly women like Akira do not believe they have the power to demand the high-quality care services that middle-class parents paying market rates feel they can demand. And because the low-income mothers I interviewed felt powerless in this way, they distrusted that they could ever get good care from a formal center, just as they suspected they would be mistreated by other representatives of formal organizations such as caseworkers and bosses. The belief many of the women shared that only kin should watch children probably related as well to this kind of distrust. It indicates a feeling that if one is powerless to control how one is treated by formal organizations, the safest approach is to turn to one's own community, where those with limited power can protect each other.

Other mothers seemed to base their distrust, at least in part, on what could best be described as a "moral panic" that gripped the United States in the 1980s and early 1990s, when day care centers and other sources of care for children were suspected of physical, psychological, and sexual abuse of children.[12] This was illustrated most clearly by the McMartin Preschool scandal, in which preschool staff were said to have impossible powers such as the ability to fly and were accused of a bizarre range of mistreatment of children, including performing satanic rituals on their young charges in underground tunnels on the school's grounds. Even though the mother who initiated the charges was later revealed to have suffered from schizophrenia, and even though the longest and most expensive trial in U.S. history was unable to produce a single conviction, the McMartin case cast a long shadow of doubt for parents anxious about women's entry into the labor market and the potential effects on children placed in the care of others. The news and popular media, capitalizing on this fear, have in the intervening years shown a series of sensationalized stories about the abuse of children when cared for by people other than their mothers.[13]

Catalina's reference to "something happen in the news" and Beverly's mention of a segment about abusive babysitters on the television show *Maury* both indicate that stories distributed through the media influence mothers' distrust. Two other women made vaguer references to a general fear about dangers to children that lurks in the cultural zeitgeist. Shandra did not trust an "outsider" because "so many things have happened in the child care," and Renee mentioned that "so much stuff be happening to people kids these days."

While mothers were probably right to be suspicious of some caretakers, the belief that outsiders are always more dangerous than kin is not supported by research, which finds that children experience more harm in the care of friends and family than in formal child care centers.[14] It was Justine's friend who photographed her naked son, and it was Ronnie's cousin who hit her child with a belt, not staff members of child care centers. Low-income mothers probably do not have access to data about rates of abuse and neglect in various kinds of child care provision. They thus must rely on their own experience, the experiences of their close network ties, and more general sources of information such as the media. This last source may not always be one that reliably helps mothers reach their goal of ensuring their children's well-being.

Aside from not having access to the research showing the relatively higher rate of abuse and neglect by relatives than by staff in formal centers, why might mothers trust relatives more than others with their children? The theoretical literature on trust suggests several reasons. We know from the literature that people are more likely to trust those they know well, those whose motivations they know and endorse, and those who they believe share their interests.[15] The women I interviewed indeed were more likely to trust their family members as child care providers because, in sharp contrast to "outsiders," they felt they knew family members and their motivations well and believed that relatives shared their interests in their children's well-being.[16]

As has been documented in national studies, there is nothing unusual about the women I interviewed—low-income mothers in general are more likely to rely on relatives to provide care for their children than to use other sources of care.[17] Some of this reliance on relatives has been shown to relate to cost and availability. Studies demonstrate that before welfare reform and its expansions in child care funding, low-income mothers had great concern about their ability to cover the cost of child care.[18] In part because of this concern, many women opted to use relatives or other network members for child care when available, since they were often willing to provide care at low rates or even for free.[19] After reform, some of the cost issue has been alleviated, although child care subsidies remain below market rates and accessing and maintaining subsidies can be difficult.[20] Subsidies lower parents' costs but do not necessarily lower problems they face in managing child care issues.[21] Poor mothers in the post-reform era still rely heavily on informal network-based care,[22] although in order to fully meet work and family demands many mothers must piece together a variety of child care sources.[23] The need to combine multiple sources of child care is especially great for mothers who have varied work schedules that include nonstandard hours.[24]

In addition to their comfort with family members, some low-income mothers may use relatives' care because relatives face their own barriers to entry into other forms of employment and are thus more available in these cases.[25] The use of network-based care, however, can impose its own problems in terms of insufficient availability, stability, and quality of care.[26] Given these issues, some scholars propose that we need to provide greater support for the use of a variety of methods to meet poor women's child care needs.[27] Despite all of these practical concerns documented by other studies, the reason given most often by the women I interviewed for why they preferred to use relatives for child care was that they trusted relatives the most.

INCREASING MOTHERS' TRUST IN CHILD CARE CENTERS

The best way to improve mothers' trust in child care centers is to make structural changes in the child care market that improve the trustworthiness of centers. The child care policy built into welfare policy is more focused on moving mothers into the labor market, however, than it is on improving the quality of child care available. Reformers suspected that many recipients just needed a push to get into the labor market and to address all the problems that were keeping them out. Given that so many recipients moved into jobs and off the welfare rolls, they were, in a sense, right. An important question, though, is what the costs of this forced labor market transition may be. Child care subsidies are primarily a work support, providing parents the means to enter the child care market as purchasers of services. The ability of subsidies to positively affect children's development is less clear.[28] Several mothers discussed feeling forced to use child care they did not trust, sometimes to the detriment of their children's physical, and perhaps psychological, well-being. In fact, scholars have recognized that the two goals of child care policy—maternal employment support and child development—compete with one another.[29] Currently, the vast majority of the money available through the federal Child Care and Development Fund (CCDF) goes toward the direct provision of child care subsidies to support mothers' ability to enter the labor force, with a significantly lower proportion of funds being used for grants or contracts to develop child care program slots. Only 4 percent of the funds are earmarked for quality improvements in care.[30] Yet children in poverty have been found to benefit more from high-quality care services than children living above the poverty line, and access to such care in low-income communities is uneven.[31]

Since mothers will continue to distrust low-quality care, increasing both the absolute amount of CCDF funding and the proportion of that funding that goes toward quality improvements is probably the most important policy approach to boost trust. Given the potential advantages of building mothers' trust in formal child care centers, it is also worth the effort to devise creative ways to expose low-income mothers to formal centers so that they may learn to trust them over time. Centers that operate in transparent ways and that openly communicate with parents will be most likely to earn trust.

Forcing mothers to use care they do not trust is a troubling aspect of welfare reform. An afternoon with Dolores Rios, interviewed before reform, made clear why it is so difficult for low-income mothers, especially those living in low-income neighborhoods with visible street crime, to turn their children over to others' care. On one of my visits with Dolores, her eight-year-old daughter Lili asked her mother if she could walk me out. "Only to the gate, no further," came Dolores's reply. At the edge of her apartment building's courtyard, Lili stood on the big iron gate and swung herself out onto the sidewalk, buying an extra five feet or so of freedom while technically not breaking her mother's rule. "See that lady?" she asked me excitedly while pointing to a figure seated on a bench across the street. "She's a prostitute." Like any eight-year-old, Lili was fascinated by the world around her, and that was her mother's greatest fear. Dolores did not see how she could take a job that would leave Lili and her other children without her watchful eye.

If child care is viewed simply as a barrier to work, the claim that welfare reform addressed the child care problem that Dolores and Lili highlight is probably right. However, on the basis of the accounts of the mothers interviewed after reform in this study, women struggle just as much to find care they can trust for their children after reform as they did before reform. A more nuanced notion of success—one in which children are reliably nurtured while their mothers are at jobs—has apparently not yet been met, despite reformers' promises.

FIVE

"You Can't Put Your Trust in Men"

GENDER DISTRUST AND MARRIAGE

If you bad when you not married, what make me think I'm
gonna change you when you do get married? . . . If there
ain't no trust, ain't no love, then there's no relationship.

—Tanya Barker

Darlene Harris, an African American mother of a two-year-old son, was
twenty-two years old when I interviewed her in 1994 before welfare
reform. She had the poise of someone much older. Darlene spoke with
determination about wanting to become a nurse and own a house. If she
reached these goals, it would be in spite of the difficulties put in her
way by her son's father. She had spent four years with James but had
finally extricated herself from daily life with his erratic behavior and its
associated financial and emotional drains. Their breakup, however, did
not free her completely from his interference.

Darlene's main complaint about James was that his drinking and drug
use sapped him of any sense of responsibility for her or her son's financial needs and that it created havoc in their household. For almost a year
of their relationship, he did not work at all. She worked forty or fifty

hours a week and paid all of the rent during this time. She also became pregnant. She was thus relieved when James managed to get a good job at a hospital. "Now I'm thinkin', you know, 'He got a nice job. He gonna pay all the rent,'" she explained. But disappointment returned when he ended up losing the hospital job because he would stay out late drinking and miss work. Darlene was eight months pregnant when James got fired. On top of that, in the middle of January in Chicago, James sold Darlene's only coat because he needed the money. Eventually, James got a fast-food job, where he worked at the time of our interview and where Darlene suspected he would always work. "I guess that's where he always gonna be," she said with a bit of disgust in her voice.

Darlene's frustration grew more and more intense because not only did James fail to bring income into the household while she was pregnant, but he often had friends over who expected her to supply them with food and drinks. "I would come home, he got a house full of his friends and drinking everything. It's twelve o'clock at night, you know, 'Can't even one of y'all meet me at the bus stop?' One night I came home and I went off . . . I just cleared everybody out. . . . I was like 'No, y'all got to go.' Ate up all the food, you know. 'What you bring home from work?' and stuff like that." Finally, Darlene left James, who then became increasingly abusive, largely related to his jealousy about the possibility that she might be with someone else. He broke into her apartment on several occasions, once throwing a chair through the window. After that incident he was sent to jail, but he was released when Darlene succumbed to pressure from his family to drop the charges. He also once broke the windows of their son's babysitter's house because he thought Darlene was inside. The babysitter then quit, leaving Darlene in a bind for child care when she worked. Luckily, her grandmother filled in, but her grandmother had asthma and lived in a housing project where Darlene did not feel her son was safe.

The thought that she might have married James, as they had sometimes discussed, was disturbing to Darlene. "Me and his father talk[ed] about marriage a lot, before I even got pregnant, but I'm glad I didn't do that. . . . Now he can say, 'Well, I got a baby by you' and this and that. If I was married to him, he [would say,] 'You my wife.' You know, that would mean something else he would have to hang onto." The last thing Darlene wanted to do was give James more control over her life.

Welfare reform's goal of promoting marriage, or at least healthy relationships between children's mothers and fathers and the involvement of fathers with their children, did not lead Mia Fields, interviewed after reform, to feel much differently about the father of her four children than Darlene felt about James. Dushawn was a drug dealer turned drug user who got so addicted he could no longer function as a dealer. To make matters worse, the law had caught up with him and he was on house arrest so had little opportunity to bring any money into the household. At that point, he began taking Mia's paycheck for himself. As the mother of three children, and pregnant with a fourth at the time, Mia was desperate.

She described the day that she prayed to God to be released from the burden Dushawn posed. To her great surprise, the next day law enforcement agents came to her home, accused Dushawn of having been "out of bounds" (breaking the rules of his house arrest), and took him into their custody. Mia explained that she could attribute this event only to her prayers, since Dushawn had never left the house. "The next morning, God as my witness, it was the sheriff at my front door. I'm in there cooking pancakes for me and the kids. [The sheriff] came and got [Dushawn] and told him he was outta bounds. I swear, that man had not left the house, period. . . . I didn't cry, I did not shed one tear, and I looked up at [God] and I said, 'Boy, you is one powerful guy.'"

Since then, Dushawn had been in and out of prison, most recently for a six-year period. At the time Mia and I first spoke, he had been out for a year and had come out no longer hooked on drugs. He still contributed nothing financially to the household, and Mia would not have anything to do with him herself, but he did see the children. The children, however, hurt that their father often promised to pick them up for an activity and then failed to show up, were not sure they felt any differently about Dushawn than their mother did. As Mia reported, "Don't do my kids like that, 'cause they, you know, they trustworthy kids. If you say you gonna do something, they look for it. You know, 'cause that's what I gave 'em. If you can't do that, let me know. 'Cause that take a lotta effect on a child, and then you lose your trust with 'em too'cause they thinking, 'Well, you lied that time, so I don't know if I'm gonna get ready today.'" Mia did not trust a lot of people, but she distrusted Dushawn the most. Her attitude was "We're a stress-free household—leave us alone!"

By the time I met Mia she had met another man she called her "friend," though he was clearly more. She smiled when she talked about him. She described him as wonderful and trustworthy but refused to marry him even though he had asked several times. He was employed and helped her with her kids, taking them for haircuts and out to eat. Still, she would let him into her life only so far. Her philosophy was that you needed to protect yourself and your children by not trusting anyone, even the apparently trustworthy, too much: "I care about him, it's just I'm so used to my own time and I have my own life, the way I set it up and with my kids. . . . We do a lot of things together, but it's just, marriage is not something I think I want to do, and then later on it might not work out. So I didn't want to put the pressure on myself." Mia tied her view on marriage to a larger view on trust and protecting oneself. After her difficult experiences with Dushawn, she developed a barrier between her household and the outside world. This protective shell was to keep out the potentially untrustworthy, which included just about everyone. As she continued right after her discussion of marriage above, "That's the type of person I am, and that's the way I want my girls to be. I want them to be independ[ent] and not too sociable. And if you talk to one of them, they will actually tell you they do not have friends, they have associates. All my kids say, 'My friend is my mother. Anybody else is associates to me.' I'm glad they got that attitude, 'cause right now today you really can't trust no one." Having "associates" was fine, but letting anyone move beyond that level of acquaintance was too risky for Mia.

Darlene and Mia's experiences were far from unique. While many other mothers in both time periods had less dramatic reasons to distance themselves from the fathers of their children, distance between children's parents was the most common state of affairs. Some women had become involved with new men since the disintegration of their relationships with their children's fathers, but, like Mia, they often kept these men at a certain distance. Some of the women did marry or cohabit with their first or later children's fathers or with new partners met after their children were born. However, the relationships between many of the low-income women interviewed and their partners or potential partners were so marked by distrust that they failed to result in long-term cohabitation or marriage. As such, the women's families looked similar to those in the Fragile Families and Child Wellbeing Study, which followed close to five thousand children in large U.S. cities from their birth to age five years. (Three-quarters of the children were born to unmarried parents, hence the term *fragile* to capture the families' increased likelihood of dissolution and experience of poverty.) In that study, only 51 percent of children still cohabited with their fathers a year after the children's births. By the time the children were five years old, almost two-thirds of them no longer lived with their fathers.[1] Table 1, discussed below, shows the partnership status of the women I interviewed at the time of the interviews.

In their book *Promises I Can Keep: Why Poor Women Put Motherhood before Marriage*, Kathryn Edin and Maria Kefalas point to distrust in men as a major explanation of why the 162 women they interviewed in Philadelphia and Camden, New Jersey, chose not to marry the fathers of their children.[2] Multiple other studies have also highlighted the ways gender distrust marks the romantic relationships of low-income couples and interactions of low-income men and women more generally.[3] Thus the distrust in men reported by the women I interviewed is not unique to the samples of women I drew. Similar pronouncements of distrust have been made by women in a variety of studies.

At times, the women I interviewed spoke of men's lack of trustworthiness in general. But mostly they told stories of how they had learned to distrust men through their prior involvements with men who proved untrustworthy in specific ways. A good number of mothers in both time periods blamed abusive, dangerous, belittling, or simply unsupportive former husbands and boyfriends for derailing their lives. The experience of having opened themselves up in such intimate relationships only to be treated badly in return led some women to swear off men entirely and others to be wary of letting the men with whom they became romantically involved too deeply into their family lives. While some of this caution was about protecting their own hearts and minds, much of it was driven by the desire to protect their children both physically and emotionally from men they feared capable of violence, neglect, or psychological cruelty. Mia Fields's gamble to take tentative steps toward a new relationship was paying off in that she enjoyed the company of her "friend" and he helped her with her children. Other women did not know if they would similarly benefit and often did not want to take the chance. Their reluctance may have cost them opportunities for financial help and emotional fulfillment. On the other hand, if their suspicions were well founded, it may have protected them from the chaos that relationships had brought in the past.

Welfare reform aimed to promote marriage and the involvement of fathers with their children. But the policies it initiated did not address the nature of men's and women's perceptions of and interactions with each other. Nor did welfare reform alter any of the structural bases of these perceptions, such as the increasingly low wages low-skilled men could garner in the labor market, the dramatic increase in the past several decades in the government's use of incarceration as a crime prevention strategy, and the meager level of cash assistance payments that have made it hard for mothers to absorb unemployed men into their households.[4] Without addressing the nature of gender relationships and the structural elements that promote distrust in them, it is unlikely that more superficial policy changes, such as those of welfare reform, will be effective in promoting permanent unions.

This chapter begins by outlining what welfare reform did to try to promote marriage and paternal involvement and discussing the fact that quantitative evaluations of reform show these policies to have had little effect on family structure. I argue that welfare reform policies did not effectively promote marriage because they did not address distrust between women and men or the structures that create it. The chapter thus proceeds to demonstrate women's high level of distrust in men both before and after reform and to discuss how that distrust is produced through women's experiences with their romantic partners. This part of the chapter may seem to readers far afield from the topic of welfare reform, and that is the very point: reform policies did not address the production of women's distrust of their potential romantic partners. From this study of women, I can report only on women's distrust of men. But researchers studying low-income men find high levels of men's distrust in women as well, which welfare reform also did not address.[5] The chapter concludes with a discussion of the structural forces that undergird gender distrust and the policies that could ameliorate them.

WELFARE REFORM AND THE FAMILY

Marriage has become increasingly rare among low-income parents, and many children are born to unmarried parents.[6] One of welfare reform's key goals was to increase the marriage rate and lower the nonmarital fertility rate by promoting marriage and paternal involvement. For some policy makers, this set of goals probably involved beliefs about the immorality of nonmarital childbearing and cohabitation.[7] For others, these goals may have been primarily about marriage as economic behavior. If indeed married parents produce more income between them and share resources more efficiently, they are less likely to need welfare for survival.[8] Thus marriage might produce both economic gains for the partners and cost savings for state governments. Greater material resources for the parents might also translate into positive outcomes for children. However, both the stories of the women I interviewed and the work of other scholars provide evidence that the potential marriage partners for low-income women do not always bring economic resources into families and can even be an economic drain on them.[9]

Attempting to Change Low-Income Families

Before welfare reform, only single parents could receive cash assistance through the previous program, Aid to Families with Dependent Children (AFDC).[10] Reform reduced this disincentive to marry by allowing married couples to receive assistance from the new program, Temporary Assistance for Needy Families (TANF). However, both spouses' incomes are considered in determining eligibility for TANF, so women married to employed men are not eligible if husbands' earnings raise the family above the eligibility limit. If both spouses are employed, meeting the income limit for eligibility is that much less likely.

Through offers of federal funding, post-reform welfare policy also encourages, but does not require, states to promote marriage through relationship-training courses. When the TANF program was reauthorized in 2005, the Bush administration pushed for and won approval of $150 million (a relatively small amount by federal spending standards) to introduce the Healthy Marriage Initiative (HMI), which includes Healthy Marriage training programs for low-income parents. Healthy Marriage programs teach listening, problem-solving, and anger management skills as well as the value of commitment to one's partner as a strategy to manage life's challenges. Training programs vary in length from single half-day sessions to weekly sessions lasting several months.[11] Given the relatively small budget for these programs and the fact that only some states have chosen to develop them, marriage promotion programming for parents has seen as much, if not more, action in rhetoric as in actual implementation and spending allocation. Illinois is one of the states that chose not to offer Healthy Marriage programs. While my respondents were usually encouraged by caseworkers to make their relationships work and to think of marriage as a goal, they did not attend Healthy Marriage programs. These programs in other states, however, have not met with much success in changing marriage and nonmarital fertility patterns.[12] The challenges the women I interviewed faced in their relationships suggest why these programs may not be sufficient to meet their goals.

The federal government has also attempted to lower nonmarital fertility rates by offering financial bonuses to states that succeed in doing so. States have used these funds in a variety of ways. Some have focused on addressing teen fertility through abstinence education programs offered in schools, after-school programs, or other settings through which teens can be reached. Some have funded state health departments to work on linking access to contraceptives and family planning information to primary medical care. Others have tried to reach potential fathers through community programs that promote responsible fatherhood. Finally, close to half of the states initially adopted the family cap, the policy discussed in both chapters 1 and 2 that denies additional cash assistance for children born to women already receiving assistance for other children. Since the family cap has been found to have little effect on fertility, Illinois, which originally adopted the policy, dropped it shortly before I began the post-reform interviews.

In addition, the reform legislation requires women applying for public assistance to legally establish the paternity, meaning the identity of the fathers, of their children. Legislators hoped that formal paternity establishment might lead to greater paternal involvement with children and the benefits, both economic and noneconomic, that such involvement could bring. Some legislators might also have hoped that the legal connection between parents might lead to joint family formation and marriage.[13]

A more immediately practical implication of the policy is that establishing paternity enables the states to offset the cost of welfare by collecting child support payments from fathers. Such awards, which vary across cases but are typically based on a percentage of a noncustodial parent's earnings, mostly serve to pay back the state for expenditures on cash assistance. Only the first $50 a month is passed on to the custodial parent, usually the mother. The remainder of whatever the noncustodial parent pays in child support goes to the state. However, if an award is large enough, a mother can be better off receiving child support directly from her child's father and forgoing the cash assistance, which would be in welfare offices' interests, since they are under pressure to reduce their caseloads. Being named as a father to the state, however, can have negative consequences for fathers, since it exposes them to the garnishing of their wages and what may feel like harassment from the state. Mothers must often choose between hostile treatment by fathers for cooperating with the state and hostile treatment by caseworkers for not cooperating with the state.[14]

Marriage promotion rhetoric and policy are controversial for several reasons. Most notable is the message that other family forms and nonmarital sexual activity are immoral. Some critics of marriage promotion see this position as being unduly judgmental, disrespecting single-mother families, and suggesting that women's only potential economic (and social) salvation is through men. The assumption that marriage brings economic benefits to women and children is also questionable. While marriage is positively correlated with income and wealth, it is not yet established indisputably that the relationship between marriage and wealth is causal.[15] If this correlation applies to individuals selected into marriage by their ability to earn income or their access to wealth, or to individuals who wait to marry until they are in solid economic positions, then it may be inappropriate to expect that the unmarried, if they too were to marry, would reap the economic rewards that the married enjoy. Low-income women may be particularly unlikely to improve their lots through marriage, since the men they meet are mostly also low income and many are unemployed.[16] Indeed, the decision not to marry is for some low-income women a defense against being pulled further into economic hardship by adding another mouth to feed to the household.[17]

Mandatory paternity establishment is also controversial.[18] The most serious concern is that it will expose women and children to domestic violence if it reintroduces men who are perpetrators of violence into their lives. Domestic violence prevention advocates campaigned successfully to amend paternity establishment rules to exempt women who can demonstrate that paternity establishment would put them at risk of domestic violence.[19] Concerns remain, however, that exemptions are too hard to obtain. Less dramatically, there is concern that paternity establishment creates hostility toward mothers from fathers who become subject to wage garnishing by the state for child support payments.[20] Such hostility is counterproductive to the goal of reuniting parents with each other and with children. State involvement may also interrupt successful informal arrangements between parents, replacing them with more formal, less cooperative exchanges, which again may drive parents and children further apart rather than bring them together.[21]

Finally, there are concerns for the well-being of the men. To the degree that the fathers of low-income children are low income themselves, they may be barely surviving economically.[22] Child support awards may create additional economic hardship, and failure to pay may expose fathers to jail time. These outcomes too are unlikely to enhance the chances for family reunification. The economic pressures on fathers may also drive them into the underground economy, where earnings are not documented and thus cannot be garnished by the state. These concerns for the fathers may not seem as important as the fathers' financial responsibility for the children and the children's need for child support payments. However, since only the $50 per month "pass through" goes to a child if the child is on a welfare grant, the financial benefits to children and their mothers are not large.

No Increase in Marriage

Regardless of these controversies, most would probably agree that an environment hospitable to marriage for those who desire it is a good thing. The question is whether the marriage promotion rhetoric and paternity establishment policies of welfare reform have the power to promote lasting unions. Jacob Klerman's chapter in Grogger and Karoly's thorough review of welfare reform evaluation research shows strikingly little, if any, effect of the policies initiated by welfare reform on either marriage or nonmarital childbearing.[23] The marital status patterns among the women I interviewed reflect the results found in the more representative quantitative studies that Klerman reviews. Very few of the women in either time period were still romantically involved with the fathers of their first children, and only a minority were involved with the fathers of later children.

Table 1 shows the marital and partnership status of the women at the time of their interviews.[24] Almost half of the women before reform (42 percent, or eleven out of twenty-six) and more than half of the women after reform (65 percent, or forty-five out of sixty-nine) had never been married (and were not cohabiting). Only one woman (4 percent) before reform and five women (7 percent) after reform were married. The same numbers (one before reform and five after reform) were not married but were cohabiting with a partner. While it is not shown in the table, some women (29 percent, or five out of twenty-six before reform and 31 percent, or twenty-four out of sixty-nine after reform) who were

Table 1   Marital and Partnership Status for Women Interviewed before and after Reform

Marital/Partnership Status[a]	Before Reform	After Reform
	% (number in parentheses)	% (number in parentheses)
Single, never married, not cohabitating	42 (11)*	65 (45)
Cohabiting, not married	4 (1)	7 (5)
Separated	19 (5)	9 (6)
Divorced	31 (8)*	12 (8)
Married	4 (1)	7 (5)
Total	100 (26)	100 (69)

NOTE: While the study data are not from random samples, the table follows a common practice of using statistical tests to show how large the differences are between the pre- and post-reform samples without making claims of formal statistical significance.

a. Tables of marital and partnership status typically include a category for "widowed." None of the women were widowed, but one woman before reform and nine women after reform had children with men who subsequently died. While some of these women were still romantically involved with the men at the time of the men's deaths, none were married to the men.

*p < .05.

neither married nor cohabiting had some degree of romantic involvement with a man. But the women were hesitant to let these men too far into their lives. Thus, as we might expect from the results of the quantitative evaluations of reform's effects, the policies reform initiated to promote marriage and nonmarital fertility were not reflected in high rates of marriage, childbearing within marriage, or attachment to the fathers of children for the women in this study in either time period.

ISSUES OF DISTRUST IN GENDER RELATIONS

Among the women interviewed, the vast majority were no longer with their children's fathers. Their descriptions of these discontinued relationships spanned a wide range. Some of the relationships had been fleeting—a few as brief as one night, but most a bit longer than that.

The fleeting relationships ended as most fleeting ones do. They were based on very little attachment to begin with, and hence very little had to happen to initiate their dissolution. A simple discovery that the two people involved had no real attraction, had little interest in each other, or annoyed each other was enough to end the relationship. Some of these fathers stayed involved with the children, or at least the fathers' mothers or other family members did. Many did not.

The longer-term relationships, which ranged from a year or two to a decade or more, ended for a variety of reasons. A few women were left by their partners and were stunned by their disappearance. Some partners just grew apart as time and age progressed, leading to a separation but leaving neither partner with any great animosity. Other women felt driven to extricate themselves from relationships that had become dysfunctional, in some cases doing so to save themselves and their children from untenable or even dangerous circumstances.

Among the small minority of the women who were still involved with the fathers of their first children, only a few of these women described these relationships in positive terms. Many more had complaints, some quite severe.

Learning through Experience to Distrust Men

Most women recounted ways in which they had learned to distrust men, not because of an abstract concept of men in general but because of direct experience with specific men. Many in fact told stories of having placed too much trust in a certain man too soon, only to learn, painfully, that the trust was misplaced. They then commented that this experience had led them to distrust men in the future in order to protect themselves and their children.

It took Juanita Soto (whom we met in chapter 3) nine years and one hospital stay to shake off Manny, whom she had married and divorced, and with whom she had had three children, but she was finally free. His sentencing to a ten-year prison term for drug dealing was her ticket out from under his control. "It was kind of a load off really. 'Cause I was kind of living paranoid. I was scared of him." Juanita described Manny as initially romantic but as gradually becoming someone else. He "talked down" to her and made her question her own worth. She attributed a nervous breakdown and a psychiatric hospital stay to the stress of the relationship: "To tell you the truth, Manny has always been . . . he was a nice person, but when he chose the drug he changed into a bad person which was like the devil. From that point on he just kept down-talking me and making me feel dumb and just drowning that in my mind. Drowning it and drowning it . . . 'Oh, you ain't going to accomplish nothing. You're nobody. You're so stupid. Look at how . . . you don't even know how to talk. You don't even know how to read.'"

After Manny's imprisonment, despite her loneliness, Juanita was led by her experience to abstain from engaging in relationships with men. She explained,

> I wouldn't want to get married again, to be honest with you. . . . It's probably why I'm by myself, 'cause I don't trust men. They . . . they scare me. In fact, they're so dominat[ing] and loud and . . . it's like they just don't want you to succeed. . . . So, I don't think so. Maybe if I get old, somebody will take care of me. [Laughs.] But right now, I'm not looking for nobody, I'm not. . . . I don't have anybody on my mind. I'm just trying to make it for myself and my kids. Especially for them. . . . I want their lives to be better than what mine was.

Koyana Woods, interviewed after reform, had similar experiences. She was married for fifteen years to the father of four of her six children. She did not realize when they married that he had a drug problem. Through his addiction, he became violent, at times threatening her to give him money for drugs. It took her a long time to get out of the marriage. Despite this experience, after her divorce, she allowed herself to become involved with another man. She felt she could tell this man anything and that he was the love of her life, but he left her for another woman. She told me that she would never become involved romantically with a man again.

Juanita's and Koyana's experiences were not shared by all of the women in the study. Some mothers reported cordial or even supportive relationships with former partners and the fathers of their children. Some mothers had little involvement with the fathers of their children but did not blame the fathers. Instead, they explained that these men were either too young at the time of the children's births or too burdened by troubles of their own to carry out paternal responsibilities. A few women blamed themselves for the failure of romantic relationships.

Even so, Juanita's and Koyana's experiences were far from unique. While some women found ways to trust partners again (some with success, some again disappointed), the learned distrust of many led them to decide they were better off alone with their children. As Tanya Barker said when explaining why she had not accepted her boyfriend's marriage proposal, "If I can't trust you now, I'm gonna trust you later? If you bad when you not married, what make me think I'm gonna change you when you do get married?"

The vast majority of the women's discussions about why they distrusted men surrounded specific incidents from their past interactions with partners. But there were a handful of exceptions when women indicated a generalized distrust in men, that is, a view that men were an untrustworthy group, that was not based on their own or another woman's specific experience.

As Ronnie Simpson, a woman interviewed after reform, said when asked to rate her trust level in her partner in whom she—unlike most other women—placed enormous trust, "He's supposed to be a ten, but I give him a nine and a half. You can't put your trust in men. Men put you down, so I give him a nine." Shermaine Jackson, another woman interviewed after reform, echoed Ronnie when she said that she trusted the father of her children with the children but that she herself did not trust him because he was a man and she did not trust men in general.

Aspects of Relationships That Teach Distrust

Women lost trust in their partners along several dimensions. Some partners were untrustworthy as financial partners. These men failed to bring money into the household, demanded money from the women, or even sabotaged women's efforts to improve their lot. Some partners were untrustworthy as

lovers. They slept with other women or they provided no emotional support or intimacy. Some partners were untrustworthy as fathers. They did
not financially or emotionally support their children. Some partners were
dangerous because they themselves were violent or because they exposed
the household to those who might do harm. Some partners disappeared
from family life through choice, through imprisonment, or through death.
Many women found that their partners created disruptions that made life
chaotic and sometimes almost too difficult to bear. In the majority of cases,
these disruptions led to severing of the relationship.

MONEY

Resources, including money, were painfully scarce for almost all of the
mothers. Partnerships presented the potential for increasing resources'
supply, but they also exposed women to the possibility of competition
for or denial of resources. It was the inability to know which way the balance would tip that made partnerships a financial risk. Some women
were sure that partners would drain resources and thus avoided relationships or needed to be convinced to open their hearts and their homes.
Other women dove headlong into a relationship, sure that it offered the
promise of a better life, only to be bitterly disappointed when instead the
relationship robbed them of the few resources they already possessed.

Money, and all it represented, was a key location for the development
of women's distrust. Sharing financial resources and responsibilities or
otherwise acting as a unified economic unit can be seen as one sign of
bonding in a relationship. Many of the women's relationships were notable for their lack of financial integration, even when the partners cohabited or were married to each other. These partners often did not seem to
act as a fiscal team; they were more like two independent agents constantly eyeing each other to protect what was theirs or perhaps get what
they thought should be theirs. Many women indicated that they knew
little of how their partners spent their money. For instance, Salma
Hernandez filed separate taxes from her husband of two years and did
not know whether her husband paid child support to his children from a
previous relationship. Some women's partners took money from them;
some partners made money but never shared it. Other forms of financial

irresponsibility included partners who failed to look for or show up at jobs or who demanded that the women financially support them.

Many women discussed current or past partners' failure to make economic contributions to children and the household at large. Some described partners draining the household of financial resources. Some women attributed this financial drain to men acting selfishly or wanting to control them, some to men's own dire economic circumstances due to unemployment, and some to men's drug and alcohol problems. Some men were incarcerated or had been during parts of the relationship. Incarceration restricted men's economic participation in households, although it did not necessarily eradicate it, as some men, especially those with continuing involvement in the drug trade, sent money to their partners while incarcerated.

Jennifer Rodriguez, interviewed before reform, struggled with her partner Marco's drug use and problems maintaining employment. Marco was the father of her two young children. As one of the few women still involved with the father of her children, she was heavily invested in making the relationship work. However, despite her love for Marco, she was close to the end of her rope and knew that she might not be able to stay with him. She described Marco as a "third child" and highly "dependent" on others.

> He's real dependent. Like, right now he's upset because he doesn't have a job. And that's all he complains about. And he does go out and apply a lot, but he doesn't get called, and he gets real discouraged. . . . He's a good worker, he's a real good worker. Any job he does, he'll do it as best as he can. And then something will happen with the car, he can't get there or something. Right now, he's pretty much waiting for his brother to get him a job somewhere. He's looking, but he wants his brother to get him in. He's dependent, he's real dependent.

Jennifer suspected that Marco had returned to his previous heroin use, though he angrily denied her accusations. His unemployment led him to become increasingly depressed, and he often stormed out of the house, scaring both Jennifer and the children. Jennifer was unsure about the future of her relationship. "I don't know about my boyfriend. Because I am willing to give him up, if he's not going to straighten up with that problem. Because I don't want my children to grow up in that. If things work out, I don't know. I don't know if we'll ever get married, because it's kind of scary to get married and then have things not work out."

Jennifer's problem thus was not that she did not value what a committed relationship could bring. She did not need a marriage promotion program to encourage her to invest in her relationship. She was already trying very hard to make her relationship work. The problem extended far beyond Jennifer and Marco to the labor market that had no room for Marco and the drug trade that offered to help him escape his resulting depression. The welfare reform policies that were soon to come down the road did not attempt to fix either of those structural features of Jennifer and Marco's environment. Despite the problems, Jennifer recognized that at least Marco wanted to contribute to the household. Other women's partners or former partners did not express the same desire.

Women interviewed after reform also described the financial drain on their resources posed by their current or former partners. Alpha Walker said that her ex-partner, the father of her youngest child, would ask her for money but did not provide her with anything in exchange. Sometimes she gave in because she knew that if she gave him things he might hang around a little and spend time with the children. But she mostly thought she should resist his requests. "He [want] some beer. I don't drink beer, I ain't gonna buy no beer. Then I find myself [doing it] just sometime just to really have him around with the kids. 'Cause [men] seem to do more if you try to be there for them more, you know. If I say, '. . . Okay, I'll go to the store and get this beer,' . . . then we sit down and he be there a while. He cut the kids' hair and everything. But if I ain't got nothing to offer, sometime he gone about his business." Alpha found herself continually frustrated. She worked hard to raise her kids on her own without any help from her ex-partner and did not feel she owed him anything. She would have felt better about her ex-partner's requests if he had asked for money to help him get on his feet. "I'm like, 'Well, I think I'm doing good to raise my kids by myself. I don't need you. I don't need you to do anything, so I'm not gonna continue to give you nothing. You know, if you come to me and tell me, "Well I just got a job and I ain't got no bus fare to get there. [Can you] help me . . . till I get paid?" That be something I see myself trying to do for you. But no, not somebody who just wants me to buy some beer. You better go on.'"

While money can be a source of tension for all couples, very tight financial circumstances raise the stakes. The paternity establishment requirement for welfare recipients after reform provided an additional source of tension, especially if men felt they could not afford to pay child support and women felt they could not afford to live without it.

Wakeisha Jefferson's daughter's father lived in Mississippi. In general, Wakeisha had no real strong animosity toward him, and she took her daughter to visit him from time to time. He had informally, but minimally, helped out financially. Wakeisha attempted to routinize this informal arrangement by asking him to send her $150 every two weeks. He agreed but then failed to actually make the payments. So when Wakeisha eventually applied for welfare and was told she would need to establish paternity, she did not feel bad to have to do it "the hard way." Eventually, the father received a letter with a court date. He called Wakeisha and angrily asked her about the letter, but she pretended she did not know how they had found him. Despite his anger, she felt he had gotten what he deserved, especially when the court awarded child support payments that were higher than her initial informal request. "I said, 'Just send me a hundred and fifty dollars every two weeks,' and he didn't even do it. I'm like, 'Okay, now you can pay more than that outta your pocket.' 'Cause the actual hundred and fifty dollars every two weeks [was less] but he didn't wanna do it so he's gonna pay more."[25] Eventually he accepted that attending the court date was his responsibility and the hostility surrounding the incident died down.

Flor Ramero's experience with establishing paternity and a child support award was less successful. She was initially put off by what she considered the welfare department's invasiveness when they insisted on knowing who the father of her daughter was. She actually was not sure herself of his identity, but since the department threatened to deny her assistance without a name, she gave them the most likely candidate. He was summoned to court for a paternity test but did not show up for his court date. In lieu of the test, the court simply set a child support award.

When the potential father learned that the court would be garnishing his wages, he quit his job. At the time Flor and I spoke, he owed over $20,000 in back payments but had never paid any support.[26]

Unlike Wakeisha and Flor, Jane Pearce was able to evade the department's request to establish paternity by saying that she did not really know the father well or his last name. She feared that naming the father of her children would actually interrupt her current arrangement, which resulted both in a substantial amount of financial support paid informally and in the father's involvement in his children's lives. He bought the children clothes, paid Jane money, and was an active presence, even though Jane had since married another man. Jane said, "He has always been there for his children, so I never had to turn him over. . . . He probably would have felt like . . . I was going against him." Jane felt fortunate that her children had a responsible father, and the last thing she wanted to do was make him feel that she was taking aggressive legal action against him.

> I don't have a problem with my children father. He buy school clothes every year and shoes throughout the whole year . . . so I think that he do a whole lot and you don't find a lot of fathers out there that does that. You know, most of 'em, they just get the kids and then they're gone. . . . I thank God every day that I lucked up on a good one. I call it lucked up. I was blessed that time to find a good one 'cause you don't find too many men that stay in they children life. They just get the baby and then they gone.

Jane felt that the very policy designed to bring fathers back into the lives of children would actually push her children's father away. Her comments highlight how little the paternity establishment policy takes into consideration the dynamics between children's parents. Note that she said, "I never had to turn him over," indicating that naming the father of her child would have felt to him like a criminal accusation and punishment. Unlike so many other women, Jane actually trusted her ex-partner and saw the policy as trying to force her to break the trust she shared with him.

SABOTAGING OF WOMEN'S EFFORTS TO IMPROVE THEIR LOT

Women's distrust in the fathers of their children or in other romantic partners around financial issues extended past the men's own, often unsatisfactory, financial contributions. Some women complained that men sabotaged their efforts to work or attend school. Some women suspected that this was because their partners feared that the women's entrance into the public sphere would allow them to find other men or because it made men with little education or attachment to the labor force feel inadequate.

Iliana Dominguez lost one of her jobs because her partner pressured her to accept collect calls from him at work. Her boss caught her once and let it slide but when she caught Iliana a second time, she fired her. Ellen Graham's partner was more disruptive. He would offer to babysit their daughter while Ellen worked but would then get drunk so that at the last minute Ellen could not leave her daughter with him. She eventually lost her job for not showing up without giving sufficient notice.

Grace James's husband wanted "a traditional stay-home wife who took care of the house." At first, Grace did not mind fulfilling this role and was happy to stay home with their young son. But as her husband's drinking intensified, he began to want company. He pressured her to join him and brought his friends over to drink. She felt he was dragging her down, turning her into an alcoholic, and creating a disordered home life for her and their son. Eventually she had to leave. She described what it was like to leave him: "Well, it was hard. But it was a relief too, because I didn't have to worry about him coming home all the time at night and want to turn the radio up, stereo, two or three in the morning, sky-high, and all that junk. Or bring his friends and 'Get up and go fix my friend a sandwich,' and all this type of stuff at two and three." Grace reported that the role of traditional wife became much less appealing as she saw her husband's envisioned job for her as one of servitude, not freedom. Suddenly, it felt as if her husband was holding her back and that she needed to invest better in herself.

While Iliana, Ellen, and Grace were interviewed before welfare reform, Earline Major had similar problems after reform. Her children's father would also fail to come through with promised child care at the last minute when she needed to go to work, and as a result she too lost her job. Earline was convinced that he used this tactic as a way to punish her for not letting him move in with her and to try to force her into changing her mind. She explains,

You can't live here, you can't live here. You're not working. I can't have you living off me, you know. 'Cause I'm working and I'm receiving very little food stamps because I was working. And the little food stamps that I was having and the food I was stretching to feed me and my kids can't possibly feed a man. A man eats twice as much as a woman. So, I'm like, "You just can't be here." So, he got upset about that and he decided that "well, this was how I'm gonna repay you back for not looking out for me. I'm not gonna watch my kids." And I eventually lost my job, calling off a lot, not on time, being tardy.

Earline's inability to trust her children's father to be a reliable child care provider and what she saw as his attempts to manipulate her eventually led her to break up with him. The fact that her cash assistance and food stamps could not stretch far enough to feed him as well as herself and the children also played a role.

TREATMENT OF CHILDREN

What was probably most important to women in both time periods for building trust in the fathers of their children or other romantic partners was how the men treated their children. Much of this relates closely to the discussion of money, since helping to financially support children was a key part of being a good father to most of the women. However, the women considered other factors as well, such as time spent with children and appropriate ways of interacting with children. The women did not approve of men who used drugs or drink when in charge of children or who were inattentive or harsh with children.

Alice Smalls, interviewed after reform, placed no trust in any of her three children's three different fathers, describing them as bad fathers when they were around who then became completely absent fathers. But her high level of trust in her boyfriend was based largely on his treatment of her children. "Yeah, he's been there a long time. We still together, and he treats my kids just like they be . . . his," she explained. Alice had been incarcerated for a short period and her boyfriend had been engaged in her children's lives during that time, earning her trust. At the time of our interview, her boyfriend was incarcerated himself, but he maintained his involvement with her children both financially and emotionally. He proposed marriage in letters from prison, and, because she had such a high level of trust in him as a father figure, she was considering accepting.

Wakeisha Jefferson, who was also interviewed after reform and who discussed issues about child support payments earlier in this chapter, immediately began to talk about her ex-partner's performance as a father (rather than his interaction with her) when asked if she trusted him. Unlike Alice and many other mothers, she actually approved of his parenting. "I give him an eight. I know he won't hurt his son, I know that. I know he wouldn't do nothing and he bring him back in one piece, take him and bring him back safely, nice, be still nice and clean how he left. I give him a nine, eight and a half, 'cause I know he wouldn't do nothing to hurt him. He, if he do something wrong, he spank him or whatever, I know that, but I give him like a eight and a half."

The women interviewed before reform discussed the same standards for judging the trustworthiness of the fathers of their children as the women interviewed after reform did. Nakida Brown trusted her daughter's father a lot more than her two sons' fathers because "he do what he supposed to do and then some. He has helped out a lot." Her sons' fathers did not contribute at all financially or emotionally. In turn, Nakida did not let them see their children. "'Cause they not helping me, they don't have no right to come and see 'em. They think her daddy [Nakida's daughter's father] is they daddy."

Allison Smith placed no trust in her children's father, whom she described as abusive. Instead, her trust went to her boyfriend for his sensitive understanding of and respect for the dynamics of her household. "He won't argue in front of the kids at all 'cause he said he doesn't want the kids to think that he arguing they mother. Things that he don't like, he wait and he'll tell me when they not around."

Some women said they had no idea where the fathers of their children were. These fathers' complete lack of financial, emotional, or other care-taking involvement with their children led most women to describe them as untrustworthy as fathers. Other fathers were active presences in their children's lives, and women often gave them credit for good parenting even if they did not find them trustworthy in other areas. Newer partners who performed as social fathers to children not biologically their own also earned enormous trust from the women.

At times the women's conversation about their partners and former partners was so dominated by tales of conflict over money, responsibility for children, and other issues that any expectation that romantic partnerships might bring emotional benefits fell by the wayside. The women discussed intimacy and love, and even sex, so infrequently that it almost felt as if these were luxuries their overly stressed, sometimes even desperate, situations could not afford. Yet one aspect of intimacy remained a major topic in our conversations as a source of loss of trust, and that was sexual infidelity. Many women reported their partners' unfaithfulness. Some were distraught over it, and others chalked it up to "men being men" and considered it just another reason not to trust men in general.[27]

Rasheba Stokes lost trust in her partner after he was unfaithful to her, but she separated his romantic trustworthiness from his trustworthiness in other realms. She was still with her partner after eleven years. "He's a man. He been doing his manly things, cheating and whatever. . . . I could rely on him, I just don't trust him, far as you know, being faithful, but I can rely on him as far as checking me out or being there for me and my kids. I just don't rely on him to be there for me, you know, romantically. . . . We have our good days, good years and we have bad days, bad years. This is one of the bad years." In a sense, Rasheba's general lack of trust in men to be faithful allowed her to trust her partner in other ways. Clearly, it seemed more important to Rasheba that she could rely on her partner to help her and her kids in pragmatic ways than that he be trustworthy in terms of sexual or, in her words, romantic fidelity.

Rafaela Fuentes was one of the few women to discuss feelings of intimacy or tenderness with a partner. Those feelings occurred when she first started dating a man and was not immediately convinced she wanted to be with him. After a particular night when he comforted her after a nightmare though, she changed her mind.

One night that I had stayed with him, I had such a bad nightmare, and it was like he came and comforted me, and I felt so good. We didn't do anything that night. It was just him comforting me, and a week later he [asked] me, "What made you change your mind about me?" And I said,

"The fact that you didn't force me to do anything and the fact that you comforted me when I needed it. . . ." I told my sister he didn't try, . . . and she was like, "Are you serious?" and I go, "He was a gentleman."

Rafaela's and her sister's surprise that a man would be loving and supportive in this way reveals just how rare this kind of intimacy had been in their relationships.

A few sexually unfaithful men added insult to injury by choosing to have an affair with a woman in their partner's own social circle. Amber Potts discovered that her partner was sleeping with a woman she knew from work. While she was upset and did break up with her partner, she claimed that she did not really leave him because of the affair but because of his financial irresponsibility. Lupita Delgado and Cecilia Alvarez also caught their partners in relationships with women they knew, in this case from their neighborhoods. Gabriela Garcia's son informed her that her husband was having an affair with the children's babysitter. She did not take the news as calmly as some of the other women. "I fired the babysitter, of course, and then I tried to shoot him, but the safety was on." Her husband did not pursue any legal action. Kate Lawrence said she was still devastated from discovering her ex-husband's infidelity with a friend and that on a scale of one to ten of how much she trusted him, she rated him a zero.

VIOLENCE

Another major source of distrust in men, both children's fathers and other partners, was domestic violence. While some women reported single incidents of a man displaying a violent outburst, for some who spoke of it violence was a consistent threat hanging over their heads. Some women were the victims of domestic violence so severe that they ended up in the hospital with physical or psychological effects. For these women, violence controlled their actions and created constant fear.

Often, the women reported that a man's violent tendencies had not been apparent when the couple first became involved but only came out later, often coinciding with a partner's increasing drug and alcohol use. Juanita and Darlene, whose experiences with domestic violence are discussed above, both attributed their partners' violence toward them to the partners' drug or alcohol addictions. Both women described extricating themselves from their relationships (in Juanita's case, a marriage) as lifting an enormous weight from them.

I interviewed Linda Waters before reform. She was a twenty-six-year-old African American mother of four with a stately manner. Throughout our conversation, she routinely needed to reposition the ear piece of her eyeglasses that kept popping out from behind her left ear. Somehow her battle with her ill-fitting eyeglasses seemed to symbolize her frustration in dealing with her husband, whom she described as abusive and draining her of resources.

Linda distrusted her husband, who she claimed spent most of his time with other women or on the streets but came home long enough to insist she give him a good portion of her welfare check and to threaten her with physical harm if she complained. She said that he also threatened to turn her into the welfare office and tell them that he was living with her (before reform, a married woman cohabitating with her husband could not legally receive standard welfare payments) if she did not give him the money available through the child care subsidy. According to Linda, her husband did not work, provided no help for the bills, had a girlfriend on the side, and spent most of his time in the streets. Linda said, "I'm afraid of leavin' him, 'cause if I leave him, he'll kill me and my kids." She said that when the police had come to their home about the domestic violence, her husband knew how to talk to them and the police often took his side.

Violence was also an important source of distrust for women after reform. These women's experiences are best illustrated by Melissa Jacobs, a twenty-eight-year-old white mother of three who said that she finally knew she had to leave the father of her third child when she was about five months pregnant. "He said, 'I bet you that isn't even my child you're carrying,' and came at me with a baseball bat. I said everything in my power. At that point I knew that I needed to do what I needed to get out of it." This was not the first incident of violence for Melissa. She continued,

> I wasn't with him but I think like six or seven months, and all that went down during that time, and that's when I realized enough was enough,

and I saw where it was leading, and I said no. I turned around and went to a friend's house, found out that he was stealing stuff out of my house. I called the police to find out what leg I had to stand on, took my kids, had my brother come and get me. . . . So I left my kids there [with my brother], and I went back and then he came at me, put a gun to my head, told me, "I should kill you right now."

Somehow Melissa got away from him that time, but she did not get away from him permanently until after she became pregnant. What was different about Melissa from many of the other women who reported domestic violence was that her experience did not keep her from later trusting the father of her second child, to whom she was married at the time of our interview. Melissa expressed plenty of distrust in others, most notably one of her siblings, whom she suspected of heroin addiction. But she trusted her husband, or, as she said, "He's my husband, I better trust him!" His acceptance of all three of her children as his own, even the one she had had with another man during a period when they had broken up for a while, made her trust him.

While welfare reform theoretically funded services for women victimized by abusers and offered exemptions from work requirements for women in need of such services, Wanda Bailey, interviewed after reform, was shocked that when she went to a meeting with her caseworker with two black eyes the caseworker said nothing. The caseworker simply carried on with the routine matters of the typical caseworker-client meeting. Wanda thought that caseworkers were supposed to help with domestic violence, but she did not see any evidence of it that day. This is a case where a policy that recognized some of the realities of the women's relationships actually did exist, but it was not implemented.[28]

Some of the women who did not report outright violence indicated that they still found men frightening. They described men as loud, large, and aggressive. Men's activities, particularly if they were engaged in the underground economy, and especially the drug trade, brought others into the household, some of whom were even more frightening. They also brought the police into the household. All of these outsiders, both partners' associates and police, threatened any sense of sanctity and safety of the home and made the women feel vulnerable to chaotic forces outside their control, though in some cases the entrance of the police was regarded as a blessing.

Many partners who brought danger into the home through activity in the underground labor market ended up in jail. Other men fell victim to the risks of male youth and died young in car accidents or shootings. Ten of the women (one of the twenty-six interviewed before welfare reform and nine of the sixty-nine interviewed after reform) had children with men who had since died. Men's violence, participation in the underground economy, and other risky behaviors thus sometimes resulted in their absence from women's lives.

Despite the general climate of gender distrust among the low-income women interviewed, this distrust was far from universal. Some women found new men in their lives in whom they placed a great deal of trust. And some women maintained trust in the men with whom they had their first children. Yet most of the women had lost trust in the fathers of their first (and sometimes later) children. Disappointed, women went on to take one of two paths. Some had become resigned pragmatists with no expectation that future relationships or men could be any different and hence no plans for a partnership down the road. Others remained dreamers, optimistic that the right man would come along and that there was hope for a romance that could become a reliable and fulfilling partnership.

UNDERSTANDING GENDER DISTRUST
IN LOW-INCOME COUPLES

The women's discussions of why they distrusted men were firmly grounded in their own experiences with past relationships. These experiences of abandonment, of financial hardship, of lack of paternal involvement with children, of infidelity, of belittlement, and of violence produced their distrust in men. It was not that they never were willing to trust a man. In fact, part of the problem was that the women might have been too trusting as they began their romantic lives.[29] They were quick to place trust in men who, for whatever reason, proved unable or unwilling to be trustworthy partners. We do not know for sure what led women to make these choices, whether it was youth and immaturity, raw sexual attraction, low self-esteem, perception of no other options, desire to escape their families of origin, or something else. Whatever it was, it led to the downside risk of trust. Distrust then resulted from misplaced trust. Here and there, the women made more generalized statements about men, such as Rasheba Stokes's comment, "He's been doing his manly thing, cheating or whatever," indicating that she believed it was just in men's nature to cheat. But any such generalized views of men's nature did not stop the women from initially trusting men, nor did they explain, or explain fully, the women's eventual distrust in men, which was grounded in specific experiences of feeling mistreated.

The distrust voiced by the women I interviewed resonates with women's distrust in men documented by other researchers. Edin and Kefalas discuss distrust as a major factor in women's decisions not to marry the men who father their children.[30] They too cite men's failure to make economic contributions to children and households, infidelity, and violence as the roots of women's distrust. Estacion and Cherlin also make the case that while low-income women espouse "generalized distrust," what they act upon is contextualized distrust—or distrust based on specific experience with specific men.[31] Joanna Reed finds that low-income women's relationships often break up over the kind of behaviors among men that I document here.[32]

Since I interviewed only women, we hear only their side of the story. But we know from researchers who interview low-income men that they also voice a high level of distrust in women. Kevin Roy shows that men suspect that women want them only for their money and ignore their sincere attempts to create affective bonds with their children.[33] Some of this distrust starts early, in adolescence. In his ethnography of teenaged boys in low-income Boston neighborhoods, David Harding shows that boys distrust girls because they suspect that all the girls are interested in is their money and (ironically given the women's beliefs) that some girls only want to use them for sex.[34]

Putting all of these findings together, we see that boys and girls and men and women in low-income communities often take an adversarial position toward each other. Each thinks the other is out to use them—for money and for sex—and each believes the other disregards their efforts toward any kind of meaningful relationship.

Once again, it is easy to see the role that low-income women and men's position in the macroeconomy and other larger structures plays in producing experiences that teach them to distrust each other. Low-income men's foreshortened educations and weak labor market positions mean it is hard for them to financially contribute to their partners' and children's households. As many scholars have argued, such men may disappear from family life out of frustration and shame.[35] They also may feel pushed into the underground or drug economies, which bring with them the turbulence so many women find unsettling.[36] The U.S. criminal justice system, which, starting in the 1970s, began to emphasize punishment over rehabilitation and thus led to rapid growth in the penal system, shuttles many of the men who take this route into the prison system.[37] Finally, the men's anger at their lack of power in mainstream society may erupt in the violence that terrifies their partners. Violence can also serve as a strategy for survival on the streets for young men living in concentrated poverty neighborhoods.[38]

Low-income women are similarly blocked from labor market success. Since they tend to be the primary caretakers of their children, their need to find sources of income to augment meager earnings or welfare benefits is acute. The real value of welfare benefits has fallen as state increases in benefits have failed to keep up with inflation. Men's suspicions that women just want money thus may reflect women's drive to provide for children when both the welfare system and labor market produce inadequate funds.[39]

The relationship between structural position in the macroeconomy and gender distrust may also take on more subtle forms. As discussed in chapter 1 and elsewhere in the book, being at the bottom of the stratification system makes one prize respectful treatment, since those without power face constant attacks on their dignity and since dignity is one of the few precious possessions one owns. Feeling that someone is simply out for sex or money without offering commitment in return is an attack on one's dignity and leads one to distrust the attacker.

In the settings of the welfare office and workplace, the women's position at the bottom of a structural hierarchy and its associated lack of power made them sensitive about perceived disrespectful treatment by caseworkers and bosses. Here the situation was compounded by the fact that both parties—women and men—were situated at the bottom of the macrostructure and both might be perceiving the same disrespectful treatment and responding with distrust. This mutual distrust might ricochet back and forth, reinforcing and escalating gender distrust to levels so high that successful, permanent unions would become difficult, or even impossible, to achieve.

PROMOTING REAL CHANGE IN GENDER DISTRUST

The women interviewed described partners' unreliability as economic contributors, as emotional supports, as fathers, as sexually loyal partners, and most dramatically, as safe presences. This unreliability bred distrust, which worked against the formation of lasting unions. Reform's attempt to address unreliability through rules that tie parents together in superficial ways has done nothing to address the likely underlying causes of such unreliability. As such, the policies welfare reform brought are ineffective in truly supporting lasting unions. The women interviewed for this study in the mid-2000s, approximately seven or eight years after the implementation of reform, did not describe their relationships with the fathers of their children or with the men with whom they were involved much differently from the women interviewed when potential reform was just a debate.

How could one policy ever be expected to change so complicated a process as family formation when so many other factors—the labor market for both men and women, gender norms, the drug trade, the judicial system, wage levels, the delicate nature of attraction and repulsion, romantic expectation, anger, and interpersonal trust—remain out of reach of the policy lever? Perhaps a more coordinated, no doubt more expensive, set of policies that would truly change the context in which the players find themselves would be more effective.

One crucial way to build women's trust in men would be to promote policies that would improve men's labor market position, which would also create attractive alternatives to both drug use and drug sales. Investment in women's labor market opportunities would also help, both by giving them more options to avoid abusive men and by widening their social networks through which they might meet more economically stable men in whom they might place greater trust. Edin and Kefalas also point out the potential value of programs that encourage young men to delay fathering children until their late twenties, when they "age out" of criminal activity.[40]

These structural changes offer greater promise for real change than most relationship-training programs. There is nothing wrong, in theory, with programs to help people build stronger and more constructive relationships. These programs are bound to fail, however, if they are mandatory and preach to unwilling ears or if they are led by inadequately trained personnel who deliver only superficial intervention.

While I firmly believe that addressing labor market opportunity would go a long way to improving trust between women and men, it is probably not a panacea. We see gender distrust emerging in early adolescence before young men encounter the inhospitality of the labor market and before (most) young women are saddled with financial responsibility for children. Perhaps these young people are aware of the limits on their professional futures, but there are probably other sources of this early gender distrust. This book does not explore what those may be, but one may be a strict adherence to traditional gender norms and the cartoonish images of each other that result. In her book on the gender attitudes of children raised during the 1980s wave of women's entry into the labor market, Kathleen Gerson argues that families that exercise "gender flexibility," an openness about who does what in family life, are the most successful ones.[41] Children raised with flexible notions of gender roles thus may grow up to take less adversarial and more cooperative stances toward their partners.

SIX "I Trust My Mother and No One Else"

TRUST AND DISTRUST IN SOCIAL NETWORKS

We are a close family. As a matter of fact, I have a brother that lives on this same block with me . . . and a sister who lives on the next block. Another brother who lives in the next block. And then the rest is kind of like scatter throughout over Chicago, but we see each other often. I have a sister that lives in the suburbs, but I see her every Friday. And we all call each other. As a matter of fact, the only calls I get are from a brother or sister. So we are very close, because my mom had one brother and he lived far away from her and she would always tell us how important it is to keep up with your family.

—Bernice Alexander

I just wanna release a lot of pressure and now I have no company. At first, I used to have a house full of people just coming over constantly. Now I don't have to worry about that. I can get a good night's sleep. . . . And I feel like, "Okay, it's all over now. You can get back to your life and let me get back to mine." . . . I just want more structure for my kids, that's why. I don't want all that nasty stuff around.

—Georgia Burke

I trust my mother and no one else.

—Koyana Woods

Lashawna Owens depended on her family, and they depended on her. She moved freely through her social world trusting that her family and her community provided a safe and supportive environment for herself and her eight-year-old son, Dante. Lashawna's mother was her main source of child care. Her mother, who lived nearby, came over in the morning to take Dante to school, picked him up from school, and stayed with him until Lashawna got home from work about an hour later. While Lashawna did not directly return the favor to her mother, she did regularly watch her niece and nephew in order to help her sister out. In turn, Lashawna had gotten two jobs through leads from her sister. These exchanges built or perhaps reflected trust. Lashawna asserted, "I trust my family one hundred percent. They are my family, I totally trust them."

Dante's father was an involved and reliable father even though Lashawna was no longer romantically involved with him. The two had no formal visitation agreement, but Dante floated between his parents' two households without any apparent tension or stress. Dante's spending time in his dad's house started when Dante was just a baby. "He would get him on weekends, keep him for a week, two weeks, three weeks. He was getting my baby. So I was cool. I didn't have no problem." Lashawna's trust in others extended to her neighbors and friends as well. In the summer, when Dante was not in school but Lashawna's work hours remained the same, her parents were nominally in charge of him. But much of the time Dante moved through the neighborhood playing with various friends. "He'll be outside. He go to whoever house he want to go." Lashawna described a social network full of supportive resources and a community rich in social capital. She found both invaluable for balancing the requirements of employment and single parenthood.

Iliana Dominguez described a much different world. She was holding on by her fingertips and there was no one she trusted to lift her off the ledge. She was raising her two children by herself. The fathers of her children provided no support and she felt better off without them. It had taken her a long time to disentangle herself from involvement with her younger child's father. She described him as needy and abusive. Iliana lived with her grandmother, whom she described as "mean." Her grandmother was threatening to kick her out of the house because she had not paid rent for the past two months. Iliana explained, "My daughter was getting sick, so I lost all my vacation time and my sick time and I didn't pay my grandmother rent for two months because I didn't have the money. You know what it is, two weeks without working and then you go back to work and then all these appointments. Well, she didn't understand that. She's like, 'No, I want the money. I want my money. I want my money, money, money.' This woman is money hungry, period."

Iliana's mother lived nearby, but Iliana had no contact with her. Iliana said there were just too many hard feelings over her mother's not having been there for her when she was a child—her mother had often left her in the care of her "mean" grandmother. Her mother had a new partner, a woman with two teenage children, and was sharing all of her resources with her partner's children. "I'm jealous that my mom is not in my life, but as far as having her alive and being happy, I'm glad that she is, because you know she needs to be happy." Iliana felt there was no one she could trust, there was no one she could rely on for help, and she was very much alone.

Lashawna and Iliana represent two extremes among the women I interviewed. Some were embedded in social networks rich in support, while others faced very challenging lives all alone. In reviewing the literature on degree of trust and social capital in low-income communities in her book *Lone Pursuit*, Sandra Smith discusses conflicting findings over whether such communities are marked by social cohesion and support or by social disorganization and alienation.[1] The women I interviewed provide evidence of both circumstances in both time periods. Some women, both before and after reform, were like Lashawna and described networks that were a lifeline. Mothers, sisters, brothers, cousins, and sometimes friends acted as partners in raising children, in sharing emotional support, in providing goods, and in keeping each other sane during hardships. Women with social network members who helped in these ways trusted such members of their networks implicitly. Many women found themselves rich in these relationships, and despite the struggles of parenting in poverty, their trust in these others kept them from feeling alone.

At the other extreme, some women, again in both time periods, were more like Iliana and felt alone as alone can be. Some had experienced abuse or rejection by their families. Some had been mistreated by friends who had exposed not only the women themselves but also their children to harm. These women learned to distrust others and retreated into a protective shell, shielding themselves and their children from those who might wreak havoc, but also blocking out any potential source of network-based help.

This chapter differs from the chapters on the welfare office, the workplace, child care providers, and romantic partners in that the women told many more stories of trust in the interaction partners who populated their social networks than in their interaction partners in the other four settings I have discussed. When asked whom they trusted most, the vast majority of women at both time periods named a mother, sister, cousin, or friend. But the women told stories of strong distrust as well, and those who had learned to distrust network members found the untrustworthiness they perceived particularly painful since it struck so close to home. Still, women trusted their network members to be reliable and come through for them more than those in any other setting. This trust was most often tied to network members' offering them support in the form of the goods and services that helped them survive and sometimes even get ahead. When women distrusted network members it was most often because they drained the women's households of resources or created disruptions in the women's lives. Many of the structural conditions I have discussed in chapter 1 and other parts of the book contributed to the burdens that women's social networks placed on them. The cuts in the social safety net, the erosion of wages at the bottom of the labor market, the burgeoning drug economy, and related forces created an environment in which not only the women were struggling but many of their network members were struggling as well. Shared hardship often led to situations in which some network members became a burden to others.

WELFARE REFORM AND SOCIAL NETWORKS

Welfare reform instituted no specific policies related to social networks. This reflects the fact that reformers held an individualized conception of what kept women out of the labor market. They saw the root of the problem as being individual women's traits, such as their lack of job training, inability to pay for child care, and insufficient "personal responsibility." Welfare reform did not take into consideration demands placed on women by network members in need, which other researchers found to limit work activity before reform.[2] It thus did not treat the conditions at the community level that contributed to the neediness of those surrounding individual women.

The fact that reform created no policies addressing women's social networks does not mean that it had no intentions regarding networks. To the contrary, one of the underlying philosophies of reform was that it was not government's job to permanently support those in need. Instead, reformers believed, it was the job of communities—of friends, of family, of neighbors—to support each other. By removing the entitlement to cash assistance benefits and creating time limits on those benefits, government was giving the message that it was time for social networks to step in to fill the void.

WOMEN'S INTERACTIONS WITH SOCIAL NETWORKS BEFORE AND AFTER WELFARE REFORM

The experiences of the women in this study were mixed in terms of whether social networks did indeed fill the void for them created by reform's scaling back of financial support. The women interviewed after reform did draw more on their networks for the kinds of resources that helped them survive than women before reform did. Their networks were more likely to give them money, other nonmonetary goods, and help with child care than the networks of the women interviewed before reform. Thus at least some of the post-reform women could say that their networks helped them at a time when cash assistance from the state was limited.

To give a sense of these patterns across the two groups of women, I coded their qualitative interviews according to several aspects of their interactions with their social networks. This allows me to show, in table

2, percentages of the women in each time period who described various kinds of interactions with their networks.[3] Since this is a small qualitative study, we do not know if these figures would be reproduced in more representative data, but they are helpful for illustrating clearly what the differences are between the women interviewed in the two time periods.

As we see in table 2, 29 percent (or nineteen women) of the post-reform women discussed frequently receiving money from their network members, whereas only 4 percent (actually just one woman) before reform did.[4] After reform, 34 percent (twenty-two women) said they frequently received other goods, while only 13 percent (three women) before reform did. Finally, two-thirds of post-reform women (66 percent or forty-four women) said they received a lot of help with child care through networks, whereas only 33 percent (eight women) before reform did.

Clearly, the women I interviewed after reform were drawing more on their networks for basic needs to get by than the women I interviewed before reform. If indeed that difference were to be reproduced in representative data, one might conclude that social networks did fill some of the needs created by both welfare reform's cut to benefits and the new work requirements that led to a greater need for child care.

However, that is only part of the story. As Iliana's story illustrates, not all women interviewed after reform had strong social networks—or network members they trusted. Some women were extremely isolated and did not have access through networks to the kinds of resources that could help them replace lost support from the welfare system. Also, many women had network members they greatly distrusted. These network ties *drained* them of resources. They took money and goods from the women and created chaos in the women's households. Women at both time periods reported having friends and family members who were destructive in these ways, but women after reform were actually *more* likely to report being drained by network members that they considered untrustworthy.

Table 2 shows that 27 percent (eighteen women) after reform reported having at least one network member who was currently significantly draining her and her household of resources, whether by taking money

Table 2   Women with Various Network Resources or Burdens by Time Period

Network Resource or Burden	Before Reform	After Reform
	% (number/total cases in parentheses)	% (number/total cases in parentheses)
Frequently receive money from network members	4 (1/24)**	29 (19/66)
Frequently receive nonmonetary goods from network members	13 (3/24)*	34 (22/65)
Frequently receive child care from network members	33 (8/24)**	66 (44/67)
Network members currently heavy burden on resources	8 (2/24)*	27 (18/67)
Network members formerly heavy burden on resources	13 (3/23)**	52 (33/63)
Most recent job gotten through network tie	65 (15/23)**	39 (26/67)

NOTE: Participants were asked to discuss all network resources and burdens that they experience; hence table columns do not total 100 percent. A few interviews did not include discussion of all of the network resources or burdens. Percentages were calculated from the number of interviews containing discussion of the topic. After each percentage, the table shows in parentheses the number of women experiencing the resource or burden out of the total number with interviews covering it. While the study data are not from random samples, the table follows a common practice of using statistical tests to show how large the differences are between the pre- and post-reform samples without making claims of formal statistical significance.

*p < .10; **p < .05.

and goods or creating a great deal of chaos in her household. Only 8 percent (two women) before reform reported a current situation in which they were being significantly drained in these ways by a network member. When asked about whether network members had drained their resources significantly in the past, over half (52 percent or thirty-three women) of post-reform women indicated yes, as compared to only 13 percent (three women) of pre-reform women.

These differences, again if they were reproduced in representative data, might reflect that, by cutting benefits not just to individual women but to the population of low-income families, welfare reform created financial stress on a community-wide level that rippled through women's social networks.[5] Also, after reform, the most advantaged women (in terms of education, skills, and job readiness) left the welfare rolls first, leaving behind a more disadvantaged population of welfare recipients.[6] It is possible that these more disadvantaged women had social network ties to more disadvantaged people, who in turn imposed more burdens on the women and drained their resources further. Table 2 also shows that the women interviewed before welfare reform were more likely to have found their most recent job through a network member (65 percent or fifteen women) than were women after welfare reform (39 percent or twenty-six women). This fact, coupled with the fact that women before reform were less likely to report being drained by people in their networks, suggests that the women before reform may indeed have had networks that were more advantaged (particularly in terms of labor market success) than those of the women interviewed after reform.

In summary, the women interviewed after reform were more likely to draw on networks for the kinds of social support that help people get by. But not all of the women had networks they trusted to come through in this way. Also, even though post-reform women got more of the kinds of help that enabled them to get by, they simultaneously also had more network members who were draining them of resources.

Welfare reformers wanted women's social networks to take over some of the government's role in supporting low-income mothers and their children. But all reform did to make that happen was to cut women's benefits, thereby creating an incentive for women to seek help from their networks instead. Welfare reform did not invest in communities in order to make the networks in those communities more likely to be able to help (or less likely to drain women's household resources). It did not make changes to the structural characteristics of the labor market that I discussed in chapter 1 that would help the employment prospects of network members. Improving network members' labor market outcomes would also probably increase network-based resources and decrease network-imposed drains on women's resources. Furthermore, welfare reform cut benefits not just to the women but to many of their network members, who thus were probably in as much need of help from the women as the women were in need of help from them.

In the next section of the chapter, I return to the women's narratives, showing in detail the nature of their interactions with network members they trusted and network members they distrusted. We see in these narratives that women trusted network members who shared resources and distrusted those who drained their resources. I then discuss ways we might understand trust and distrust in networks and how we might promote trust in network ties.

ISSUES OF TRUST AND DISTRUST IN SOCIAL NETWORK MEMBERS

In addition to the differences on average across the two time periods shown in table 2, there was great variation across women within each time period in experiences with social networks. Both before and after reform, some women described deep trust in network members, others described deep distrust, and still others described both. In the following sections, I explore the nature of both trust and distrust in network members.

Trust in Network Members

Bernice Alexander, an African American woman interviewed before reform whom we met in chapters 2 and 4, had ten siblings living in Chicago. She placed enormous trust in all of them.

> We are a close family. As a matter of fact, I have a brother that lives on this same block with me . . . and a sister who lives on the next block. Another brother who lives in the [next] block. And then the rest is kind of like scatter throughout over Chicago, but we see each other often. I have a sister that lives in [the suburbs], but I see her every Friday. And we all call each other. As a matter of fact, the only calls I get are from a brother or sister. So we are very close, because my mom had one brother and he lived far away from her and she would always tell us how important it is to keep up with your family, and her mom died at a very early age.

Bernice said that she and her siblings relied on each other for survival and that they all helped each other out whenever they could. For instance, she regularly watched her brother's children since he was also a single parent. Bernice did have some close friends, but she said she did not trust them as much as she did her family members. "'Cause I mean, even though we help each other out or whatever . . . everybody got some sneaky points to them."

As Bernice spoke, I continually found my eye drifting to the large beautifully carved wooden bed that sat in the center of her living room. Bernice, like Juanita Soto and other women interviewed, did not have enough bedrooms in her apartment for herself and her children. Like Juanita, she had made the living room her bedroom while the children shared the one bedroom. I finally found a moment to ask Bernice about the beautiful bed's origin. A proud smile spread across her face as she told me that her brother had carved it for her himself. Her family members indeed gave her a lot, as the elegant bed filling the living room attested.

Danielle Adams, whom we met in chapter 4, also trusted her family. Interviewed before reform, she had left welfare for a job paying a relatively high wage as a temporary sanitation worker with the city. Danielle placed enormous, and exclusive, trust in her immediate family members. Resources flowed between her and her highly reliable mother and two sisters, making life manageable for all four women. Her sister watched her five- and twelve-year-old children when she worked. Danielle and her sisters and mother all lived within a block or two of each other and always had. "Whenever one of us moves, the other three always seem to follow," she explained. For the six or seven months prior to our interview, Danielle's oldest sister and her sister's three children had been staying with her in a two-bedroom apartment. Danielle trusted her sister with the children, and her sister trusted Danielle to provide material resources and pay the rent.

Danielle's ability to trust her sister and other family members supported her entry into the labor market and allowed her to maintain employment. The financial resources she was able to pass on to her sister in the form of housing and other goods constituted a form of network reciprocity that fed the system.[7] Resources were tight once they were spread across both sisters and their children (seven people in total). But the benefits were high: Danielle never described feeling alone or insecure.

Several other women, like Danielle and her sister, trusted network members to such a degree that they shared households. When I met Mariah Vincent before reform, she had been living with her friend Lani for seven years. Lani and Mariah were both single mothers. Though they were not romantically involved with each other, their relationship functioned like a traditional marriage in that they made joint decisions about long-term plans, raised their children together, and ran the household as a single unit. They also shared household expenses and tasks. When I asked Mariah how they shared the cost of groceries, for example, she said, "Whenever we need stuff, whoever has the chance to go to the store just goes." I pressed her, since she had one child, a thirteen-year-old son, and Lani had four children. I wanted to know whether adjustments were made for the fact that she had a family of two while Lani's was a family of five. "No, I don't watch it like that. If we need milk, I buy milk. I don't say, 'Your kids drank so much milk, so you pay so much.'" As Mariah explained, "These kids were raised together. They're like brothers and sisters."

Both women had been welfare recipients, but Mariah had left welfare for a job eighteen months before I interviewed her and had been thriving in it ever since. Mariah's employment represented the success of a long-term life plan the two had developed together. To prepare for employment, Mariah attended classes at a job-training center. Her training culminated in her obtaining a GED. During the time she was in school, Lani watched the children and did a greater share of the household work, with the idea that later Mariah would help her go to school and work. In the past, Lani had held jobs and Mariah had watched the kids while she worked. Each woman trusted the other to reciprocate in their exchange of domestic duties, income, and time to invest in schooling. This trust had been invaluable to Mariah in making her journey from welfare recipient to full-time worker in a stable job that she loved.

Bethany Grant, whom we met in the Introduction, similarly trusted her friend Sheena. In fact, the two women's households had been linked in a variety of ways, even combining when times were particularly tough. Bethany and Sheena moved to Milwaukee together seeking a safer environment and more generous welfare benefits. There they had separate apartments, but they navigated the labor market together, usually finding jobs in the same companies. When their work hours did not overlap, they watched each other's children. Bethany also had a boyfriend at the time who watched her children. When I asked Bethany about why one of her jobs cleaning hotel rooms had not worked out, she explained, "I had my boyfriend, he was babysitting then or they would go down to Sheena's house, which was only a block up. . . . I think I worked there for like, four months. And, the only reason I quit was because we were going through some problems with her kids and what-not, and me and my boyfriend got on some bad terms, and I didn't have no reliable babysitter." The commitment of the two women to each other's households is revealed by Bethany's statement "We were going through some problems with her kids." Sheena's problems were Bethany's problems. When I met Bethany, the two women had since moved back to Chicago and were temporarily living together in a two-bedroom apartment. Bethany had three children living with her, and Sheena had five. In addition, Sheena's grandchild, nephew, and great-niece often stayed in the household. The apartment was a tight squeeze for thirteen people but better than the alternative of homelessness.

> We're in a two-bedroom apartment . . . but, it's something that got to be done, because don't neither one of us just want to be out on the street. So we trying to help each other. In the process, I went with her yesterday to look for some apartments. She went today to look at one of them that me and her went to. And she think she might have it. . . . I hope everything work out for her, because like I say, she need to be on her own and raise her kids. Just like I need to be on my own and raise mine. It's just at that point things was happening, and we didn't have nowhere else to turn.

Bethany's and Sheena's trust in each other produced a valuable benefit for them both: the ability to stave off homelessness. Their cooperation helped both women house their family members, care for their children, and pursue employment. As we will see below, not all women trusted network members who, like themselves, were in financial crisis. Some women suspected desperation would lead these people to steal from them or to compete for resources in other ways. Bethany's and Sheena's willingness to trust—and, most importantly, the fact that each of them proved trustworthy to the other by not stealing or fighting for resources—enabled them to cooperate with housing and child care, which in turn saved them both from homelessness and similar crises.

The high degree of trust that Danielle, Mariah, and Bethany placed in their networks was also visible in some of the women after reform. Charmaine Wallace trusted her family members completely. She lived with her grandfather, who covered all household expenses (including the house itself) and helped support Charmaine and her young son. Her mother and sister lived nearby. Charmaine was close with both women. Together, these three family members covered Charmaine's child care needs while she fulfilled the training and work requirements of welfare. When asked how much she trusted each family member on a scale of one to ten, Charmaine responded for all of them, "Eleven or twelve." She had no doubts that her grandfather, mother, and sister considered her and her son's interests to be their own interests. She was fully confident in their performance as child care providers and in the reliability of their support of her both materially and socio-emotionally.

Wakeisha Jefferson, also interviewed after reform, similarly ignored the limit of ten on the trust scale I gave her. We were discussing an older man in his seventies in her neighborhood who was a pastor. He had taken Wakeisha under his wing and looked out for her. She began going to his church with her parents when she was five years old. At the time of our interview, when she was twenty-four, he felt like a member of her family. In fact, she thought of him as a father figure and trusted him more than she did her own father. When I asked her to rank how much she trusted him on a scale of one to ten, she replied,

Oh, I give him a twenty. . . . That's like my daddy. I do anything for him. I love him. . . . He does more [than my daddy]—not to put my daddy down—he does more. He's like my daddy. It's like I said, I known him since I was five and I used to look at him all the time and I wanted him to be my daddy and now he attached to my son and he does anything and everything for him. . . . He took him to Toys R Us last Christmas. He just picked out what he wanted and he got it. He got the big basketball rim thing and he got a leapfrog [an electronic educational toy]. He got a lotta little toys and it was just, he just did it.

Wakeisha put less trust in her own father, with whom she had lived until her parents separated when she was ten. "My father [is] mean, he mean a little bit. . . . But he all right. He all right, I'm just gonna put it like that." When her father helped her in the ways that the pastor helped her, it was unusual. "He took me grocery shopping the other day. I was so surprised." Wakeisha trusted the pastor more, both because he could be relied upon to provide resources and because of the symbolic meaning of those resources. His readily sharing them demonstrated his devotion to her son. It was a way of showing that he was invested in her son's interests.

Distrust in Network Members

The great deal of trust some women placed in their network members does not mean that trust in networks was universal. Some women at both time periods had friends or family members whom they deeply distrusted. We met Darlene Harris, a woman interviewed before reform, in chapter 5 and learned about her distrust of her son's father, James. Darlene lived alone with her child and was deeply distrustful of many people in her network. She made an exception for her grandmother, who helped her with child care, but for the most part she did not even trust her family members. At twenty-two, she had worked, with only one interruption during her pregnancy and her child's early infancy, at the same cashier job since high school. Through experience, she had learned that life is a lot tougher when you are involved with people who are destructive to you, and she was committed to living a life independent of such intrusion. To do so was not easy. It took a concerted effort because many of the characters who had inhabited her early life were just the type of people she wanted and needed to avoid.

She had been raised primarily by her mother and stepfather, whom she described as an abusive man who regularly embarrassed and beat his children and stepchildren and was verbally cruel to his wife. All three of her stepfather's children ran away from home, and eventually, right before her senior year in high school, Darlene did too. At the time of our interview, because of this history, she had little contact with her mother. "My mother and I are not real close," she explained. She moved to her father's house, but he soon moved to Mississippi. To finish high school in the area, she moved in with her aunt and uncle. When her uncle died, she moved out and lost touch with her aunt (who was related only through marriage to her uncle). By that time, she had become involved with James, whom she had met one day in the park. She told me that she would regularly say, even jokingly to James himself, "I wish I had just kept walking by that day in the park." She became pregnant and had a miscarriage. A year or so later, she became pregnant again and had her son. Shortly after, she left James.

Most of Darlene's life had been spent living in contentious households. From childhood to her first serious romantic attachment, her domestic relationships had been marked by negative encounters. From these interactions she concluded that others could not be trusted, and she vowed to put a safe distance between herself and them. For the first time, Darlene was finally living a relatively autonomous life. She lived alone with her young son, had steady work, and was trying to create a calm life for herself and her baby.

Nicole Fleming, also interviewed before reform, was one of the many women who trusted some of her network members and distrusted others. She was committed to her mother and deeply distrustful of her brother, her nephew, and others in her family who she said were substance users and dealers. Her mother owned her own home but, in Nicole's eyes, was a virtual hostage in it, at the mercy of her family members entrenched in the underground economy of the drug trade. Out of devotion to her mother, Nicole had recently demanded that her brother, whose drug addiction made his behavior erratic, leave his mother's house and come live with her, and he had done so. Her act was not in any way a sign that she trusted her brother. It was her distrust of him that led her to want him out of her mother's household.[8]

Her inability to trust her brother caused Nicole two major problems. First, because he had no means of financial support for himself, she had to support him in order to have any chance of keeping him away from the moneymaking options of the street. Since Nicole herself was unemployed and receiving welfare, doing so meant she needed to keep living with her employed boyfriend even though she wanted to leave him. Second, Nicole wanted to get a job so that she could give her mother money and could eventually live without her boyfriend's paycheck, but she was afraid to leave her children alone with her brother given the unpredictable way he behaved. Her distrust in her brother was one of the main problems in Nicole's life, but she was certain that trusting him would bring no benefits. She had learned that her brother, or at least his behavior under the influence of drugs, was not trustworthy, and she was sure she was right not to take a risk on him.

Nicole's distrust did not lie solely in her brother, and her removal of him from her mother's house had not eliminated her mother's problems. Other members of Nicole's family were also involved in the drug trade, and they too wreaked havoc in her mother's house. Nicole described how her nephew (who was her mother's grandson) mistreated her mother:

> My poor mother, she's living in that house and not one of them helps. My nephew . . . just got out of jail for dealing drugs. [He and his friends] went into my mother's house. They raided her house. They tore her house completely apart. We spend all this money to get him out of jail [and] he raids the house. He gets two jobs and he doesn't give my mother a dime! And he's living with her and now he has a baby. He doesn't even speak to her. And they in her house. They eatin' her food. It makes me more determined to do what I have to do. I'm the only hope that my mother has.

While we do not know how Nicole's brother and nephew would behave if they were in a different environment, Nicole attributed their lack of trustworthiness to the drug trade. As I suggested in chapter 5, the fact that many young men have few if any opportunities for stable employment in the mainstream economy and are thus enticed into drug sales and sometimes drug use probably results in untrustworthy behavior.[9] Structural forces are thus the likely root of trust problems in such cases. And the women who learn not to trust those involved in the drug trade may be avoiding vulnerability rather than missing opportunities.

Many of the women interviewed after reform also expressed distrust in network members. Georgia Burke's distrust similarly related to the structural forces that produced gang formation and criminal activity. Georgia was a mother of seven who so impressed the counselors at her job-training program with her diligence that she was able to convince them to hire her full time. This transition from program participant to program employee was unprecedented, and her ten-dollar-an-hour wage and benefits package were rare for graduates of the program.[10]

Georgia's present circumstances were very different from those of her earlier years, during which she had been in a gang. She had been incarcerated and later cleared of murder charges. Georgia claimed, and the court was convinced, that because she had no prior convictions on her record her fellow gang members had set her up to take the fall for the murder in order to save the guilty member, whose multiple convictions would have resulted in a long mandatory sentence. Upon her release, she dropped out of the gang and felt that she needed to get away from the gang members she no longer trusted. She also felt that she needed to break away from the rest of her social network if she was ever going to succeed in the labor market and make a better life for her children.

> I learned now. I don't really let my friends come over to my house or nothing. They call me stuck up, but I really don't care. . . . They don't have jobs now and . . . they call me stuck up because I be telling them that "You oughta get you all a job." 'Cause I'm not gonna be waiting on no one for my check. [She is referring to a welfare check here.] I rather get me a payroll check that has my name on it. And they like, "Well, she act like . . . she thinks she this." But then they don't know how to do a résumé, don't know how to do nothing, and I have to help 'em.

It was so difficult for Georgia to extricate herself from the gang and from her network of friends that she eventually felt she needed to move across the city to make a clean break. As she explained, her move brought the peace she sought.

> I didn't wanna confine myself into like no hole. I just wanna release a lot of pressure, and now I have no company. At first I used to have a house full of people just coming over constantly. Now I don't have to worry about that. I can get a good night's sleep. I used to have bags under my eyes when I was coming here [to work]. . . . And I feel like, "Okay, it's all over now. You can get back to your life and let me get back to mine." . . . I just want more structure for my kids, that's why. I don't want all that nasty stuff around.

Gang life requires cooperation among members. When she was younger, Georgia was willing to cooperate because she trusted that her fellow members had her back. This turned out not to be true. She thus became much less trusting. She needed to create a barrier between her household and the chaos she knew her network members could create. While such a barrier might have blocked the inflow of certain resources, Georgia felt it more important to protect herself from disruptive people who drained her resources.

Julie Callahan, whose TANF application process was described in chapter 2, distrusted her sister. Since the two siblings shared an apartment, her distrust was a daily stressor. Because Julie at twenty-three was four years older than her sister, it had fallen to her to be the financial manager of the house. Her sister paid her two hundred dollars a month, and Julie had been buying all of the household goods and paying all of the bills.[11] When it became clear to Julie that two hundred dollars constituted less than half of the monthly expenses and Julie requested more, Julie's sister refused. She also did not pay Julie back whenever Julie lent her money. Julie's sister worked, making nine dollars an hour, so Julie did not understand why she was paying more than half the expenses when she was unemployed and had a newborn.[12]

Julie's distrust in her sister was so high that, despite money being tight, she went out and bought a small refrigerator for her room and a padlock for her bedroom door. She stopped buying food for her sister and began to stock the refrigerator in her room with the food she and her children needed and locked the door when she went out. Julie's story is similar to one told by Tahiera Jackson, a pre-reform mother, whose suspicions that her roommate was stealing money from her made her nervous about leaving the apartment for work. Julie described living in the same apartment with someone you do not trust as exhausting. Interestingly though, she did trust her sister to occasionally babysit for her children.[13]

Koyana Woods perhaps made the most dramatic statement of distrust in those around her. She declared simply, "I trust my mother and no one else."

Trust and Distrust Reflect Contributions to and Drains on Resources

The women's stories of whom they trust and whom they distrust show the importance of network members' contributions to and drains on their resources for fostering trust and distrust. In their narratives, women described positive resources delivered through networks as invaluable and network-based drains on their households, whether in the form of excessive resource demands or household disruption, as catastrophic.[14] All women, at both time periods, were more likely to say that they trusted their network members if they received supportive resources through them and were more likely to say that they distrusted network members who placed burdensome and nonreciprocal demands on them, whether material or psycho-social.[15]

It is difficult to determine the origin of these relationships among trust, distrust, and contributions to or drains on resources. We do not know whether the offer of resources builds trust (while draining resources builds distrust), or whether the temporal order is the reverse and those who place trust in others open the pathway to resource sharing. Perhaps it is a little bit of both. Some women's descriptions of their withdrawal from social interaction, however, such as Georgia's retreat from the network ties that landed her in jail, certainly seem to be responses to an untrustworthy environment rather than preemptive strikes against network members who might in actuality have been supportive.

UNDERSTANDING LOW-INCOME MOTHERS' EXPERIENCES WITH THEIR NETWORKS

Compared to women interviewed before reform, women interviewed after reform were more able to draw on their networks for the resources needed for survival: money, goods, and the child care that enabled them to meet work requirements. Welfare reformers' desire to move responsibility from government to private networks thus is reflected in this way in the lives of the women I interviewed. Whether the women after reform drew more on their networks simply because they were in more need or because their networks were more forthcoming with offers of help in the face of this need (or out of a desire for reciprocity should they too need help) is unclear. What is also unclear is what kind of toll this offering of resources took on the women's network members who might, like them, have been facing hardship due to the diminishing welfare state. It is also concerning that while after reform a greater proportion of women drew on their networks for resources that helped them get by than did women before reform, a significant proportion of women even after reform did not receive such resources through their networks. Also, while more women used networks to help them survive after reform, fewer used networks for job leads to help them get ahead than women before reform did.

Social scientists use the term *social capital* to refer to the resources that flow to people through their social networks. Social capital is an input that, just like financial capital, can be invested to reap rewards.[16] As Sandra Smith discusses, there has been much debate in the literature on whether low-income communities are best characterized as socially organized and rich in social capital or socially disorganized and devoid of social capital.[17] Carol Stack's classic ethnography *All Our Kin* made a strong case for social organization. Ann Roschelle's *No More Kin*, obviously titled in reference to Stack's work, throws doubt on Stack's claims.[18]

On the basis of the findings here, I argue that it is a mistake to conceive of a single kind of low-income community. To the contrary, the women I interviewed lived in communities vastly different from each other's. Some respondents were indeed embraced by a supportive web of network ties, while others were so isolated that they have no network support. There was also a great deal of variation in trust in social networks, largely related to the degree networks offered support or drained resources.[19] In addition, many women trusted some network members while distrusting others. Some women even trusted a network member in one realm, say providing child care, but not another, say respecting one's property. As we saw, Julie locked up her food so her sister would not take it but let her sister babysit her children.

Poverty scholars interested in the role of social capital in low-income families' well-being have discussed two different kinds of social capital.[20] "Bonding" social capital consists of the resources that those who are close to each other (such as family and good friends) share. Such resources, like money, borrowed household items, and child care, help people get by from day to day. "Bridging" social capital is made up of resources received from more distant social network members who often participate in different social worlds and are not as close to the recipient.[21] These resources, such as job leads, help people get ahead.

As table 2 indicates, while some women at both time periods described having access to a great deal of bonding social capital, women after reform actually drew on their networks more frequently for the kinds of resources that helped them survive: money, goods, and help with child care. Women before reform, however, were more likely to benefit from bridging social capital, as is evidenced by a higher proportion of them getting their jobs through network ties.

Of course we do not know if this shift to more reliance on bonding social capital is particular to the women I interviewed at the two time periods or whether it is true of the larger population of low-income women in each time period. If indeed the experiences of the women I interviewed reflect wider patterns, the patterns are not surprising. Welfare reform has resulted in a more disadvantaged group of aid recipients, as the most advantaged have left the rolls.[22] This more disadvantaged group probably needs more help from their networks. Furthermore, if their network members, like them, are more disadvantaged, these people may be less in a position to offer job leads. Also, the fact that women before reform were encouraged but not, for the most part, obliged to find employment may mean that they were less likely to pursue employment aggressively through all means available and more likely to become employed only when jobs presented themselves through networks.[23] The women interviewed after reform, on the other hand, rarely described finding jobs through network ties or seeking information about jobs from family and friends. This may be partly due to the new welfare rules, which, in Illinois and many other states, require women to begin their job searches almost immediately after applying for cash assistance. This requirement does not allow time for the process of finding jobs through networks to unfold. The women interviewed after reform were thus more likely to pursue the job leads provided (and sometimes enforced) by the job-training centers that contracted with the state.

The post-reform women's greater receipt of the resources associated with bonding social capital (money, goods, and child care help) is puzzling in some ways. If indeed post-reform women's networks contained more disadvantaged members, it is counterintuitive that they would provide more money and goods than earlier women's networks did. Post-reform network members probably had less money and fewer goods to spare than pre-reform network members did. This assumption is supported by the fact that women after reform were more likely than pre-reform women to report that people in their networks were draining resources from them. What was probably happening, then, was that in the face of shared hardship network members were turning to each other for the resources needed for survival and that despite scarce resources networks were rising to the occasion given the increased need. Network members may also have made more resources available in order to support norms of reciprocity that they felt were necessary for their own survival.[24]

Providing child care is a little different from providing monetary and nonmonetary goods, since one can offer it without having material resources, and if one is paid for child care services, offering it actually garners material resources. The dramatically higher usage of child care services through networks reported after reform was most likely driven by women's higher employment rates and hence need for child care, but also possibly by network members' need for the money that flowed through child care subsidies, meager as it may have been. As discussed in chapter 4, very few women after reform mentioned child care as a barrier to work, whereas the vast majority of women before reform brought up child care as the primary barrier to work. Perhaps child care was less problematic after reform because women were tapping their networks more than they had before reform, and because their networks were also more willing to serve.

As in the case of the other contexts treated in this book, we see that much of the women's trust or distrust in their networks was based on direct experiences with their friends and family members. Women in both time periods documented the deep connections they had with others and the high level of trust they placed in them because they knew from experience they could rely on them. Women also told of how they had learned the hard way that some network members could not be trusted to come through for them and actually might instead have hurt them. Just as was true for romantic partners, sometimes the women placed great trust in network members only to learn later that their trust had been misplaced.

Sometimes, however, women's wariness served as preemptive protection. When Koyana said that she "trust[ed] her mother and no one else" she was announcing a strategy for managing life in what she saw as the risky world around her. Her strategy was to keep others at arm's length, trusting only if others' trustworthiness was fully proven. Again, I argue that the women's macrostructural position at the bottom of the stratification system undergirded both their encounters with untrustworthy network members and this preemptive use of distrust as armor.

The women's disadvantaged position in terms of income, educational opportunities, and labor market prospects meant that most of their network members were also low-income people, typically living in low-income neighborhoods. These friends and family members were thus also scraping by and were at times driven to extreme acts out of financial need or utter frustration. Some network members got sucked into the drug trade or substance abuse, or acted on opportunities to steal money or food, or walked away from their responsibilities as parents, siblings, or children. And sometimes these acts imposed enormous burdens and hardship on the women I interviewed. It was the deprivation the women shared with their network members at the bottom of the income distribution that made the women particularly likely to experience these burdens that taught them to distrust, even when they used that distrust preemptively.

FOSTERING TRUST IN LOW-INCOME WOMEN'S SOCIAL NETWORKS

For low-income women to maximize support from others, they must first be surrounded by those who are trustworthy and then be willing to trust them. Neither of these two steps is easy to promote through policy, but there are some approaches that might help.

First, it is important to remember that the policy changes wrought by welfare reform apply not just to individual women, like the women I interviewed, but also to many of their network members—sisters, cousins, neighbors, and friends. Welfare policy's demands thus tax not only individuals but also entire networks and communities whose members all may feel the increased pressure of a diminishing social welfare safety net.[25] There is currently no political will to reverse course and expand the safety net. In fact, the recession that began in 2008 instead led to further cutting of social welfare benefits, despite the increased need for them brought about by rising unemployment and poverty. But expanding the safety net would probably reduce distrust stemming from the kinds of burdens that financially strapped network members impose.

Similarly, increasing funding and—equally important—creative ideas for community investment would ease the disadvantages of networks. Neighborhoods injected with increased opportunity for bridging social capital development through either mixed-income housing, partnerships between community groups and residents, or other means have been shown to have some positive outcomes for community members.[26]

Finally, though again not in keeping with political will, more flexibility in what counts as a family for the purposes of defining a welfare "case" would enhance the cooperative family systems created by women like Mariah and Lani who took turns being in the labor market and being home taking care of all of their children. Since currently each parent (and associated children) is a case, each parent receiving cash assistance faces work requirements and time limits. There are few opportunities for mothers who both receive cash assistance to join forces and work as a single family unit with one woman in the labor market and one home watching the children.[27] This arrangement worked so successfully for Danielle and her sister and for Lani and Mariah. The more incentive network members have to support each other in these ways, the more trust will be built. But it is very hard for mothers who both face work requirements to join forces in this way. Welfare reform aimed to shift responsibility for helping low-income families from the government to parents' social networks and communities, but by treating women as isolated individuals it missed opportunities to reinforce the bonds that tie networks together.

Conclusion

During his 1992 presidential campaign, Bill Clinton pledged to end "welfare as we know it."[1] Many thought he had done so when, in August 1996, he signed welfare reform into law. This book has told the stories of low-income mothers living under welfare as we knew it before reform and as we know it after reform. Undeniably, there have been changes. Today's welfare system, which Susan Schiller encountered when she last applied for benefits, has different rules than the one Bethany Grant faced. Bethany and all of the other women interviewed before reform knew that they always had a safety net should they ever need it, even if its benefits were small and its bureaucracy was difficult to navigate. Susan and her contemporaries had no such assurance. Even with the dramatic downturn in the economy that began in 2008, our most vulnerable families have almost nowhere to turn if they exhaust their time limits on cash assistance benefits. This fact in itself represents an important structural change faced by all low-income families.

Even so, welfare as we know it looks a lot like welfare as we knew it before. Certainly the lives and challenges of those moving through the welfare system have changed little. Low-income mothers still live in a set of social contexts whose structural arrangements are much the same (and in the same national culture in which they are blamed for their own plight).[2] They still go to caseworkers who are operating without the resources or incentives to fully help. They still work in jobs with little reward and under supervisors who can easily replace them. They still have few options for good child care. They still encounter men rendered unreliable by their own structural barriers to employment and with whom they share a mutual distrust that begins early on, perhaps even before adolescence. They still vary in their ability to tap social networks for survival and in their obligations to help network members even worse off than themselves.

The ways these arrangements shape social interactions in each of these contexts promoted distrust for many before reform and has continued to do so for many after reform. Since taking action in the face of uncertainty (which is almost always present) requires a leap of faith, distrust stalls action. Low-income women may well be held back by their low education levels, their limited work skills, their personal demons expressed through drugs or alcohol, and other individual traits, but this book has shown that their action is also inhibited by their distrust of others. This production of distrust is largely unchanged with the advent of welfare reform. Distrust is learned through direct experience, experiences reported by others, the news media, rumor, and other informational outlets. It may also be worn reflexively by some as protective armor. But that does not negate the fact that much of the distrust is based on direct experience undergirded by structural factors. Much of the trust literature focuses on the benefits of trust. It is a lubricant for social action.[3] It eases business practices and exchanges of all sorts.[4] It is inherently entwined with social capital, an invaluable resource for producing safe communities, connections to the labor market, political clout, and survival strategies under economic stress.[5] True, those who trust are deemed risk takers, but many gains require the taking on of risk.[6] Unfortunately, however, in many women's experience risk does not produce rewards.

Few groups, if any, are more in need of the benefits potentially generated by trust than low-income families, particularly those headed by low-income women who participate in the welfare system and low-wage work. This is especially true in the age of welfare reform, when the safety net has shrunk in size and durability and the economy is unpredictable. These mothers and their children are acutely vulnerable. Yet despite their need for the benefits of trust, many low-income mothers express high levels of distrust.[7] Many are suspicious of both the institutions and the individuals around them, reflecting in part the suspicion that greets them.

One response to their predicament is to say that they need to become more trusting, to take the risk of trusting those around them in order to capitalize on the potential social capital that such trust could bring. But this simple prescription ignores the much more complex experience of many of these families that has led them to their suspicions. The view of low-income families as distrustful masks a complicated dialectic of trust and distrust in which trust placed in the untrustworthy produces distrust, and distrust then forestalls trust. Furthermore, mothers may simultaneously distrust some but place deep trust in others or even trust and distrust the same person in different contexts.

Documenting and understanding these patterns directs our attention away from individual mothers' ability to trust and toward the structural circumstances that construct their experience and thus their learned distrust as well as their use of distrust as a preemptive means of protecting themselves. And part of the complexity of the issue is that the experience of living at the bottom of the structures I have described—at the very low end of the income distribution, in neighborhoods of concentrated poverty, and as seekers of welfare and low-wage jobs rather than providers of them—where one feels both judged and uncertain about one's standing may promote distrust even when such distrust moves one further from one's goals.[8]

Mothers in both time periods made statements such as "I trust no one" or "I have associates, not friends," indicating that they kept others at arm's length as they struggled to survive and care for their children.

Such assertions protected their self-respect, which many mothers felt was under constant attack by dismissive caseworkers and bosses, by disloyal romantic partners, and by network members who took from them without asking.[9] But despite these assertions of caution, many of these same mothers reported past events in which they had risked relying on others and had gotten burned. Thus many mothers had developed their self-protective stance of preemptive distrust out of earlier experiences when they had placed trust in others whom they later deemed unworthy of that trust. This study provides evidence that trust is, at least in large part, learned through experience rather than simply a personality trait or an expression of values.

Such learned distrust occurred across many arenas. For some women, romantic partners were a primary source of distrust. For others, though their experience was more rare, distrust in other network members—family, friends, neighbors, or others—was most pronounced. Some women lost faith in child care providers. Some women's strongest distrust was in employers or in welfare caseworkers. And for many, distrust spanned several of these relationships, so that multiple interactions were marked by suspicion. The relevance of distrust is thus not limited to one type of outcome in one specific context. Distrust is a dominant feature in low-income women's lives in a wide variety of contexts, including those involving interactions with formal institutions and interactions with informal personal contacts.

The main message of this book is that both policy makers and poverty researchers need to pay more attention to the role of distrust in low-income mothers' lives. Skeptics may point to women's individual traits, rather than what happens between them and others, as predictive of their outcomes. Of course these individual traits have effects, but they do not tell the whole story. Women in my samples who varied across race, ethnicity, age, education, years of welfare receipt, employment history, number of children, and a variety of other traits all told stories of distrust shaping their behavior. Others may argue whether it is distrust that matters or other issues about the environment such as the low wages and poor working conditions in low-skill jobs or the lack of available high-quality child care. My answer to them is that the issue is not whether distrust *versus* these other factors matters: these other factors *are* the very structural factors that I argue produce distrust. Distrust is a mechanism that exacerbates the negative effects of these structural factors on low-income families' lives. Low wages and poor working conditions create hardships for families because they keep them in poverty. But in addition, they produce distrust in employers, which results in job turnover and thus further hardship.

One of the key insights that trust researchers give us is that trust and distrust matter. Trust allows people to act in the face of uncertainty and to access the opportunities provided by taking risks. Distrust blocks opportunity. However, trust offers benefits only when interaction partners are trustworthy. When they are not trustworthy, distrust protects from harm. As Russell Hardin, a leading scholar studying trust, so eloquently states, "Trust is functional in a world in which trust pays off; distrust is functional in a world in which trust does not pay off."[10]

Many of the women in this book believe they live in a world in which trust does not pay off a lot of the time. Many of the stories they tell clearly support their belief. Few would argue that trusting physically abusive partners, neglectful child care providers, or bosses who lock workers into workplaces overnight has benefits. But from some of their stories it would seem that some opportunities could have been lost on account of distrust. Avoiding formal child care centers because of sensational stories in the media on child abuse may not move the mothers toward their goals of safe and nurturing care for their children, especially when the alternative is putting them in care situations that are unregulated and prove dangerous.

The puzzle, then, is that trust and distrust may both be functional for the mothers at different times and that it is hard for them to judge which situations call for trust and which for distrust. We saw instances in which the mothers encountered those who were not trustworthy but trusted them nonetheless, only to learn distrust from the experience. We also saw instances when the mothers did not trust and possibly lost out on opportunities to move ahead, to help their children's development, or simply to be less lonely. Where should the line be drawn to maximize exposure to trust's benefits and minimize exposure to its harms? It is hard to know the answer.

Not all of the mothers were so gifted with street smarts that they avoided trusting the untrustworthy. For some mothers it might be helpful to boost their self-esteem and educate them about their rights so that they make trust decisions that will pay off and avoid those that will not.

. But, even if such measures might be effective in some cases, putting the onus solely on the mothers themselves to make beneficial trust decisions would be misguided. Instead, it is important to address the other side of the coin: the untrustworthiness of those with whom the women interacted. Some of the women's interaction partners were so untrustworthy that their behavior was criminal, or should have been. Cracking down on abusers of all sorts—whether employers who treat workers inhumanely or boyfriends who use violence—is an obvious first step. But more can and should be done.

Throughout the book, I have looked to the possible structural roots of the untrustworthiness that the women encountered. For example, I have identified the role that the organization of the welfare office may play in giving caseworkers and welfare recipients opposite interests and making caseworkers, who are rewarded primarily for keeping their caseloads low, cavalier about women's right to certain information and benefits. Addressing these structures would go a long way to decrease untrustworthiness and the distrust it foments. Structural change is difficult, and often the political will to do it is lacking or nonexistent, but it would make social policies more effective and would improve the conditions of low-income women's and children's lives.

Not only would structural changes reduce the untrustworthiness that women encounter in their interactions with others, but they would also probably reduce the distrust that women bring preemptively into their interactions with others. This kind of distrust has the potential to keep women from accessing opportunities. It also can escalate mutual distrust with interaction partners, since, sensing the women's distrust, caseworkers, bosses, boyfriends, and others may respond in kind by developing distrust of their own. As a result, interactions go sour, demonstrating to the women that their distrust was indeed well founded and encouraging them to distrust in the future as well. Women's preemptive distrust (which some might call a "chip on their shoulder") probably stems from living life at the bottom both of the macrostructure of the U.S. stratification system and of more proximate mesostructures such as welfare offices and workplaces. The stigma of the relative powerlessness of these structural positions leads some women to feel that they need to protect themselves in interactions with those who hold power over them. And even if interaction partners are peers, sometimes resources are so scarce that competition results and distrust is again protective.[11]

Some might argue that what I am calling preemptive distrust stems from culture rather than structure. A new literature on culture and poverty argues that the political backlash against the culture of poverty thesis has led academics to abandon entirely any discussion of culture in poverty research, to the detriment of understanding life in poverty.[12] This literature rejects the culture of poverty notion that those in poverty have a different set of values passed down through the generations. Instead, it suggests that low-income people employ certain cultural practices as strategies for surviving poverty. Some might characterize preemptive distrust as a cultural practice that helps low-income mothers cope with the challenges they face. I do not object, but I see a firm limit in cultural practices' explanatory power. I warn that attention to cultural practice, while warranted, can distract from the underlying structures that are the root causes of low-income women's outcomes.

It was their disadvantaged position in a host of structures that rendered the women I interviewed both vulnerable to untrustworthy interaction partners and preemptively suspicious of those they believed did not share their interests. Thus I would argue strongly that the structure is the first thing to fix. At the end of a book documenting the cultural practice he describes as "the code of the street," a violent form of self-protection in low-income neighborhoods, Elijah Anderson calls for the reestablishment of "a viable mainstream economy in the inner city."[13] I similarly believe structural forces are the basis for any cultural practices of distrust and that structural change is the solution, even though the reinforcement of structural barriers by cultural practices is what makes the situation so complex.

TRUST AND POWERLESSNESS

The stories I have told are largely about the problem of trust in the face of relative power inequities.[14] This theme is most evident in the contexts of the welfare office and the workplace, where low-income women are subordinate to their caseworkers (and the state they represent) and employers (and the workplace institutions they represent). The women need their caseworkers to get benefits. They need their employers to get paychecks and, if they are receiving welfare since reform, to meet work requirements. Caseworkers' jobs depend on the existence of clients as a group, but caseworkers do not need any particular individual clients. They are rewarded for moving clients off the rolls, not for retaining them or serving them well. Employers of low-wage workers similarly need a pool of workers but rarely need any worker in particular. Because low-wage work requires little in the way of training or hard skills, employers rarely make investments in workers and hence face little cost if workers quit or are fired. Other workers can simply be hired in their place.[15] The power dynamics between formal child care centers and parents are less clear. But parents are certainly vulnerable in child care settings because of their children's vulnerability. In addition, as formal organizations, child care centers may be associated in women's minds with other institutions in which they feel powerless. Women may thus feel they have more control with informal network-based providers.

Women's experience in the context of romantic partnerships is not by definition one of powerlessness, but many women report that romantic partners exert power over them through physical and psychological intimidation.[16] Of course, women are not solely victims. Some may give as good as they get, and men may have their reasons to feel powerlessness against women's control over children or other issues.[17] Still, many women in both time periods described feeling powerless in their romantic relationships.

In the context of the interviewed women's personal social networks, subordination to one's interaction partners was less of an issue (though still present in cases where dominance through abuse and other means occurred), but I would argue that powerlessness played a different role.

Since the majority of the women had networks filled with people who were similarly disadvantaged, women knew that everyone was desperately scraping by to survive. While there were plenty of stories of cooperation as a survival strategy, there could also be a sense in which everyone was out for themselves. Thus the women were not necessarily powerless vis-à-vis their interaction partners, but the extreme disadvantage of everyone in the group could promote distrust and failure to cooperate.[18]

One way to think about trust and power (or powerlessness) is in terms of Hardin's concept of encapsulated interests, by which he means that one interaction partner's interests are advanced when, along the way, she pursues the other's interests as well. The greater the asymmetry of power, the less likely it is that the more powerful interaction partner will encapsulate the interests of the less powerful one and the more likely it is that the less powerful partner will distrust the more powerful one.[19] This appeared frequently to be the case for the women I interviewed when they interacted with various others.

Karen S. Cook critiques the trust literature for having little to say about the role of power in trust relations.[20] She further argues that we know little about the circumstances under which trust occurs in the context of powerlessness, though she surmises a set of important circumstances. She writes that "the conditions that lead to trust in the context of power inequality have not been specified clearly but may include transparency, fairness, and procedural justice, among other factors beyond the clear demonstration of trustworthiness by both parties."[21]

The conditions that Cook hypothesizes will promote trust in the face of power inequity were absent in many of the settings I studied. For example, since many women in both time periods did not understand what the welfare rules were or how the welfare office operated, the welfare office had not successfully achieved transparency. Many women believed that they were inappropriately denied benefits and so did not believe that caseworkers practiced procedural justice—or that the processes within the organization were conducted fairly. It is possible that caseworkers were fair and did practice procedural justice but that they did not clearly communicate what they were doing and why. Such communication failures would be part of the lack of transparency. Women at both time periods similarly believed that some (but not all) employers were unfair and failed to practice procedural justice.

Also absent were structures that could substitute for trust, such as contracts or legal assurances of outcomes that would give the women confidence to act even if they did not trust their interaction partners.[22] Carol Heimer even argues that distrust is the first step toward trust.[23] She explains that when actors do not trust their interaction partners, there is pressure to create the kinds of structures to which Cook refers.[24] Once these are created, actors feel confident to engage with others. This exposure to others can, over time, teach actors that these others can be trusted (if indeed they prove trustworthy).

The problem for low-income families is that the terms of their interactions with welfare offices, workplaces, and others offer few mechanisms that substitute for trust and thus little opportunity to engage despite their distrust. They have few if any guarantees of outcomes even if other actors turn out to be untrustworthy. The lack of such guarantees keeps them from being exposed to the possibility of trustworthy behavior and learning to trust as Heimer envisions. Welfare reform's removal of a federal entitlement to welfare benefits and the decline of the labor movement and union protection have further removed the existence of legal guarantees that could operate as a substitute for trust. These guarantees are long gone and very unlikely to return, but if more of these protections were in place, perhaps distrust could lead to trust as Heimer suggests. However, the social interactions enabled by such protections would lead to trust only if the interaction partners indeed turned out to be trustworthy in their behavior. If social interactions served only to bring the women into contact with untrustworthiness, continued distrust would result, and for good reason.

DISTRUST IN EACH OF THE FIVE CONTEXTS

The Welfare Office

In both time periods, women reported frustrating interactions with caseworkers who sometimes failed to produce benefits that the women believed they had a right to receive. As a result, many women both before and after reform distrusted their caseworkers, especially when it came to offers of benefits designed to entice them into the labor market. They believed only in the sticks of mandatory policies.

In the pre-reform world, this distrust probably slowed welfare exits because women feared that leaving welfare for a low-wage job without the assistance of work supports would be too costly. If women's assessments of their caseworkers' trustworthiness were wrong, their hesitancy to respond to voluntary work incentives cost them potential chances to improve their socioeconomic situations and to be free of the stigma attached to welfare receipt. If, however, they were right and the street-level practice of caseworkers was to fail to make good on promises of work supports, then women's distrust did not result in missed opportunity. In the post-reform world, the women's distrust led them to be responsive to the work requirements, since these policies were in line with women's view of caseworkers as driven primarily by their aim of reducing caseloads.

The Workplace

Both before and after reform, events at work convinced many women that they would not be treated fairly by their supervisors in the future. Such beliefs often led them to quit their jobs, frequently without first attempting to address perceived mistreatment.

The similarities across time may be surprising, given the greater work incentives introduced after reform. But welfare reform did not do anything to change the relationship between employers and employees, the social organization of workplaces, or the structure of the low-wage labor market. Nor did it do anything to change the larger culture in which the women lived, a culture that blamed them for their circumstances and led them to take a defensive posture.[25] Reform also could not change the impulse to resist mistreatment, to save face, or to escape threat. Once one considers these limitations of reform, the fact that workplace conflict continues to be a major source of job turnover is more understandable.

Women's distrust of their employers kept them from attempting to work out conflicts, which led to high turnover in jobs. Placing greater trust in employers might have produced longer tenure in jobs, but only if employers were responsive to women's concerns.

Child Care Providers

Women interviewed after reform were much less likely to describe child care as a problem than women interviewed before reform. The greater availability of child care subsidies coupled with the increased pressure to find child care led many post-reform respondents to find some kind of care for their children in order to meet reform's work participation requirements. However, women interviewed before and after reform shared the same difficulty in finding child care providers they felt they could trust. Again, this lack of trust often stemmed from past experiences in which women came to see their trust as having been misplaced. Some women were also influenced by sensational media stories about children's abuse in care facilities.

Before reform, distrust in child care providers stalled or interrupted some women's participation in the labor market. After reform, women had fewer choices to remain out of the labor market, and this led some women to use child care that they felt put their children at risk. Other women, feeling they had no trustworthy child care options, made the decision to try to survive without either welfare or earnings. Distrust in formal day care centers may have led some women to give up opportunities for care in which their children would actually have been safer and have had more child development opportunities than they had in more informal care settings.

Romantic Partners

Many women reported experiences in which partners were unreliable in terms of money, involvement with children, fidelity, or safety. Most dramatically, some women told stories of violence. While a good portion of the mothers went on to have men in their lives in the future, many kept these men at arm's length and were hesitant to cohabit or marry. Their reluctance may have cost them opportunities for financial help and emotional fulfillment, but only if the next man would have been trustworthy.

Social Networks

Much sociological work celebrates the bonding social capital that close ties with kin produce and, in particular, its value in the survival strategies of those in poverty.[26] Indeed, many of the women interviewed prized such productive relationships. However, social interaction with family and friends was also a source of strain for women who learned the hard way that they could not trust everyone in their networks.[27] As a result, some of these women withdrew from social life. This withdrawal isolated them and their children from the harms, but perhaps also the potential benefits, of social interaction.

TRUST AND TRUSTWORTHINESS IN LOW-INCOME MOTHERS' LIVES

Through the social policies we have enacted, we as a society have said we want low-income mothers to enter the labor force. They too value what a firm footing in the labor force could bring: financial stability, self-esteem, role modeling for children, and the opportunity to move to safer neighborhoods. But it is not easy to successfully transition into the labor market alone. It was not easy before reform, and the modest work supports put in place as part of reform have not made much improvement.

The cooperation and support of others including caseworkers, employers, child care providers, romantic partners, and extended kin would go a long way toward easing the burden placed on low-income mothers struggling both to care for their children and to meet the dictates of welfare reform. However, to access this support, mothers would have to trust these other actors. They would have to take a leap of faith and believe they would be treated fairly and safely if they risked making themselves vulnerable to these others. For many of the women in this study, this risk was great and had often been taken with disastrous consequences. As a result, many mothers deemed trust too dangerous and instead developed a distrustful stance toward the outside world. Many of the low-income mothers trying to transition completely from welfare to work concluded that distrust was functional in their world. To the degree that they were right, it would be mistaken to argue that their distrust cut them off from potential social capital and other opportunities that would offer employment and economic well-being. Instead, the untrustworthiness of those individuals and institutions around them negated the development of and ability to access such opportunities. Yet we do see examples of those for whom taking the risk of trusting helped in surviving poverty and the demands of welfare reform. For example, Mia Fields, whom we met in chapter 5, was beginning to let a new, very supportive man into her life despite her past difficult experiences with the father of her children. Such stories raise the question of how much potential opportunity is lost through the creation of distrust.[28]

Given the downside of misplaced trust, however, the best way to promote the development of trust and its associated benefits would be to work on increasing trustworthiness—making welfare systems accountable, instituting fair labor practices, investing in well-trained child care providers, creating more drug treatment options for those addicted and wreaking havoc on their families, developing more economic opportunities for those who currently drain the resources of their network members for economic survival—rather than simply focusing on promoting more trustful natures in low-income mothers themselves. Trustworthiness builds trust.[29]

On one of my last visits with Dolores Rios, an aspiring chef, she told me that her dream was to win the lottery and then start her own restaurant where she would have an apartment upstairs. "That way I could come down at 11:00 at night and do stuff and not worry about the kids, 'cause they'd be right there." After a pause, she wistfully said, "Someday." Dolores's dream was no different from that of many Americans—to be financially secure, to have satisfying work, to be independent, to spend time with family, and to be free from worries about children's safety. In this book, I have argued that the gap between reality and dreamed-of outcomes for low-income women—and by extension, probably for all of us—is widened not only by what happens within us but also by what happens between us and by the distrust it sometimes creates.

APPENDIX Research Methods

In this appendix, I describe the various stages of the study. I begin with a brief overview of the intellectual inspiration for the two rounds of interviews. I then move on to a discussion of the development of the interview protocols, the recruitment of study participants, the nature of the interviews and my rapport with the interviewees, the coding of the interviews and analysis of the data, and the writing of the text.

INTELLECTUAL INSPIRATION

As discussed in the Introduction, this project began as a doctoral dissertation. I had been steeped in the literature on pre-reform "welfare dynamics," which investigates low-income families' movement on and off the welfare rolls. Two of this literature's findings intrigued me: a high proportion of low-income mothers moved off the welfare rolls into employment fairly quickly, and a high proportion of mothers who did so eventually returned to welfare.[1] I became interested in what made low-income mothers decide to and be able to transition from welfare to work and what made their transitions to work so difficult to sustain.

The welfare dynamics literature provided some answers to these questions by identifying several key individual traits (such as age of youngest child and number of children) that predict welfare exit. Clearly individual traits matter. But I suspected that factors beyond individual traits mattered too. I thought that aspects of women's environments and their connections to others might make it easier or harder to exit welfare and sustain employment. My supposition stemmed from my reading of the economic sociology literature, which demonstrates that social interactions and, to use Mark Granovetter's term, "embeddedness" in social contexts affect economic action.[2] I wanted to explore the kinds of social interactions and contexts that were relevant for low-income women's economic actions of welfare receipt and employment. The program participation and labor market surveys used in the welfare dynamics literature do not typically measure these factors (and they are not easily measured in quantitative data). I set out to conduct qualitative interviews with low-income women and to ask them about their experiences in the contexts that seemed most relevant to me: the welfare office, the workplace, the child care market, romantic partnerships, and social networks of friends and family.[3]

These interviews revealed that indeed the women I interviewed had many social interactions in these five contexts that played a role in their choices and their abilities to move from welfare to work and to stay in jobs. As I describe in the Introduction, only after the pre-reform interviews were completed did I begin to see what was most salient about the social interactions the women had in the five contexts: many of these interactions were marked by distrust. Thus when I became interested nearly a decade later in how women were faring since reform, I set out to look much more pointedly at the role of distrust in low-income women's lives.

INTERVIEW PROTOCOLS

One of the key benefits of qualitative research is that it can produce rich data in study participants' own words. To capitalize on these benefits, I strove for a conversational tone in interviews that both aided rapport and allowed participants to pursue topics they deemed important. At the same time, I wanted to collect data on a consistent set of topics across participants. I thus developed, at each time period, an interview protocol that covered everything needed for the study, but I was flexible about how the interviews proceeded, allowing conversations to take their natural course. Sometimes this made conducting the interviews challenging, since it forced me (and the research assistants who joined me in conducting the second round of interviews) to keep track of what was covered and what still needed to be covered while still listening carefully and being responsive to the interviewee.

The pre-reform interview protocol was significantly shorter than the post-reform protocol. Since reform had not yet occurred, there were no questions to ask about reform's many new rules, though I did ask about the existing rules. In addition, I asked no specific questions about trust before reform, since the importance of trust became clear only once I analyzed the pre-reform data. The pre-reform interview protocol asked a series of open-ended questions about each of the five contexts of interest. It also collected demographic data and a detailed welfare, work, partnership, and fertility history. Finally, it asked in-depth questions to tap participants' understanding of welfare rules.

Here I used a method taught to me by Howard S. Becker in my graduate school qualitative methods course: I played dumb. I pretended I had little understanding of welfare rules and asked participants to explain them to me. After doing so, if they did not mention a particular rule that was important, I began to ask more specific questions about the rule to ascertain whether they were aware of it and what their understanding of it was. This approach both produced a more accurate sense of their impressions of various rules and aided rapport, since it did not seem as if I was the authority testing them on their knowledge. And of course, it turns out I was not the authority, since I learned a lot about the street-level practices of caseworkers from the study participants.

Developing the interview protocol for the second round of interviews was complicated. I needed to cover the same ground as I had before reform in order to compare the reports of the two sets of women, but I also wanted to address distrust more specifically. I understood that if I asked only specific questions about distrust, it would threaten my ability to compare post-reform with pre-reform interviews when specific distrust questions were not asked. My solution to this problem was to begin the interviews with questions similar to those asked in the first time period and then to move in the direction of asking more specific distrust questions. Thus I asked participants to tell me about their experiences with caseworkers or with boyfriends or other people in other contexts, just as I had done in the pre-reform interviews. Once these discussions ended, I asked more specifically how much they trusted or distrusted each of these people and why. I also asked whom they trusted the most and whom the least.

Another challenge was that I needed to cover the new welfare reform rules, which are much more extensive than the pre-reform rules and hence made the interviews long. I never came up with a good solution to that problem. Luckily, most participants were remarkably patient despite the length of interviews.

RECRUITMENT OF STUDY PARTICIPANTS

The book is based on in-depth qualitative interviews with a total of ninety-five women in Chicago across the two time periods (twenty-six women before reform and sixty-nine women after reform).[4] The majority of the pre-reform respondents were identified through two different Chicago job-training programs. Most participants in these programs attended mandatorily in order to meet requirements dictated by the Family Support Act of 1988, reducing the chance that participants were self-selected to be particularly interested in employment. In addition, a few interviewees were identified through the Effects of Violence on Work and Family project, a survey conducted with a random sample of eight hundred women living in a Chicago neighborhood.[5] Post-reform respondents were found through two different job-training programs and four other more general not-for-profit agencies providing services to low-income families in Chicago.

Both before and after reform, I spent time at the job-training or social service agencies, and staff introduced me to program participants so that I could describe the study and ask them if they were willing to participate. In most cases these introductions were informal and occurred one-on-one with individual women. One exception occurred at a post-reform job-training center whose staff introduced me more formally to an entire classroom of women during one of their training sessions. I could immediately tell that this approach was a mistake in that it gave the impression I held a position at the job-training center itself, which I later learned was distrusted by many of the women present. Participants appeared suspicious of me, and I received pointed questions about my motives, particularly from Mia Fields and Dionne Anderson. I was thus surprised when later each agreed to the interview and even more surprised when they were among the most forthcoming participants. I thus got a taste firsthand of a form of preemptive distrust. But somehow I passed their test, probably by asking questions in such a different manner than caseworkers and job training counselors did, and they risked opening up to me.

At the time of the interview, the women either were receiving cash assistance (in the form of AFDC before reform and TANF after reform) or had left the welfare rolls in the past several years. The inclusion of past as well as current recipients allowed investigation into women's experiences as they exited welfare and entered the labor market, as well as women's experiences while on the welfare rolls. It also ensured that I was not recruiting only current recipients, who were more likely to be in the middle of long spells of welfare receipt and hence more disadvantaged than others.[6] All women had at least one child under the age of eighteen at the time of the interview, since they would not otherwise be responsible for minor children and balancing the demands of motherhood and other responsibilities. Also, those without a minor child would not have been eligible for welfare. Interviews with the pre-reform sample took place in 1994 and 1995, shortly before welfare reform was passed. Interviews with the post-reform sample were conducted a decade later, in 2004 and 2005.[7]

The objective of the recruitment strategy was to ensure that the two samples covered a broad spectrum of women with welfare experience during both time periods, rather than to identify a representative sample of current and former welfare recipients at each time period. In the book I am thus describing similarities and differences between the two samples I interviewed rather than those of the greater population of low-income mothers. Throughout the book, I compare the women I interviewed in the two different time periods. The reader should remember, though, that these comparisons are based on small and nonrepresentative samples. At times, I indicate the proportion of women who did or thought something at each time period, but again, these figures are meant only to characterize my samples, as we do not know if they represent a broader population. That said, collecting the in-depth material presented in the book on factors difficult to capture in representative survey data would have been impossible without the kind of approach I have used.[8]

Table A1 shows descriptive characteristics for the two groups of women in the two time periods. For the most part, the groups of women I interviewed in the two time periods did not differ dramatically from each other in terms of basic demographic characteristics. Compared to the women interviewed before reform, those interviewed after reform did include a higher proportion of never-married women and a somewhat higher proportion of African Americans. (The race difference did not meet statistical significance, though significance is of limited meaning in small nonrandom samples.) In addition, not surprisingly given time limits and work requirements, a higher proportion of post-reform respondents were off welfare, and, of those off welfare, women interviewed after reform had been off for more years than those interviewed before reform. Given the changes in welfare policy and accompanying changes in the composition of the welfare rolls between the two time periods, all of these differences between the two groups of women are expected and reflect what actually happened for the population at large. The two groups are fairly similar across other characteristics.

One might ask whether the differences that do exist between the samples in terms of race/ethnicity and marital status pose challenges to the conclusions I draw in the book. I do not believe so. One of the things welfare reform did was to induce similar changes in the *population* of welfare recipients. Hence, when one is asking whether women with current or recent welfare receipt after reform have levels of distrust similar to those of women receiving welfare before reform, it is appropriate to use samples that changed as did the population. However, it is true that we do not know from these samples whether women with identical characteristics would have the same experiences before and after reform. That

Table A1 Characteristics of Pre-Reform Sample, Post-Reform Sample, and IFS Study

Characteristic	Pre-Reform	Post-Reform	IFS (Cook County TANF recipients)
	1994–1995 (N = 26)	2004–2005 (N = 69)	1999–2000[a] (N = 874)
RACE/ETHNICITY[b]			
Latina, % (number)	50.0 (13)[c]	36.2 (25)	14.0
African American, % (number)	42.3 (11)	53.6 (37)	87.0
White, % (number)	7.7 (2)	10.1 (7)	11.0
Other, %	—	—	2.0
EDUCATION			
HS diploma, % (number)	23.1 (6)	30.4 (21)	—
HS diploma or GED, % (number)	38.4 (10)	40.5 (28)	—
Mean highest grade	10.2	10.8	—
Median highest grade	10	11	—
FAMILY STRUCTURE			
Never married	42.3 (11)*	65.2 (45)	65.0
Mean no. of children	2.5	3.3	2.5
Median no. of children	2	3	—
With children age < 6, % (number)	53.8 (14)	47.8 (33)	—
AGE			
Mean years of age	32.4	32.3	31.8
Median years of age	34	34	—
WELFARE STATUS			
Currently receiving AFDC or TANF, % (number)	84.6 (22)**	63.8 (44)	100.0
If off AFDC/TANF, mean years since last received	1.98*	4.70	—

JOB HISTORY

Currently employed, % (number)	26.9 (7)	29.0 (20)	—
Mean no. of jobs ever held	4.2	4.8	—
Median no. of jobs ever held	4	4	—

NOTE: While the study data are not from random samples, the table follows a common practice of using statistical tests to show how large the differences are between the pre- and post-reform samples without making claims of formal statistical significance.

a. IFS data from D. Lewis et al. (2004).

b. In my study, I include in the Latina group all those who claim Latina ethnicity regardless of race and exclude those who claim Latina identity from either the African American or the white group. Thus the three categories sum to 100 percent. In IFS, those claiming Latina identity are included in their respective race groups and are also shown in a separate Latina line. Thus African American, white, and other sum to 100 percent. The 14 percent Latina category overlaps with these groups.

c. Since percentages can be misleading in a small-sample study such as my own, I have included N's in parentheses after percentages for my study only.

*p < .10; **p < .05.

said, other than in race/ethnicity, marital status, and the policy-related changes in welfare receipt, the study's pre- and post-reform samples are indeed nearly identical, as table A1 shows.

To provide the reader with a sense of how the samples compare to more representative data, Table A1 also includes data from the Illinois Families Study (IFS),[9] which followed 1999 TANF recipients in Cook County (which includes the City of Chicago). I show here data collected from the IFS sample in 1999–2000, roughly the midpoint between my two study periods. The objective of my sampling strategy was not to match the IFS study, since IFS's exclusive sampling of current welfare recipients would not allow me to see women's lives after their transition from welfare. The comparative information is provided here simply as a means of illustrating how the current study's respondents compare to another somewhat comparable and more representative welfare sample, even though we would not expect either of my samples to exactly match IFS given the different goals (and hence designs) of the two studies.[10] Unfortunately, IFS did not include many of the variables I have on my samples. Table A1 shows the ones that are available. There are few if any reasons to suspect that my samples are marked by any unusual selection issues. The only notable implication of the comparison with IFS is that it suggests that my study may oversample Latinas and actually undersample African Americans. (Given that this is a small, qualitative study, oversampling

Latinas allows us to learn more of their experience.) Other than race/ethnicity, the comparison with IFS indicates that my samples are quite similar to a more representative sample.

It was important to me that my samples be racially and ethnically mixed as I was disturbed that many popular representations of welfare recipients incorrectly depicted recipients as exclusively African American. President Reagan's image of the always African American "Welfare Queen" was just one example of this. In Chicago, there is a large population of low-income Latinas, so it was not difficult to include Latinas in the samples. However, there are far fewer white welfare recipients in Chicago, so including them in substantial numbers was more difficult. Had I conducted my study in a more rural area or even in a city with a higher population of low-income whites, I would have had an easier time achieving my goal. I am pleased that my two samples do indeed include whites in proportions roughly comparable to those in IFS, but I would have liked to have been able to oversample whites as I did Latinas in order to learn more about their experiences.

The women lived in similar kinds of neighborhoods in both time periods. While poverty can be found anywhere in Chicago, the highest concentrations of poverty are in the West Side and South Side neighborhoods. Most of the pre-reform women lived on the West Side of Chicago, with just a few elsewhere in the city. The majority of the post-reform women also lived on the West Side, though more of them lived on the South Side than did the pre-reform women. Figures A1 and A2 are maps of Chicago showing where the respondents at each time period lived, broken down by race and ethnicity. The maps also show the percentage of the population below the poverty line in each census tract in Chicago. As the maps illustrate, most women in both time periods lived in census tracts with relatively high levels of poverty, although there was some variation in levels of neighborhood poverty.

INTERVIEWS

Before I began the first pre-reform interviews, I did not know how the study participants would receive me or my questions on sensitive topics. I am a white woman, and the majority of the study participants were African American and Latina. I was working toward a PhD and hence held a much more privileged class position than did my respondents. Also, I had no children at the time and did not know if my childlessness would inhibit rapport as we discussed motherhood. This was not my first experience conducting qualitative interviews with a low-income, largely minority population. As an undergraduate, I had written a thesis based on interviews with low-income adolescent mothers,

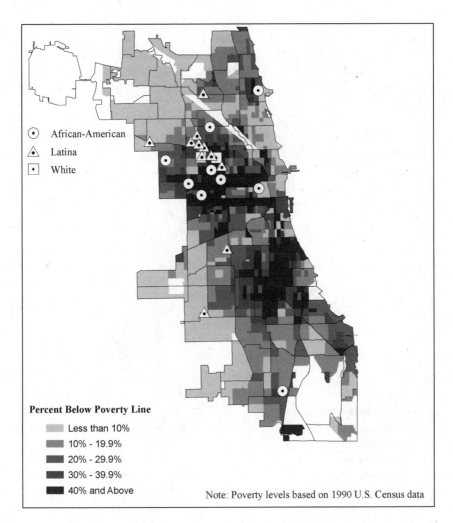

Figure A1. Pre-Reform Women's Race and Ethnicity, Residential Location, and Census Tract Poverty Level

many of whom were African American. Those interviews had gone well, and the mothers were generously open with me. However, these interviews were a little different because I would be asking about welfare receipt, a deeply sensitive topic (though perhaps, in retrospect, no more sensitive than adolescent motherhood).

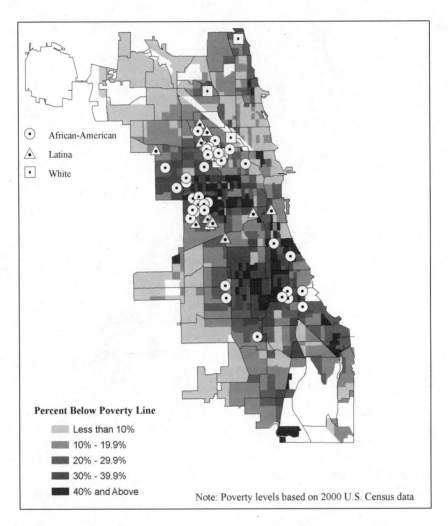

⊙   African-American

△   Latina

▣   White

Percent Below Poverty Line

Less than 10%

10% - 19.9%

20% - 29.9%

30% - 39.9%

40% and Above

Note: Poverty levels based on 2000 U.S. Census data

Figure A2.   Post-Reform Women's Race and Ethnicity, Residential Location, and Census Tract Poverty Level

I was thus relieved and deeply grateful to the study participants when they welcomed our conversations. In fact, women in both time periods showed little discomfort with or hostility toward me. To the contrary, many indicated that they enjoyed the conversations and even thanked me for taking the time to talk with them. The vast majority of participants spoke at great length. Interviews (across both time periods) ranged from one hour to an unusual five and a half hours. Most pre-reform interviews were between an hour and ninety minutes. Most post-reform interviews were between ninety minutes and two hours. Given the distrust I document in the book, the women's openness to me is at first surprising. However, it is telling about the conditions that produce their distrust. I showed great interest in the women's stories and was sympathetic about their struggles. The way I interacted with them was thus in stark contrast to the way they described their interactions with the caseworkers, bosses, and others they distrusted. As such, it appeared that the interviews did not trip their alarms and that they appreciated the opportunity to talk about their experiences to a willing audience.

There were exceptions, however. One woman interviewed before reform seemed uncomfortable throughout our interview. She was polite and answered my questions. She was not hostile, simply uncomfortable. At one point, I acknowledged that she seemed uncomfortable and asked her if she wanted me to stop the interview. She said no, it was just that she didn't like to talk about "this stuff," by which she meant welfare receipt. I moved away from that topic and wrapped up the interview quickly. A second pre-reform woman did act hostile during the interview and was the only woman before reform who did appear to distrust me. However, somehow during the interview she decided that I could be trusted and became incredibly friendly. At that point she told me she originally had thought I was a "government spy" but had then concluded that I was not. When I asked her how she had decided I wasn't a spy, she told me that I was too nice to be one. She then became very forthcoming and warm. One woman interviewed after reform just went through the motions of the interview. She did not seem uncomfortable, but she clearly was not willing to give me much of herself.

One difference between the pre- and post-reform interviews was that I had changed. I was ten years older, making me a bit older (rather than younger) than many of the study participants, a professor rather than a graduate student, and a mother of an infant. Being a professor gave me slightly more distance from the participants, but being a mother gave me much less. While before reform I had intellectually understood the women's feelings about their children and their fears about child care, after reform I viscerally felt their concerns, since they were my current concerns as well. During one post-reform interview, I brushed a piece of hair away from my face and found that it was caked in mashed sweet potato from my daughter's last meal. The woman I was interviewing and I had a good laugh over our shared knowledge of motherhood's challenges.

I conducted all of the pre-reform interviews and just over half of the post-reform interviews. Two doctoral student research assistants, Rebecca Vonderlack-

Navarro and Melissa Ford Shah, conducted the remainder of the post-reform interviews. All of the interviews were audiotaped, with the permission of the participants. The audiotapes were later transcribed. Interviews were conducted in respondents' homes, nearby public spaces, or social service agencies.[11] Study participants were paid for their time. Pre-reform participants were paid $12. Post-reform participants were paid $25, since their interviews were longer (and because of inflation over the ten-year interval). These amounts were meant to be respectful thank-yous for their time but not amounts so large that they coerced participation or cooperation.

Within twenty-four hours of completing an interview, I (or Rebecca or Melissa) wrote up extensive field notes on the interview. Before reform, I wrote open-ended notes. After reform, we used a form we devised to provide consistent presentation of information across cases. (The forms still allowed for open-ended notes to be included.) We also reread the pre-reform interviews and filled out these forms for them as well. The forms became invaluable during the writing process as a quick reference both for the basic facts of a respondent's life and for detail on her affect and reactions during the interview.

FOLLOW-UPS AND OBSERVATIONS

At both time periods, I (joined by Rebecca and Melissa after reform) spent some additional time with a few participants. We either had follow-up phone conversations or went to their houses and spent less structured time with them than during the interviews. We asked questions about how they were doing and got updates on issues raised in the interviews, but we also just hung out with the women and their children, laughing or helping with whatever domestic task was under way. I spent time in this way with three of the twenty-six women before reform. Rebecca, Melissa, and I followed up and spent time with ten of the sixty-nine post-reform women.

Given these small numbers and the fact that the degree of follow-up contact varied across women, this more ethnographic approach did not constitute a major part of the study design. Instead, the study was primarily interview based. However, the more ethnographic data were highly valuable in giving us a richer feeling for women's daily lives and some insight into how experiences unfolded over time. For instance, regular contact with Julie Callahan, who appears at the beginning of chapter 2, allowed me to understand her experience applying for welfare as it was happening. Similarly, spending time participating in the daily rhythm of life at Dolores Rios's home helped me to see her neighborhood through her daughter's eyes (when the eight-year-old pointed out a neighborhood sex worker to me) and hence to understand Dolores's fears better. Rebecca's time

with Adriana Marquez and my time with Mia Fields showed us why the placements their job-training programs found them became untenable over time. As
the two lay on couches in Tasha Blackwell's living room, Tasha's good-hearted
but relentless teasing of her friend Yolanda for being overly trusting and getting
hurt revealed Tasha's strong feelings about the dangers of trusting too quickly.

CODING AND ANALYSIS

After conducting the pre-reform interviews, I developed a set of codes related to
my dissertation topic and coded the interviews. However, those codes did not
adequately capture the concepts of trust and distrust. After completing the post-
reform interviews, I thus set out to develop a new set of codes and to code both
sets of interviews with these new codes. Melissa, Rebecca, and I drafted a code
list based on the interview protocols and research literature. We then revised the
code list after coding a sample set of interviews as a team using NVivo software.[12]
A final code list was then used to systematically code all transcripts (both pre-
reform and post-reform interviews). Transcripts were coded by the three inter-
viewers and three additional student coders. The study team also developed a
list of "attributes," the term used in NVivo for characteristics with which an
entire interview (i.e., the case) can be marked in the coding process. The attributes we used included both basic demographic factors such as education level
and more subtle factors such as a woman's level of trust in her network members. Attributes ease comparisons of cases' interview material (such as by time
period of interview, race, or employment status) and allow for the production of
summary tables of sample characteristics, such as table A1 (which was actually
produced by entering the attribute information into SPSS).[13]
   I use the NVivo attributes, imported into SPSS, throughout the book when
describing the proportion of the women who held a certain belief or had a certain
outcome or when describing the relationship between two factors. For example,
table 2 in chapter 6 shows the relationship between time period of interview and
receipt of various kinds of resources through networks. Twenty percent of interview attributes were coded by two different coders, and discrepancies were adju-
dicated by me in consultation with the coders. To prepare for coding, both of
pieces of text within transcripts and of attributes of a case overall, all coders
(including myself) coded the same subset of transcripts and through a series of
meetings decided on a uniform interpretation of how codes should be used.
   To further aid analysis, we produced a set of what we called "summaries" on
several different subjects. These included each of the five social contexts studied
in the book and trust in general. To do so, we constructed forms with items of
subtopics (experience with child support payments, for instance) to be filled in

with relevant material on the summaries' subject. We then collected into one document all of each case's interview material on the given topic (identified by the codes in NVivo). We read this material, summarized it in the form, and cut and pasted into the form relevant quotes from the interviews. These summaries were helpful in identifying cases that fit certain categories without our having to read entire interviews. They also gave more context to quotes than simply pulling the codes through a search of codes would do.

Codes, attributes, and summaries are invaluable for systematically analyzing qualitative data, but there is no substitute for reading and rereading interview transcripts, as I have done multiple times. These readings made clear to me the consistency across contexts, across women, and across time periods of the importance of distrust in low-income mothers' lives. I thus set about the task of writing the story of their distrust and why it matters.

WRITING

In her methodological appendix in *My Baby's Father: Unmarried Parents and Paternal Responsibility*, Maureen R. Waller provides a thoughtful discussion on writing as part of the research process in qualitative studies.[14] She details how the experiences of research participants are filtered through the author's perception of them and filtered once again through the author's choices of how to represent those perceptions in writing. As authors revise the writing, the argument of the work comes into sharper focus. Thus, the choices one makes in writing are indeed part of the research.

I struggled with two tensions during the writing process. The first was between benefiting from the insights to be gained from a single woman's experiences or her perceptions of her experiences and giving readers a sense of how common those experiences and perceptions were across all of the study participants. Qualitative studies on nonrandom samples are not designed to represent populations at large. They are meant to illuminate important social processes. As such, the experiences and perceptions of a single individual are telling. However, a reader may still have an interest in knowing whether those experiences and perceptions are rare or common among the study participants, even though the frequency of an experience or perception does not imply anything about such frequencies in the broader population. I managed this tension by attending to the meaning of each individual's interview carefully but checking the proportion of the full sample that shared that individual's experiences and thoughts. I often reported these frequencies with general terms such as *a few, many, some,* or *most* so as not to give too much weight to a precise proportion given its limited meaning. But when I sensed that these vaguer terms would be confusing, I did provide numerical percentages, hoping the reader would not make more of them than is appropriate. This tension was particularly acute in chapter 6, where I provided a table showing percentages of the women who had various types of interactions with their networks. I gave much thought to the inclusion of this table, ultimately deciding that it gave helpful context to my discussion of the women's experiences and perceptions of their network members.

The second tension was between making my argument about distrust clear and providing a more comprehensive representation of the women's narratives. Qualitative methods produce voluminous data in the form of thousands of pages of interview transcripts and field notes. Even if it were possible to represent those data fully, any argument about a particular social process would be lost. Because I became convinced in the course of the study that distrust played a major role in not one but multiple contexts, that distrust was an important barrier to action, and that the ubiquitous presence of distrust had been overlooked to the detriment of low-income families' well-being, I was committed to making the story of distrust stand out. When I did so, however, many other stories fell away. As I think of these stories—the deprivations that women and children experienced, the specific challenges of managing low-wage jobs and children, the impact of mothers' own childhood experiences on their adult family lives, what mothers tried to give to their children, and many more—I feel their absence as a loss. But I think I would mourn more the failure to give the importance of distrust its proper due. I will trust readers to know that while distrust was a key factor in my study participants' lives, the women were much more than their distrust—that each was an individual with her own compelling stories to tell.

Notes

INTRODUCTION

1. All names and other clearly identifying information have been changed to preserve the anonymity of study participants.

2. See Bane and Ellwood (1994) for a discussion of welfare "churning," in which cases move off and back on the welfare rolls, often because of administrative mistakes that end benefits for which recipients are still eligible. Also see Brodkin (1997, 2011), whose qualitative work documents that caseworkers cut benefits inappropriately with some frequency.

3. The Food Stamps program was renamed Supplemental Nutrition Assistance Program, or SNAP, in October of 2008. I use the earlier name because my data collection ended prior to the name change and because the term *food stamps* is still commonly used despite the name change.

4. See Brodkin's (1997) ethnography of a Chicago welfare office, in which she documents that caseworkers frequently make such mistakes. Brodkin argues that since caseworkers face no penalty when they do so, there is no incentive to

avoid these mistakes. Brodkin (2011) provides evidence that these practices have continued since reform.

5. Fukuyama (1999).

6. When I interviewed Susan in 2005, $10 an hour was equivalent to $11.73 an hour in constant 2012 dollars as adjusted for inflation using the Consumer Price Index (CPI). See the Bureau of Labor Statistics' inflation calculator available at www.bls.gov/data/inflation_calculator.htm. Throughout the book, I frequently supply both unadjusted and adjusted dollar figures, either putting both in the text or putting the constant 2012 dollar figure in a note.

7. For a thorough review of quantitative studies on reform's effects, see Grogger and Karoly (2005).

8. For example, Watkins-Hayes (2009) is an in-depth study of how caseworkers operate in post-reform welfare offices. Cherlin et al. (2002) show how post-reform welfare offices sanction (or cut off) benefits of recipients suspected of not meeting welfare requirements. Scott, London, and Hurst (2005) describe the child care arrangements of women who move from welfare to work since reform.

9. There are some notable exceptions. *American Dream: Three Women, Ten Kinds, and a Nation's Drive to End Welfare,* by *New York Times* journalist Jason DeParle (2004), is masterful in the holistic detail it provides on the daily lives of the three single mothers he follows through welfare reform. To capture that level of detail, he tells the stories of three women who are related to each other (and begins with the previous generation of their family). The trade-off is that the book, by necessity, does not address how women from a variety of backgrounds experience reform. Sharon Hays's *Flat Broke with Children* (2003) also treats multiple aspects of low-income women's lives since welfare reform in detail, though the greater focus of her book is on how post-reform welfare offices have delivered the message of reform to welfare recipients and how difficult those demands are for recipients to meet.

10. Bane and Ellwood (1994); see also Harris (1993) and Pavetti (1993). This estimate, which is actually 4.4 years, is for first "spells" (or periods of time) on welfare. Many women had repeated spells, though these tended to be shorter. Also, over 50 percent of cases who began a spell on welfare would leave it within two years. But that is because some women are likely to leave quickly, perhaps because they have higher education and work skills or because they just needed welfare to assist during a temporary emergency. Once those cases leave the rolls, others take longer, hence the longer average duration estimate of 4.4 years. Estimates of welfare duration depend on several important factors. Estimates vary depending on whether investigators use monthly or yearly data. They are also highly dependent on whether a dynamic or cross-sectional analysis produces them. Dynamic analyses watch over time for when cases enter and then leave the rolls and hence produce

more accurate estimates of the actual time that cases are on the rolls. Cross-sectional analyses ask how long the cases on the rolls at a given point in time have been on the rolls. These analyses are best for answering questions about the length of time on the rolls for the recipients the system is serving at any given point in time. But regardless of these issues, only a very small minority of cases already on welfare (or recently off welfare) in the mid-1990s would still be on welfare (or have recent enough welfare histories to fit my study guidelines) in the mid-2000s.

11.   See, for example, Blank (2002); Jencks (2002). Grogger and Karoly (2005) review a wide array of studies of reform's effects. The rolls plummeted both because recipients left welfare and because potential recipients were dissuaded from applying for benefits by the new policy's requirements.

12.   As table A1 in the book's appendix shows, there are some differences across time periods in the two samples of women. These differences reflect what happened to the population of women on the welfare rolls after reform. The post-reform sample included a higher proportion of never-married women than the pre-reform sample, as well as a slightly higher proportion of African American women. (And given the policy's time limits and work requirements, a greater proportion of the post-reform sample were off welfare and had been off for longer periods of time.) To the degree that never-married and African American women are more disadvantaged in various ways, it is possible that they would experience higher levels of distrust. However, this fact does not create a problem for the study, primarily because the difference in samples reflects what happened to the population of welfare recipients across time periods, since the policy pushed the most advantaged off the rolls while leaving behind the most disadvantaged. Thus, given that the study is of how women with current or recent welfare histories are faring since reform compared to before reform, it is appropriate to compare samples that reflect the shifting composition of welfare recipients across time. That said, we do not know how samples of exactly identical composition would compare across time. Finding such samples with qualitative methods would be extremely difficult, and I was pleased that except for marital status and, to a slight degree, race/ethnicity (and the expected policy-induced changes in welfare receipt) the two samples have comparable characteristics. See the Appendix for further discussion of the two samples.

13.   See, for example, Bitler, Gelbach, and Hoynes (2006); Courtney et al. (2005); Jencks, Swingle, and Winship (2006).

14.   Grogger and Karoly (2005); Klerman (2005).

15.   Frogner, Moffitt, and Ribar (2010) find that those who left welfare between 2002 and 2005 did less well than those who left between 1999 and 2002. For instance, 70 percent of those who left in 2001 were employed, whereas only 56 percent of those who left in 2005 were. In addition, the later leavers had lower earnings, lower education levels, and lower levels of physical health.

16. Asch (1951).

17. Zimbardo (2008).

18. Oliker (1995a, 1995b) makes this point in her pre-reform study of the importance of studying one particular context: women's social networks. She argues that welfare recipients' responsibilities to their networks help explain their labor force participation patterns.

19. In 2012 constant dollars, the welfare recipient with two children and no other income received $5,575, the minimum wage was $6.04, and the full-time year-round minimum-wage worker's earnings were thus $12,566. The poverty rate for a family of three was $18,459. Adjusting to constant dollars does not change the proportions I cite in the text: the welfare recipient still receives less than a third of the poverty line figure, and the full-time, year-round worker just over two-thirds of the poverty line figure.

20. See, for example, Bitler, Gelbach, and Hoynes (2006); Courtney et al. (2005); Frogner, Moffitt, and Ribar (2010); Grogger and Karoly (2005); Jencks, Swingle, and Winship (2006); Klerman (2005).

21. See, for example, Blank, Danziger, and Schoeni (2006); Brodkin (1997, 2011); Clampet-Lundquist et al. (2004); Edelman, Holzer, and Offner (2005); Gennetian et al. (2002); Holzer et al. (2011); Huston (2004); Kilty and Segal (2006); Lambert (2008); Lambert and Henly (forthcoming); Lindhorst and Padgett (2005); Sandfort, Kalil, and Gottschalk (1999); Seefeldt (2008); Watkins-Hayes (2009); and Western (2006).

22. DeNavas-Walt, Proctor, and Smith (2011).

23. Wilson (2009, 4).

24. Even though I do not directly observe the structural factors, no reader should conclude that I do not hold structural factors accountable or that my focus on the women's distrust indicates I see them as the ones to be fixed. To the contrary, I see the women's distrust as evidence of what structural inequality has wrought. It would have been ideal to interview women in both time periods and also to conduct case studies of welfare offices, workplaces, and child care settings and to interview romantic partners and network members in both time periods. But this ideal approach was not feasible for several reasons. First, it would have been difficult to gain the trust of the women if they knew I was also talking with their caseworkers, bosses, child care providers, boyfriends, friends, and family members. Second, since I was studying not just one arena of the women's lives but five, this approach would have been comparable to conducting five separate studies (or ten if you consider that the approach would have to be repeated in two time periods), which would have been unduly consuming of time and resources. Instead, I use the women's interviews as evidence of their perceptions of events in the five settings. I also draw on the research of other investigators who studied the settings directly.

25. Brodkin (1997, 2011).

26. Alesina and La Ferrara (2002).

27. Cook (2005); Farrell (2004); Molm, Takahashi, and Peterson (2000).

28. Hardin (2004).

29. See Gambetta and Hamill (2005) for an exception. They study how taxi drivers decide whether it is safe to pick up a given passenger.

30. Cook (2005); Farrell (2004); Molm, Takahashi, and Peterson (2000).

31. Cook (2005).

32. Hardin (2002).

33. See Rotter (1980) for a discussion of trust as a personality trait, J. Lewis and Weigert (1985) for a discussion of trust resulting from emotions or values, and Hardin (2002) for an argument that trust is learned through experience.

34. Glanville and Paxton (2007).

35. See Bane and Ellwood (2004) for a review of these studies of welfare dynamics. See also Harris (1993) and Pavetti (1993).

36. See, for example, Watkins-Hayes (2009), who conducted an ethnography of how caseworkers adapted to and delivered the new welfare rules in Boston welfare offices, and Edin and Kefalas (2005), who investigated the romantic relationships of low-income parents.

37. On romantic relationships, see Burton et al. (2009); Edin and Kefalas (2005); England and Shafer (2007); Estacion and Cherlin (2010); Hill (2007); and Reed (2007). On child care choices, see Burton et al. (1998); Zedlewski et al. (2003). On job referrals, see S. Smith (2007).

38. Oscar Lewis, a key figure in developing the concept of "culture of poverty," defines it in his classic 1966 work *La Vida*.

39. Liebow (1967).

40. Edin and Kefalas (2005).

41. A new literature on poverty and culture rejects the old culture of poverty notions about the intergenerational transmission of *cultural values* and focuses instead on how *cultural practices* may help us understand the experience of living in poverty. David Harding, Michèle Lamont, and Mario Small edited a volume of the *Annals of the American Academy of Political and Social Science* entitled "Reconsidering Culture and Poverty" in 2010. In it, they discuss how the political backlash against the culture of poverty thesis, especially as represented in the Moynihan Report, led academics to abandon discussion of culture in relation to poverty for fear of being accused of "blaming the victim." (Wilson [1987, 2009] makes a similar argument.) This literature argues that culture provides people with ways of interpreting their surroundings and strategies for successfully negotiating those surroundings. For example, David Harding (2010) argues that adolescent boys in low-income neighborhoods use tight affiliation with their fellow teenage male neighborhood residents as a survival strategy for managing the threat of

violence. Some might characterize the preemptive distrust I mentioned above as a cultural practice. I discuss this issue further in the Conclusion. See also Bourdieu (1977) for his discussion of the relationship between the structure of what he called a "field" and the "habitus" or taken-for-granted dispositions that people develop in relationship to and as a strategy for managing the constraints of a field.

42. One of the post-reform respondents moved from Chicago to a suburb north of Chicago by the time I met her, although much of the interview covered her years in Chicago. All the other women lived in Chicago.

43. The majority of the pre-reform respondents were identified through two different Chicago job-training programs. In addition, a small number of them were identified through the Effects of Violence on Work and Family project (see Lloyd 1997), a survey conducted with a random sample of eight hundred women living in a Chicago neighborhood. Post-reform respondents were sampled through two different job-training programs and four other more general not-for-profit agencies providing services to low-income families in Chicago.

44. Please see the Appendix for more detail on the samples and the study methodology. Table A1 gives descriptive statistics on the women interviewed in each time period. The Appendix discusses how women in the two time periods compared to each other and to more representative data.

45. I was also able to observe the workplace of two of the post-reform respondents. See the Appendix for more detail on these additional sources of data.

46. See Kirschenman and Neckerman (1991), who interview employers discussing how they estimate which workers will perform well and which will not.

1. WELFARE REFORM AND THE ENDURING STRUCTURAL ROOTS OF DISTRUST

1. Handler and Hasenfeld (1991); Katz (1986); Patterson (2000); Piven and Cloward (1993); Reese (2005); Skocpol (1992). The historical discussion below draws heavily from these sources as well as Quadagno (1994). See Iceland (2003) for a succinct summary of the history.

2. See Handler and Hasenfeld (1991); Katz (1986); Patterson (2000); Skocpol (1992).

3. Handler and Hasenfeld (1991); Katz (1986); Patterson (2000); Skocpol (1992).

4. Hays (2003) and Wacquant (2009) both argue that welfare reform was guided by a cultural notion that low-income people should be punished for their undeservingness. See Ellen Reese's book *Backlash against Welfare Mothers: Past and Present* (2005), which also makes this argument and shows its historical roots.

5. Skocpol (1992).

6. This national program was called Aid to Dependent Children (ADC).

7. Patterson (2000, 58).

8. Fraser (1987); Gordon (1990); Mink (1990); Sapiro (1990); Quadagno (1994).

9. See Bobo (1991) and Kluegel and Smith (1986) for evidence that the public is less supportive of social programs that serve African Americans than they are for other groups, such as all those in poverty without any race specified.

10. Quadagno (1994, 117).

11. Reese (2005).

12. See Fraser (1994), who develops the terms *maternalist* and *universal worker* to describe differing conceptions of the welfare state.

13. Charles Murray's book *Losing Ground: American Social Policy, 1950–1980* (1984) makes this argument. See Fraser and Gordon (1994) for a critique of such arguments. They examine the history of the word *dependency* and argue that it is used to blame and stigmatize low-income, especially African American mothers.

14. DeParle (2004).

15. See DeParle (2004) for a more detailed account of the bill's passage. On the resignations, see Vobejda and Havemann (1996).

16. Benefit levels were (and still are) set by the states, and thus there is a great deal of state variation. At the time Bethany was interviewed, a single mother of two in Illinois received $377 ($567 in 2012 dollars) a month in AFDC payments. I provide the figure adjusted to 2012 dollars so the reader can have a sense of the buying power of the benefits, but note that AFDC/TANF benefits are not adjusted for inflation automatically. These benefits increase only when state legislatures vote to increase them and only by the amount the legislatures decide to approve.

17. PRWORA imposes a federal maximum lifetime limit of five years of cash assistance. While states may choose to be less generous, none can be more generous while using federal dollars to fund their TANF programs. Some states have chosen to use state dollars in order to be more generous. For instance, during the time of the post-reform interviews, Michigan allowed recipients who hit the five-year lifetime limit to continue to receive cash assistance funded by state dollars (but later abandoned this practice). Illinois used state funds to pay the cash benefits to recipients who worked at least thirty hours a week (although this was later raised to thirty-five hours). This rule allowed recipients with this degree of labor market participation to "stop the clock." PRWORA also allowed states to exempt 20 percent of the caseload from work requirements and time limits. It is up to states to determine what conditions make a recipient so difficult to transition into the labor market that she should be exempt from work requirements and time limits.

18. There may, however, be other support programs to which Susan could turn. For instance, if she or one of her children were to become disabled, she

could apply for SSI, a federally run program that is more generous than TANF. Many states have transferred their most needy cases from TANF to SSI in order to get them off the state-run welfare rolls and onto the federally run program.

19.   PRWORA imposes a federal maximum of two years of receipt without labor market activity. However, almost all states require work activity (job training, subsidized jobs, private employment, or some other activity that counts as "work") much sooner, some even immediately upon application for TANF. PRWORA does allow states to exempt from work requirements a portion of their caseload who are deemed unable to work. In addition, states have the option of adopting the Family Violence Option, under which they screen TANF applicants for the presence of domestic violence, refer those experiencing violence to services, and exempt them from work and other requirements that the violence prevents. Lindhorst and Padgett (2005) find evidence that the Family Violence Option is not always properly implemented.

20.   The $342 amount is $401 in constant 2012 dollars. TANF benefits are not automatically adjusted for inflation, however. See note 16 for further discussion.

21.   Susan was thus a member of what is now being called "the disconnected" or the "no welfare, no work" group in policy circles. Little is known about how this group survives. Several of the women I interviewed were "disconnected." They survived largely through a combination of living in public housing and thus not having to pay rent when they had no earnings; food stamps (later renamed SNAP); financial help from boyfriends, friends, and family; and use of food pantries and organizations that provide clothing to low-income families.

22.   Many critiqued PRWORA on the basis of this possibility. However, PRWORA's implementation was followed by such a dramatic decline in the welfare rolls that most states initially ended up with large portions of their block grants unused. Those years were prosperous ones, however. During the Great Recession, which began in 2008, and the following long recovery period, state budgets have been strapped, and many are making cuts to social spending.

23.   R. Smith (2006). Beginning in August 2003, the family cap was no longer applied to new TANF cases in Illinois. The family caps on existing cases were phased out over an approximately eighteen-month period to ease the state's bureaucratic and fiscal burden of ending the policy.

24.   These women's experiences navigating the welfare bureaucracy are interesting. Because they themselves were not eligible for benefits, their children were "child only" cases, meaning the family received a cash assistance portion for the child but not for the mother. Since the mother did not receive TANF, she was not required to fulfill any of the work requirements. Furthermore, it is actually illegal for undocumented immigrants to work in the United States. However, the women I interviewed who were undocumented immigrants say that their

caseworkers did not seem to fully understand this and still pressured them to find work even though it was illegal for them to become employed.

25. Cherlin et al. (2002).

26. One other important change brought about by reform is that states now have much greater control over their TANF programs. It is mistaken to say that cash assistance to low-income parents and their children used to be a federal program and is now a state program, but welfare reform gave states much more autonomy in choosing how to run their cash assistance programs than states used to have. Before reform, states controlled some aspects of their programs, such as the income limits for eligibility and the level of benefits themselves. After reform, the federal government almost completely turned over the running of TANF to the states. While federal guidelines are still imposed on the states, states now design the basic structure of their welfare program. There was always state variation in the generosity of cash assistance benefits, but there is now state variation in almost every aspect of cash assistance programs.

27. For examples, see Bell (2001); Bitler, Gelbach, and Hoynes (2001); Blank (2001); Moffitt (1999); Schoeni and Blank (2000); Wallace and Blank (1999); Ziliak et al. (2000). To examine whether reform has achieved its goals, many large quantitative studies have taken one of three approaches. Some have used census data, longitudinal survey data, or administrative records to analyze changing employment, program participation, and marriage patterns (often capitalizing on state variation in implementation date or program elements to identify welfare reform's causal role). Others have used random-assignment experiments in which public assistance recipients are assigned to either a treatment group, which must operate under reform requirements, or a control group, which experiences no change in policy rules (see Bos et al. 1999). Another line of work, often more descriptive in nature but crucial for documenting what has actually happened to families who exited welfare after reform, are the "leaver" studies, which track outcomes among former recipients after they exit the welfare rolls (see, for example, Acs and Loprest 2001; Sandra Danziger, Carlson, and Henly 2001; Sheldon Danziger et al. 2002; Loprest 1999; Seefeldt 2008).

28. See the review by Blank (2002). For example, Schoeni and Blank (2000) find that, controlling for the economic boom of the late 1990s, welfare reform resulted in significant caseload declines, an increase in the number of weeks worked, and an increase in earnings. Using data from the Three-City Study, a multimethod study of the well-being of families in low-income neighborhoods in Boston, Chicago, and San Antonio, Moffitt (2003) finds that policy elements such as work requirements, sanctions, and diversion (providing lump-sum assistance instead of enrolling cases in the cash assistance program) predicted both welfare entry and welfare exit between 1999 and 2001.

29. Blank (2002).

30. See Grogger and Karoly (2005) for a thorough review of welfare reform studies on a wide variety of outcomes. The volume includes a chapter by Klerman (2005) on welfare reform's effects on marriage and childbearing.

31. Jencks (2002).

32. Hays (2003). See also a thoughtful and complimentary review of Hays's book by Natalia Sarkisian (2005).

33. DeParle (2004, 155–56).

34. One difference between these qualitative studies and some (but not all) of the quantitative studies is that in their estimates of reform's effects the qualitative studies focus on women with welfare histories whereas some of the quantitative studies include low-income people who have never received welfare. The qualitative studies thus do not capture any positive influence of reform on those who have never received welfare: for example, the policy changes may create an incentive to find employment even for those who have never received benefits. My study and those of DeParle (2004) and Hays (2006) are thus best suited to examining reform in the lives of those with welfare histories rather than all low-income people.

35. Bitler, Gelbach, and Hoynes (2006).

36. Bitler, Gelbach, and Hoynes (2006).

37. Jencks, Swingle, and Winship (2006). See also Kalil, Seefeldt, and Wang (2002) on hardship as a result of case sanctions.

38. Jencks, Swingle, and Winship (2006). For other studies that address the well-being of low-income families in the welfare reform era, focusing on such outcomes as health, health insurance coverage, material deprivation, and child well-being, see Chase-Lansdale et al. (2003); Sandra Danziger et al. (2000b); Courtney et al. (2005); Sheldon Danziger et al. (2002); Sandra Danziger, Carlson, and Henly (2001); DeLeire, Levine, and Levy (2006); Duncan and Brooks-Gunn (2000).

39. Frogner, Moffitt, and Ribar (2009, 2010).

40. Courtney et al. (2005).

41. Jencks, Swingle, and Winship (2006).

42. Bane (2012); DeParle (2012).

43. Bane (2012). On Bane's resignation, see Vobejda and Havemann (1996).

44. Bane (2012, 11).

45. Bane (2012) provides this figure. Note that the caseload decline began prior to reform.

46. Of course, they may be ambivalent, trusting to a certain extent but not fully.

47. Coleman (1988).

48. See Anthony (2005) for another illustration of the importance of trust. Using the example of microcredit borrowing groups, she shows that trust is

needed for cooperation, which in turn is necessary for desired outcomes such as group repayment success and award of additional loans.

49.   See Hardin's (2004) edited volume, entitled simply *Distrust*, for further elaboration on the relationship between trust and distrust.

50.   Fukuyama's (1999, 16) full statement is "If members of a group come to expect that others will behave reliably and honestly, then they will come to *trust* one another. Trust is like a lubricant that makes the running of any group or organization more efficient."

51.   Many scholars conceive of trust in this way. See, for example, Coleman (1988, 1990); Cook (2001); Hardin (2002); Heimer (2001); Kollock (1994).

52.   Sampson (2012, 19–20).

53.   See David Harding's *Living the Drama* (2010). Harding documents the strong pull of gangs and the high level of violence in low-income neighborhoods.

54.   See Heimer (2001) for a discussion of the role of vulnerability and uncertainty in trust behavior. She argues, in part, that distrust is a strategy to reduce vulnerability. I would assert that low-income families are indeed vulnerable and that their distrust in others is a strategy to reduce their exposure to potential untrustworthiness.

55.   See Ross, Mirowsky, and Pribesh (2001). They argue that distrust is more common not only in neighborhoods where threat is high but also among people who feel powerless to address the threat.

56.   Alesina and La Ferrara (2002).

57.   Molm, Takahashi, and Peterson (2000).

58.   Macy and Skvoretz (1998).

59.   Hearn (1997).

60.   Goldsmith (2005); Levi (1998); Peel (1998).

61.   As Peel (1998, 316) asserts, "For disadvantaged citizens, distrust is a rational, critical response to their actual experiences of distrustful and even destructive governance, both in the everyday delivery of welfare services and in larger-scale projects of community development, consultation, and urban renewal." Peel goes on to state, "[It] is not simply a matter of bad personal experience. Personal and collective histories are gathered into shared scripts that mythologize the distrusting state. . . . Distrust is learned, and all too often it is proved. People share stories of misunderstanding, ignorance, and occasional brutality: the indignities at the front counter, the police raid on the wrong house, the mother who killed herself when the welfare took her kids away" (320).

62.   Another way to think about respect comes from the trust literature's distinction between instrumental trust—based on whether one has confidence that one's own interests will be met by an interaction partner—and trust based on social bonds (see Levi 1998). I have already discussed instrumental trust. In trust based on social bonds, trust is based on the emotional quality of social

interactions. Those who value how they are treated along the way over and above the eventual outcomes of exchanges will trust those who treat them well and distrust those who do not. As we shall see, many women's distrust is based on the emotional experience of feeling disrespected. Whether this experience flows from direct evidence is hard to know. What is key in this conception, however, is that it is the nature of the relationship rather than individual interests that determines trust. Women who base trust on this kind of social bond (or treatment while interacting) may distrust and extricate themselves from interaction with those who do not treat them respectfully even if there is no direct evidence that particular desirable outcomes will not be delivered.

63. E. Anderson (1999); Bourgois (1995).

64. In her study of low-income African American families, Jarrett (1994) also argues that structural context affects family life.

65. Liebow (1967, 53–54).

66. See Goffman's classic book *Stigma: Notes on the Management of Spoiled Identity* (1963). I borrow Swidler's (1986) use of the term *toolkit* in this sense. See also Bourdieu's (1977) development of the concepts of "field" and "habitus."

67. Coleman (1990, 99) posits that people trust when their estimates of the ratio of the chance of gaining benefits through trusting to the chance of losing them is greater than the ratio of the size of the potential loss to the size of the potential gain. More formally, Coleman states that people trust when $p/1 - p > L/G$, where p = the chance of receiving a gain, L = the potential loss if the trustee is untrustworthy, and G = the potential gain if the trustee is trustworthy. Russell Hardin (1993, 2001, 2006) builds on Coleman's notion. He argues that trust and distrust are learned through experience (i.e., are based on experience of interactions with the trustee). He, like Coleman, views trust as a rational process, meaning one that is based on a calculation of the expected outcomes of trusting. Trust happens when experience suggests that a given person or entity can be trusted to act predictably and reliably in accordance with the truster's interests. If experience suggests otherwise, distrust will result. For these assessments to change, new experiences showing the opposite behavior are required. Because Hardin believes that trust generally pays off and hence that those who trust are advantaged over those who do not, he argues that those with early experiences with the untrustworthy are disadvantaged. These early experiences will bar individuals from trusting and reaping the rewards of trust in the future. He singles out children raised in low-income urban environments and survivors of child abuse as two groups potentially disadvantaged in this way (Hardin 1993).

68. Coleman (1990) gives the example of a banker approving a large emergency loan over the phone on the basis of nothing but trust that the particular client in question will pay it back. Gambetta and Hamill (2005) study taxi drivers' calculations about passengers' trustworthiness.

69. Decision makers may face limitations in their ability to access the information needed for successful trust decisions. This "imperfect information" represents a case of bounded rationality. When rationality is bounded, decision makers may still attempt to maximize utility, or they may be content to "satisfice" by accepting a decision that is good enough even if it is not necessarily the best one. See Cyert (1988); Heimer (1988); March (1994); March and Simon (1958). See Small (2009) for an interesting case of parents willing to trust others with their children on the basis of very little information about the specific trustees.

70. Hardin (2002).

71. S. Smith (2007).

72. Again, it is important to note that I do not examine the experiences of low-income women without welfare histories. My study does include, however, a wide variety of those with welfare histories, since I interviewed both those currently receiving welfare and those who were able to leave the welfare rolls. To the degree that after reform the most advantaged low-income mothers may choose to avoid the welfare program altogether, reform may have had positive effects I am not capturing. I thus repeat that my study addresses whether the lives of those with experience using welfare are different before and after reform.

73. Blank, Danziger, and Schoeni (2006); Holzer et al. (2011).

74. Blank, Danziger, and Schoeni (2006); Holzer et al. (2011).

75. Blank, Danziger, and Schoeni (2006).

76. Newman (1999, 62).

77. Lambert (2008); Lambert and Henly (forthcoming).

78. See Kilty and Segal (2006), in which multiple contributors argue that welfare reform focused on individual rather than structural causes of poverty.

79. Greenhouse (2004).

80. See, for example, Bourgois (1995); Bourgois and Schonberg (2009); Ehrenreich (2001); Newman (1999). Also see results from the Women's Employment Study (WES), which followed a cross section of 1997 Michigan TANF recipients longitudinally as they moved off the rolls and entered the workforce. WES is an unusual survey in that it includes variables tapping more contextual characteristics than many labor market surveys, such as perception of discrimination at work. See, for example, Sandra Danziger et al. (2000a) and Seefeldt (2008).

81. Brodkin (1997, 2011). See also Brodkin and Majmundar (2010). Sandfort, Kalil, and Gottschalk (1999) document recipient complaints that caseworkers do not treat them fairly.

82. Lens and Vorsanger (2005).

83. Clampet-Lundquist et al. (2004). Gennetian et al. (2002) and Huston (2004) show that child care subsidy benefits may be particularly difficult to access.

84. Lindhorst and Padgett (2005). The services in question are stipulated by the Family Violence Option. See also Lisa Brush's book *Poverty, Battered Women,*

and Work in U.S. Public Policy (2011) for analysis of how domestic violence has been treated in the welfare reform era.

85. Brodkin (1997, 2011).

86. Watkins-Hayes (2009).

87. S. Anderson (2002).

88. Cherlin et al. (2002). This study also finds that women experiencing domestic violence, and hence the interference of a partner, are more likely to be sanctioned.

89. Adams and Rohacek (2002).

90. See Illinois Department of Human Services, "Market Rate Survey of Licensed Child Care Programs in Illinois FY10," www.dhs.state.il.us/page.aspx?item=56055#a_toc7.

91. Zedlewski et al. (2003); Burton et al. (1998).

92. Burton et al. (2009); Edin (2000a, 2000b); Edin and Kefalas (2005); England (2000); England and Edin (2007, 2010); England and Shafer (2007); Estacion and Cherlin (2010); Hill (2007); Reed (2007).

93. Harding (2010).

94. Burton et al. (1998, 2009); Edin (2000a, 2000b); Edin and Kefalas (2005); England and Edin (2010); Estacion and Cherlin (2010).

95. Klerman (2005).

96. See Edelman, Holzer, and Offner (2005) for all of the findings reported here on low-income men's status.

97. Waller (2002, 2010).

98. Western (2006).

99. Western (2006).

100. Western (2006).

101. Carol Stack's classic work *All Our Kin* (1974) documents this before reform, and Sidel (2006) shows it continues after reform.

102. See Edin and Lein (1997) and Oliker (1995a, 1995b) for evidence of this prior to reform and Oliker (2000) for evidence after reform.

103. Brodkin (1997).

104. Brodkin (2011).

2. "THE WAY THEY TREAT YOU IS INHUMANE"

1. The government agency that oversaw the AFDC program in Illinois prior to reform was called the Illinois Department of Public Aid (IDPA). Because of the agency's name, most recipients referred to welfare as "Public Aid" rather than welfare or AFDC. Since reform, the Illinois Department of Human Services

(IDHS)—and not the IDPA—has administered TANF. However, TANF recipients and others still frequently refer to TANF as "Public Aid" and to welfare offices as "Public Aid offices." I thus use this terminology interchangeably with welfare and AFDC or TANF.

2. Hays (2003) makes a strong case that the activity in welfare offices and the practices of caseworkers reflect the dominant culture's blaming of welfare recipients for their situations.

3. In other words, the relationship is the opposite of the case of encapsulated interest outlined by Hardin (2002), in which actors trust each other because they each incorporate the other's interests into their own.

4. Given that PRWORA's primary goal is to move TANF cases into the labor market, it is hard to imagine that not so very long ago such clear work disincentives as the 100 percent tax rate on earnings and the immediate loss of Medicaid upon leaving the welfare rolls were in place. As discussed in chapter 1, President Reagan was focused on the very different goal of reducing welfare fraud. Reagan saw "double-dipping," or receiving income both from the AFDC program and from employment, as a form of fraud and wanted to discourage it. He thus pushed for the Omnibus Reconciliation Act of 1981 (OBRA81), which removed a previous small work incentive and replaced it with the dollar-for-dollar deduction from welfare grants when earnings were present. In the years prior to PRWORA, a major job task of caseworkers was to ferret out whether a recipient was working in order to dock her welfare grant or even push her off the rolls. Recipients were thus given a mixed message. On the one hand, they were encouraged to move from welfare to work. On the other, work was an activity to be punished through loss of AFDC dollars.

5. In fact, as long as families are income eligible, they are now eligible for Medicaid even if they have never received TANF.

6. PRWORA not only provided funding for the new voluntary incentives but also increased funding for some of the pre-reform voluntary incentives still in place.

7. Some women are exempt from work requirements, including those who are pregnant or have newborns, those in active domestic violence situations, and those with certain health problems. The vast majority of recipients, however, must participate in a work activity to receive benefits.

8. I use the term *client* or *recipient* to refer to women who receive cash assistance in the form of AFDC or TANF. These are the terms typically used in the literature. In the post-reform era, however, Illinois welfare offices have used the term *customers* instead to underscore that they are serving their clientele. The women I interviewed, however, never used the term *customers*. They did not feel that they were treated like customers, or at least not like valued ones.

9. Establishing a TANF client's (or her children's) eligibility for SSI is not easy, but it is fruitful both for the state government, which transfers fiscal respon-

sibility for the client to the federal government and gets a difficult-to-employ case off the state's TANF rolls, and for the client, who receives substantially more monthly income through SSI than she would through TANF.

10. These commonly used phrases were spoken by women who were identified for interviews through every source used in the study and hence had no or very little chance of having ever met.

11. In her ethnography of post-reform welfare offices in Boston, Celeste Watkins-Hayes (2009) argues that caseworkers take one of three approaches to their work. "Social workers" have a wide interpretation of their job tasks and consider meeting their clients' social and economic needs a part of their responsibilities. "Efficiency engineers" focus on proper execution of the technical requirements of the job and resist client efforts to pull them into meeting client needs. "Survivalists" reject both the social worker and efficiency engineer approaches, considering them futile. Watkins-Hayes writes, "The problem with social workers and efficiency engineers, survivalists reason, is that they care too much—either about clients or about completing work tasks perfectly. They haven't realized that it is ultimately ineffectual to embrace either orientation. The agency (or the clients) will find a way to undercut you either way, survivalists contend. The lodestar that drives every decision, every action, is doing just enough to make it to the end of each day and, eventually, to retirement" (118–19). If we assume that caseworkers in Chicago display similarly various work approaches, we can begin to understand why the women I interviewed vary in their assessments of caseworkers. Those who encounter "social workers" will have positive views of those interactions, while those who encounter "efficiency engineers" will have more negative assessments, and those who encounter "survivalists" will have the most negative assessments of all. Julie Callahan's description of Ms. Driscoll, especially Ms. Driscoll's mention of not caring because retirement loomed on the horizon, is the perfect illustration of the survivalist mentality. Watkins-Hayes's typology also highlights the structural issues that shape caseworker behavior and promote client distrust. Social workers resist the structural pressures, but efficiency engineers kowtow to the agency pressure to meet technical requirements instead of client needs, and survivalists' resignation reflects the organization's tendency and power to overwhelm (or "undercut") the actions of individual caseworkers. Like clients caught in the power of structural forces, caseworkers similarly struggle (or give up) against the dominance of the social context. See also Quane, Su, and Joshi (2009) for a treatment of caseworker discretion after reform.

12. These figures come from the 2010 Center for Budget and Policy Priorities report "TANF Benefits Are Low and Have Not Kept Pace with Inflation," by Liz Schott and Ife Finch. I adjusted figures to constant 2012 dollars using the Bureau of Labor Statistics' CPI Inflation Calculator, www.bls.gov/data/inflation_calculator.htm.

13. S. Anderson (2001); Brodkin (1997, 2011); Brodkin and Majmundar (2010); Hays (2003); Sanfort, Kalil, and Gottschalk (1999); Watkins-Hayes (2009).

14. Both the woman at the desk and the clients sitting on the bench were African American. The majority of caseworkers in Chicago welfare offices are African American. Thus African American client complaints about their caseworkers were typically not about caseworkers of a different race. My respondents for the most part did not attribute mistreatment at the welfare office to racism. One Latina respondent, however, did feel she was treated better by Latina than African American caseworkers. Because of this, she said that she had pretended not to speak English proficiently so that she would be given a Latina Spanish-speaking caseworker rather than an African American one.

15. When I asked the manager in the welfare office whose interview I mentioned above about my observations and the complaints of my respondents, she acknowledged the issue. One of her theories as to why caseworkers sometimes spoke with clients in this manner was that caseworkers actually came from socioeconomic backgrounds similar to those of their clients but had been able to successfully get a foothold in the labor market. She described their attitude as one of "If I could do it, why can't you?" One might assume that caseworker-client conflict might arise out of a difference in backgrounds, but the manager's theory suggests just the opposite. I do not know of a source that has studied the socioeconomic backgrounds of caseworkers in Chicago and so do not know if the manager is correct, but when I ran her theory by one caseworker and three job-training counselors that I met in the course of the research, they all agreed.

16. The women's reported experiences illustrate Lipsky's (1980) concept of "street-level bureaucracy," by which he means frontline workers' implementation of an organization's rules, which constitutes what the rules really are in practice. Brodkin (1997) provides evidence that her observations of caseworkers in Chicago welfare offices support Lipsky's framework. Similarly, Watkins-Hayes (2009) describes the discretion caseworkers in Boston have in implementing rules.

17. Minimum wage during the pre-reform interviews was $4.25, which is equivalent to $6.57 (if the interview was in 1994) or $6.39 (if the interview was in 1995) in 2012 dollars.

18. See Lipsky (1980) on the ways in which policy made on the "street level" is the true policy in practice.

19. This report is in conflict with discussions I have had with poverty advocates who argue that centers like accepting subsidized cases because the government's payments are more reliable than those of individual parents.

20. Brodkin (1986, 1997); Lipsky (1980).

21. Clampet-Lundquist et al. (2004) demonstrate the difficulty that recipients of TANF have in working with the welfare bureaucracy to get the work supports

that would ease transitions off the rolls. Gennetian et al. (2002) and Huston (2004) show that child care subsidy benefits may be particularly difficult to access. Lindhorst and Padgett (2005) find that battered clients often do not receive services stipulated by the Family Violence Option. Lens and Vorsanger (2005) show that administrative hearings before termination of benefits are often successful, demonstrating the illegitimacy of some terminations, but are rarely requested, perhaps in part because clients do not trust they will be treated fairly at them. In her observational work in welfare offices both before and after reform, Evelyn Brodkin (1997, 2011) has found that clients are routinely denied benefits to which they are entitled.

22.   Another reason women may discount carrots and not sticks is that the incentive value of the sticks tends to be larger than that of the carrots. While Work Pays is indeed a greater work incentive than the 100 percent tax rate on earnings in place prior to 1993, the program does not provide large financial benefits. Before reform, if a woman worked forty hours a week for five dollars per hour (a typical wage at the time), her monthly welfare grant (based on an average of 4.3 weeks per month) would be lowered by $287. The monthly grant at the time for a mother with two children was $377. A mother of two working forty hours a week at five dollars per hour would retain a monthly grant of $90. A mother with one child would lose her cash assistance benefits entirely. Thus the actual value of the Work Pays incentive is small, and for some women even nonexistent. In comparison, the cost imposed by time limits on cash assistance, one of the main sticks implemented by reform, is large. If a woman after reform were to hit her time limit, getting cash assistance would no longer be an option, and this would greatly increase the value of employment as probably the only means of bringing cash into the household. The difference between coercive measures and voluntary incentives in their scale, and thus their power to motivate, is one reason why declaring voluntary incentives ineffective is premature.

23.   While this is not a study of caseworkers, one might imagine that caseworkers use a stern demeanor to preemptively protect themselves from the demands of difficult clients. Perhaps rude insensitivity is a caseworker's protective device, similar to clients' distrust in caseworkers.

24.   See Duncan, Huston, and Weisner (2006) for a description and evaluation of New Hope.

3.   "I COULDN'T PUT UP WITH IT NO MORE"

1.   I do not know the exact year Juanita held the jobs she described, but $8 in 1994 is equivalent to $12.37 in 2012 dollars, and the minimum wage of $4.25 is equivalent to $6.57.

2.　At the time of our interview, Juanita lived with her twelve-year-old son and eight-year-old daughter. Her oldest child, a son, whom she had had when she was fifteen, was raised primarily by her parents. At the time of the interview, he was a twenty-one-year-old college student, living with Juanita's sister.

3.　The $6.25 amount in 1994 dollars is equivalent to $9.66 in 2012 dollars.

4.　Appelbaum, Bernhardt, and Murname (2003); Blank, Danziger, and Schoeni (2006); Holzer et al. (2011).

5.　E. Anderson (1999); Bourgois (1995); Bourgois and Schonberg (2009). See also Tyler (2001).

6.　E. Anderson (1999).

7.　It is important to note, however, that one had to have extremely low income to be eligible, as most states' eligibility levels were significantly below the poverty line. Also, many eligible recipients chose not to take welfare benefits even before reform, when getting benefits was less burdensome than it is now.

8.　Edin and Lein (1997); Ellwood (1988).

9.　Edin and Lein (1997).

10.　Ellwood (1988).

11.　There is some question about how strict states are in enforcing time limits. Until recently, for instance, Michigan did not have a time limit. Once cases hit the federal five-year limit, Michigan continued to support them through state funds. After the 2008 recession began, Michigan discontinued this practice. PRWORA does allow states to exempt 20 percent of cases from the time limit. Many states do grant exemptions, often on medical grounds. One way Illinois extends time limits preemptively is that it moves anyone working a set number of hours per week (this number has increased over time from thirty at the time of my post-reform interviews to thirty-five shortly thereafter) to state funds, allowing people to "stop their clocks" when they are working near full time. This policy is designed more as a work incentive than as a way to manage cases that hit the time limit. Regardless of any exemptions that individual states may grant, they are probably an exception rather than the rule. In addition, it is clear that recipients are told and believe that the time limits are real. Grogger (2002) shows that time limits induce a behavioral effect on recipients, who limit their welfare use in response. Moffitt (1999), Ribar, Edelhoch, and Liu (2008), and Ziliak et al. (2000) show similar findings. Part of the reason why may be that welfare office staff do not communicate the possibility of extensions to their clients. A report to the Administration for Children and Families of the U.S. Department of Health and Human Services states, "In trying to send a clear message, welfare staff present simplified versions of time-limit rules, typically ignoring such complexities as periodic time limits and deemphasizing the possibility that extensions may be granted" (Bloom, Ferrell, and Fink 2000).

12. These figures add to a number greater than 100 because women reported on multiple jobs and hence could give more than one reason for having left or lost jobs in the past. As discussed in the Introduction, it is important to remember that these figures describe my samples and not necessarily the population at large.

13. As in the case of pre-reform workplace conflict, post-reform women reported on multiple jobs and hence could give more than one reason for having left or lost jobs in the past.

14. See Bourgois (1995) and Newman (1999) for an in-depth treatment of the experience of low-wage work.

15. This does not mean, however, that successful low-wage workers lack a set of soft skills that support their success.

16. See Appelbaum, Bernhardt, and Murnane (2003) for elaboration of these points. Also see Blank, Danziger, and Schoeni (2006) and Holzer et al. (2011).

17. Hays (2003); Wacquant (2002).

18. Kirschenman and Neckerman (1991) show that employers are remarkably open about their beliefs about the relative performance of workers of different races and ethnicities.

19. Bane and Ellwood (1994), Edin and Lein (1997), Spalter-Roth, Hartmann, and Andrews (1992), and others clearly show that many women in the pre-reform period combined welfare and low-wage work simultaneously or routinely cycled between welfare and work. Thus it is misguided to characterize people either as welfare recipients or as low-wage workers, since many are both. The same has been true since reform, though presumably women are more likely to leave the rolls when they are employed in order to save time on their TANF clocks.

20. I do not know the exact year of the job Susan described, but $11.10 in 2005 dollars is equivalent to $13.02 in 2012 dollars.

21. Tasha was describing a job she held in 1994. When converted from 1994 to 2012 dollars, $8 is equivalent to $12.37, while $9 is equivalent to $13.91 and $7 is equivalent to $10.82.

22. McLaughlin, Uggen, and Blackstone (2012).

23. See Levine (2009) for further evidence of men's resistance to women's entrance in traditionally male jobs.

24. I do not know the exact year of the job Beverly described, but I interviewed her in 2005. The amount of $11 in 2005 dollars is equivalent to $12.90 in 2012 dollars.

25. Lambert and Henly (2012); Lambert, Haley-Lock, and Henly (2012).

26. Molm, Takahashi, and Peterson (2000).

27. Bourgois (1995).

28. Glaeser et al. (2000) also find that trust is lower when interaction partners are of different races. Low-wage workers who are members of ethnic and racial minority groups may be particularly likely to interact with supervisors of a different race or ethnic group.

29. As I discuss at other points in the book, what Elijah Anderson has described as the "code of the street" (1999) is also about the importance of garnering respect.

30. Tyler (2001) provides a theoretical frame to understand this phenomenon. He argues that how one is treated within an organization is a signal of one's status within that organization. Disrespectful treatment is an indication that one is not valued by the organization and gives a person an identity of not being important to the group. This may result in the conclusion that it is not fruitful to cooperate with the authorities in the organization. Respectful treatment indicates the opposite. As Tyler explains (2001, 290), "One key aspect of high-quality treatment is that it leads to the inference that the motives of social authorities are benevolent, caring, and, hence, worthy of trust. . . . [P]eople evaluate their position within groups by considering their treatment by authorities. . . . Identity issues influence group viability because people respond to the group through a social identity that is shaped by this information. Those who feel respected and valued by the group respond by following group rules and acting on behalf of the group, that is, by deferring to authorities." Tyler's concept of disrespectful treatment as not only producing distrust but producing an identity that is unaligned with the group helps explain why many women found that disrespectful treatment required an immediate severing of ties with the group.

31. I do not mean to suggest that the women are always making choices that further their goals when they leave a job, that employers are always wrong to terminate them, or that employers are to blame for all workplace turnover. My point is simply that turnover is not just related to factors outside the workplace but often closely tied to what occurs inside the workplace as well.

32. See, for example, Mowday, Porter, and Steers (1982). For more specific relevance to the issue of trust, see Robinson (1996).

33. See Lambert and Henly (2012) and Lambert and Henly (forthcoming) for exceptions.

34. See Handler and Hasenfeld (1997).

35. Lambert and Henly (forthcoming).

36. See Appelbaum, Bernhardt, and Murnane (2003) and Holzer et al. (2011) for evidence of these structural aspects of the low-wage labor market.

37. Robinson (1996). See also Young and Daniel (2003).

38. Lambert and Henly (2012).

4. "I DON'T TRUST PEOPLE TO WATCH MY KIDS"

1. Ellwood (1988).

2. Funding came through the Child Care and Development Block Grant program, part of PRWORA.

3. Crosby, Gennetian, and Huston (2005). Federal funding increased dramatically in the years just after PRWORA's passage but had been frozen since 2002 through the time of my post-reform interviews. For the first time since PRWORA's passage, states actually experienced a decline in child care funding from all sources overall in 2004 (Matthews and Ewen 2005).

4. Adams and Rohacek (2002).

5. Many middle-class families in Chicago were paying more than that *per hour* for care at that time.

6. Starting in July 2011, the payment to an unlicensed provider became $13.80 ($14.06 in 2012 dollars) for a full day of care, and licensed centers were reimbursed $31.77 ($32.36 in 2012 dollars) for a full day of care to a child age three or older. See Illinois Department of Human Services (2011b).

7. See Illinois Department of Human Services (2011a).

8. See Hansen (2005) for a discussion of how important the availability of network members who can help with child care is for sustaining employment not only among low-income single-mothers but also across the class structure. Harknett (2006) shows the relationship between employment and access to network support in quantitative data.

9. In 2005, when I interviewed Dawn, $9.49 was equivalent to $11.13 in 2012 dollars.

10. Some home day cares are licensed and some are not.

11. This difference in interpretation across time that is revealed by open-ended qualitative interviewing has implications for how we design and interpret surveys. For instance, survey questions eliciting child care experience need to be worded to distinguish between problems finding any kind of care and problems finding care mothers trust. Respondents answering questions that more generically refer to "problems" or "difficulties" with child care, or that ask whether child care is a barrier to work, might be interpreted (and thus answered) differently by women before and after reform.

12. See Herdt (2009) for discussion of the term *moral panic*.

13. Clearly abuse of children does occur, and bringing its existence to light has been enormously important for protecting children. But the fact remains that there is no solid evidence that abuse occurred in the McMartin case and others like it. See Talbot (2001).

14. Wrigley and Dreby (2005).

15.   See Fukuyama (1999), Brickman, Becker, and Castle (1979), and Hardin (2001, 2002) for each of these points in turn. I use the phrase "share interests" as shorthand for Hardin's argument, but my term does not quite match Hardin's concept. Hardin argues that we trust those who "encapsulate" our interests, meaning those whose own interests are furthered when they pursue our interests along the way, even if their ultimate interests are not the same as ours. Trust has also been shown to be higher between members of the same ethnic group (Nee and Sanders 2001). Relatives are more likely to share an ethnicity than nonrelatives.

16.   The ability to know others' motivations leads to higher trust (Brickman, Becker, and Castle 1979), although if these motivations prove at odds with one's own, trust decreases (Goldsmith 2005).

17.   For example, see Ehrle, Adams, and Tout (2001). Other small qualitative studies have also found this preference. See Chaudry (2004).

18.   Edin and Lein (1997); Henly (2002); Henly and Lyons (2000).

19.   Camasso and Roche (1991); Edin and Lein (1997); Oliker (1995a, 1995b).

20.   Clampet-Lundquist et al. (2004); Gennetian et al. (2002); Huston (2004).

21.   Bromer and Henly (2009); Henly (2002); Sandra Danziger, Ananat, and Browning (2004).

22.   Henly and Lambert (2005); Scott, London, and Hurst (2005).

23.   Chaudry (2004); Henly and Lambert (2005); Henly, Shaefer, and Waxman (2006); Scott, London, and Hurst (2005).

24.   Folk and Yi (1994); Henly and Lambert (2005); Scott et al. (2004).

25.   Henly (2002); Uttal (1999).

26.   Bromer and Henly (2009); Coley, Chase-Lansdale, and Li-Grining (2001); London et al. (2004); Wrigley and Dreby (2005).

27.   Lowe and Weisner (2004).

28.   Crosby, Gennetian, and Huston (2005); Adams and Rohacek (2002).

29.   Adams and Rohacek (2002).

30.   National Child Care Information Center (2005).

31.   Fuller et al. (2002).

5.   "YOU CAN'T PUT YOUR TRUST IN MEN"

1.   McLanahan (2011). McLanahan shows that the figure of 51 percent of children cohabiting with their fathers one year after birth drops to 36 percent by the time the child turns five.

2.   The women Edin and Kefalas (2005) interviewed discussed men's unreliability as economic contributors to households, desire to control women's actions, potential use of drugs or involvement in illegal activity, violence,

mistreatment of children, and infidelity as sources of their distrust. As will be shown, the women I interviewed also voiced these concerns and also pointed to them as reasons for their distrust in men.

3. See Burton et al. (2009) and Estacion and Cherlin (2010) on low-income women's distrust in men. Elijah Anderson (1999) provides a key perspective on low-income men's lives by showing how the "code of the street" encourages men to identify with peer group members rather than romantic partners and domestic life. See also Waller (2002, 2010) for fathers' perspectives on their involvement with their children and children's mothers.

4. See Appelbaum, Bernhardt, and Murnane (2003) on low-skilled men's wages; Western (2006) and Wacquant (2009) on incarceration; and Edin and Kefalas (2005) on the economic drain of unemployed men on women's households.

5. Harding (2010); Roy (1999, 2004); Jarrett, Roy, and Burton (2002); Roy and Cabrera (2009).

6. Ellwood and Jencks (2004a, 2004b); Carlson, McLanahan, and England (2004).

7. See Cherlin (2009) on American cultural attitudes concerning the sanctity of marriage.

8. Much scholarly work debates the economic benefits of marriage and other household formations—and, more pointedly, marriage compared to other household formations. Some argue that marriage brings both partners increased wealth, increased individual income and career success, and increases in other factors, such as health, that may in turn produce economic benefits (Waite and Gallagher 2000). Others argue that these benefits, if attributable causally to marriage at all, are much more likely to be realized by middle- and upper-income partners than by low-income ones (Edin and Kefalas 2005; England 2000; Graefe and Lichter 2008). Edin and Kefalas (2005) show, as do I, that some marriages and romantic relationships even produce economic hardship for low-income women.

9. See in particular Edin and Kefalas (2005).

10. Prior to reform, there was a small program entitled Aid to Families with Dependent Children—Unemployed Parent (AFDC-UP) that served low-income married unemployed parents, but the main cash assistance program, AFDC, was limited to single parents.

11. See Hawkins and Ooms (2010) and Randles (2009) for additional background on Healthy Marriage programs.

12. Hawkins and Fackrell (2010) show mixed results. Some Healthy Marriage programs have no effects, others only small to moderate ones. Klerman (2005) shows that welfare reform policies overall have had no real effect on marriage and childbearing.

13. Haney and March (2003) argue that policy makers and low-income mothers conceive of successful fatherhood in different terms. Thus policy makers' and mothers' goals for paternal involvement differ.

14. See Waller (2002).

15. Waite et al. (2000); Waite and Gallagher (2000).

16. Edin and Kefalas (2005); Graefe and Lichter (2008).

17. Edin and Kefalas (2005).

18. Sinkewicz and Garfinkel (2009).

19. See Burton, Purvin, and Garrett-Peters (2009) on the experience of domestic violence in low-income couples and Brush (2011) on how domestic violence is treated in PRWORA.

20. Waller (2002) shows that both low-income mothers and fathers believe in noncustodial fathers' responsibility to contribute to their children's financial support but that they critique the formal child support system for creating tension and hostility between parents that results in lower levels of child well-being.

21. Waller (2002) shows a preference among low-income parents for informal child support arrangements.

22. Waller (2002) also shows that low-income parents feel the formal child support system creates undue hardship for men.

23. Klerman (2005). See also the broader discussion of evaluating welfare reform in Grogger and Karoly (2005). Hawkins and Fackrell (2010) specifically evaluate Healthy Marriage programs, whereas Klerman evaluates multiple studies of the effects of PRWORA policies themselves on marriage and childbearing.

24. It is important to remember that I interviewed small nonrandom samples of women who do not necessarily represent a larger population. Table 1 is meant to describe my sample, not the populations of low-income women at each time period. The value of studies like this one is that the in-depth qualitative methods provide insight into why the low rates of marriage and high rates of nonmarital fertility documented by representative studies occur.

25. I do not know exactly when this conversation occurred, but $150 in 2004, when I conducted the interview, was equivalent to $181.92 in 2012 dollars.

26. That sum of $20,000 in 2005 dollars is equivalent to $23,462 in 2012 dollars.

27. Elijah Anderson (1999) and Edin and Kefalas (2005) also note the high incidence of infidelity in low-income couples, particularly on the part of men. Hill (2007) finds that over half of low-income couples experience infidelity, almost always on the part of the male partner. England and Shafer (2007) find that low-income women do complain about the lack of intimacy or emotional

support in their relationships. While my respondents are not happy with the low level of emotional support they receive, they are more resigned to it.

28. Lindhorst and Padgett (2005) show that the Family Violence Option, which grants women in domestic violence situations exemptions from work requirements, is often not implemented.

29. Estacion and Cherlin (2010) also note that the women they interviewed were quick to trust men who proved untrustworthy.

30. Edin and Kefalas (2005). See also Burton et al. (2009).

31. Estacion and Cherlin (2010).

32. Reed (2007).

33. Roy (1999, 2004). See also Jarrett, Roy, and Burton (2002) and Roy and Cabrera (2009).

34. Harding (2010).

35. Liebow (1967) shows how structural barriers that men face in the labor market lead to mistreatment of romantic partners and exit from domestic life. See also E. Anderson (1999); Bourgois (1995); Edin and Kefalas (2005); and Wilson (1987, 2009).

36. Edin and Kefalas (2005) illustrate this point in detail. Elijah Anderson (1990, 1999) shows the role of the drug trade in young low-income men's lives.

37. Western (2006).

38. E. Anderson (1999); Harding (2010).

39. Edin and Lein (1997) document the impossibility of providing for children's needs when one is living on welfare grants alone.

40. Edin and Kefalas (2005).

41. Gerson (2010).

6. "I TRUST MY MOTHER AND
NO ONE ELSE"

1. S. Smith (2007).

2. Oliker (1995a, 1995b, 2000); Edin and Lein (1997).

3. These comparisons across women interviewed in the two time periods are based on my analysis of the qualitative data, not on any kind of survey instrument or other quantitative assessment. Using NVivo, a qualitative data analysis software package, I coded the interviews for women's discussions of the kinds of contributions to and drains on their resources that their networks provided or posed. Once these were coded, I could compare the proportions of women who described their networks in various ways across time periods. This exercise allowed me to see and report differences across the samples interviewed at the

two different times, though we do not know to what degree these patterns exist in more representative data.

4. While I tried hard to cover a consistent set of topics in each interview, sometimes conversation strayed from a topic, as is typical for qualitative interviews. As a result, there are a small handful of cases with missing data on each of the network interactions shown in table 2. In the table I show the percentage and number as well as the total number of cases that had data on each type of interaction.

5. In DeParle's (2004) study of a close-knit network of three women as they lived through the implementation of welfare reform, it is clear that the women he studied were grappling not only with how reform directly affected them but also with the effects of reform on the other two women in their network.

6. Frogner, Moffitt, and Ribar (2009).

7. See Menjívar (2000) for further discussion of reciprocity.

8. Nicole would take in her mother rather than her brother except for the fact that the house was her mother's only asset and she did not want her to lose it.

9. See E. Anderson (1999) and Edin and Kefalas (2005), who have previously made this argument.

10. The sum of $10 in 2004 dollars is equivalent to $12.13 in 2012 dollars.

11. The sum of $200 in 2005 dollars is equivalent to $234.62 in 2012 dollars.

12. Her sister had one child who was one year old. The sum of $9 in 2005 dollars is equivalent to $10.56 in 2012 dollars.

13. As Hardin (2006) argues, trusting a person to do X does not necessarily mean trusting her to do Y. See also Hardin's edited volume *Distrust* (2004), in which he makes the correlative statement on distrust that "A distrusts B with respect to X" (1). In other words, distrust is based not just on one person's perception of another but on that person's perception of the other's trustworthiness (or lack thereof) in terms of a particular task.

14. See Portes (1998), who warns that not all social network ties produce positive social capital and urges scholars to attend to negative social capital as well.

15. More specifically, on the basis of the same kind of coding of the interview material that I conducted to produce table 2, I find that those women who received child care help, socio-emotional support, job information, or other kinds of help through networks expressed more trust in their networks. Women who received monetary or nonmonetary resources through their networks were more likely to express trust in their networks prior to reform, though oddly, this relationship was less clear after reform. Alternately, those who described their network members as draining them of resources expressed more distrust in their networks. In addition, those who had experienced some

form of childhood trauma, such as physical, sexual, or psychological abuse or the death of a parent or close relative, were still likely to place some or a lot of trust in others, though they were less likely to do so than women who had experienced no such early trauma.

16.   Coleman (1988, 1990); Portes (1998); Lin (2001); Bourdieu (1983); Putnam (2000). I base this definition primarily on that of Bourdieu (1983/1986), Lin (2001), and Portes (1998). Coleman (1988) and Putnam (2000) tend to include the outcomes that social capital might bring into the definition of social capital itself. Portes (1998) critiques this approach as tautological. Lin (2001) makes a similar critique. I have discussed here social capital as an attribute of an individual's relationships. Scholars also discuss social capital as an attribute of communities. See Putnam (2000). Robert J. Sampson uses the term *collective efficacy*, which is similar to the concept of community-level social capital but adds more dimensions. See Sampson, Morenoff, and Earls (1999); Sampson (2012). See Small (2009) for a unique argument about a different level of social capital. He argues that when people are members of an organization, they are able to access a form of social capital that is created through the organization's relationships with other organizations.

17.   S. Smith (2007). Note that Smith's focus is on low-income African American communities rather than all low-income communities.

18.   Roschelle (1997); Stack (1974). See also Sarkisian and Gerstel (2004) and Sarkisian, Gerena, and Gerstel (2006, 2007) for their investigation of race differences in network support.

19.   Sandra Smith (2007) offers a key insight into why network members in the low-income African American community may sometimes withhold one kind of resource: job leads. She argues that those who are employed do not trust their network members to perform well on the job and cannot afford to risk their reputations with their employers for network members who may not prove to be good workers.

20.   Briggs (1998); Domínguez and Watkins (2003); Henly, Danziger, and Offer (2005); Putnam (2000); Stack (1974).

21.   Briggs (1998), Domínguez and Watkins (2003), Henly, Danziger, and Offer (2005), and others refer instead to "social support" and "social leverage" to capture the concepts otherwise described as "bonding" and "bridging" social capital. Burt (2000) similarly describes two different kinds of social capital. The first is social capital that comes through "network closure" or tight-knit but self-contained networks that do not provide opportunities to bridge to other networks. The second is social capital that comes through "structural holes" in networks that allow for opportunities through the establishment of connections between disconnected segments in a network structure.

22.   Frogner, Moffitt, and Ribar (2009).

23.   Granovetter (1974) shows that jobs found through network ties are more highly rewarding than jobs found through other means. His work is based on middle-class white professional men. We do not know if the same is true of low-income mothers with welfare histories. If it is, however, having a network that can connect you to a job may be helpful not just for becoming employed but also for getting better jobs than those without such networks could obtain.

24.   Stack (1974); Menjívar (2000).

25.   Jason DeParle's (2004) treatment of how welfare reform affected three related women facing the demands of welfare reform provides support for this point.

26.   See Sampson (2000).

27.   It is theoretically possible that one woman could be employed by the other as a child care provider, could be paid through a child care subsidy, and could have her work providing child care count toward her TANF work requirement. However, in reality, this arrangement is unlikely to meet approval by caseworkers because the child care subsidy is so low ($9.49 per day at the time of the second round of interviews) that it probably would not meet minimum-wage requirements for work activities.

CONCLUSION

1.   DeParle (2004).

2.   See Hays (2003) for a discussion of how this culture is reflected in PRWORA and its implementation.

3.   Fukuyama (1999).

4.   Coleman (1988); Anthony (2005).

5.   Coleman (1988); Sampson (2000); Stack (1974); Putnam (2000).

6.   Kollock (1994).

7.   Edin (2000b); Edin and Kefalas (2005); Levi (1998); S. Smith (2007).

8.   Kramer (2004).

9.   See E. Anderson (1990, 1999), Bourgois (1995), and Tyler (2001), who all address the importance of respectful treatment in different contexts.

10.   Hardin (2002, 96).

11.   S. Smith (2007).

12.   See Harding (2010); Small, Harding, and Lamont (2010); Wilson (2009).

13.   E. Anderson (1999, 325).

14.   Molm, Takahashi, and Peterson (2000) find that trust is higher when interaction partners have equal power.

15.   Of course, this is less true when unemployment is low, as it was right after the implementation of reform. But the recession in the early 2000s and the

Great Recession in the late 2000s have made it much more true. It is also worth mentioning that while employers do not believe their workers are skilled, success in low-wage jobs may require a fair amount of "soft" skills.

16. See Edin and Kefalas (2005) and Reed (2007). Additionally, Elijah Anderson (1999) discusses the nature of low-income (and, in his study, African American) young men's need for women in similar terms to those I have used to describe caseworkers' need for clients and employers' need for workers. He suggests that while a young man needs sex with women to maintain his status on the street, he does not need the affections of a particular woman. If a woman demands too much or if the man tires of her, he can replace her with a new woman. Anderson also characterizes relationships between men and women as contests in which men try to "get over" women's sexual defenses and resist women's desires for shared domesticity.

17. Jarrett, Roy, and Burton (2002).

18. Sandra Smith (2007) makes this point in terms of sharing the resource of job leads.

19. Hardin (2002); Farrell (2004). These authors also observe that if one partner is all-powerful, then a point may be reached in which cooperation is achieved through pure domination rather than trust on the part of the less powerful actor. A totalitarian state or violent partner may achieve goals through pure force rather than winning trust, for instance.

20. Cook (2005).

21. Cook (2005, 12).

22. Contributors to *Cooperation without Trust?*, a 2005 volume edited by Karen Cook, Russell Hardin, and Margaret Levi, show a variety of situations in which such structures substitute for trust. Cook (2005, 9) explains further: "We know, however, that in highly uncertain and risky environments, transactions occur among actors that are secured either by trust relations or by some form of reliable institutional backing—where, for example, legal enforcement is swift and sure."

23. Heimer (2001).

24. Heimer (2001, 78).

25. Bourgois (1995); Kramer (2004); Tyler (2001).

26. Stack (1974); Putnam (2000).

27. See Portes (1998) for a discussion of negative effects of social capital.

28. Sandra Smith (2007) argues that it is not the absence of social capital but the absence of trust needed to activate it that explains unemployment in low-income African American urban communities.

29. Hardin (2002) discusses the importance of the distinction between trust and trustworthiness. I borrow the title of this section, "Trust and Trustworthiness," from the title of his 2002 book.

APPENDIX

1. See the overview of this literature by Bane and Ellwood (1994).

2. Granovetter (1985).

3. See Oliker (1995a) for a treatment of how the context of social networks had an impact on pre-reform women's welfare and work patterns.

4. One of the post-reform respondents had moved from Chicago to a suburb north of Chicago by the time I met her, although much of the interview covered her years in Chicago. All of the other women lived in Chicago.

5. See Lloyd (1997).

6. As Bane and Ellwood (1994) explain, if you sample people from the welfare rolls at any given point in time, you are more likely to find people in the middle of long spells (or periods) of welfare receipt than if you sample people at the beginning or end of their spells. This is simply because the longer the spell is, the greater the probability that the person will be on welfare at any given point in time. Bane and Ellwood use the analogy of beds in a hospital. Most people's hospital stays are very short, often one night. But every now and then a very severe injury or ailment keeps people in the hospital for a long time. If you go to a wing of a hospital with ten beds in it on any given day, you could find nine beds are taken with people who have been there a year and only one bed has a person in it who has been there a day. You might then conclude that 90 percent of people have hospital stays of at least a year. But what you would be missing is that one bed has housed 365 different people with one day stays over the course of that same year that the other nine beds were used by only nine people. I get more variation in my sample than if I took a cross section of current welfare cases because I interviewed people just starting welfare spells, people in the middle of spells, and people who had already finished spells.

7. I was also able to observe the workplace of one of the post-reform respondents.

8. See Small (2009) for a thoughtful discussion of the appropriate goals and methods of qualitative research.

9. D. Lewis et al. (2004).

10. It is difficult to find an appropriate data source for comparison with my samples. The IFS is far from perfect, but it is the best comparison available. The IFS data were collected after reform, so that we might expect my post-reform sample to be closer to the IFS respondents. IFS included all of Cook County rather than just Chicago and thus was likely to capture more TANF recipients who lived in neighborhoods that were not marked by concentrated poverty. IFS includes only TANF recipients, whereas my samples include both current and former recipients. IFS itself may not represent national data. Cook County probably stands in for many large cities in America, but not for rural areas and small towns.

11. In addition, two of the post-reform interviews were conducted in my university office.

12. See Bazeley (2007) for an introduction to NVivo software. The data were coded using version 2.0 of NVivo.

13. See Norušis (2010) for an introduction to SPSS software.

14. Waller (2002).

Bibliography

Acs, Gregory, and Pamela Loprest. 2001. "Final Synthesis Report of the Findings
from ASPE's 'Leavers Grants.'" Urban Institute Report to the U.S.
Department of Health and Human Services, Washington, DC. www.urban.
org/UploadedPDF/410809_welfare_leavers_synthesis.pdf.

Adams, Gina, and Monica Rohacek. 2002. "More Than a Work Support? Issues
around Integrating Child Development Goals into the Child Care Subsidy
System." *Early Childhood Research Quarterly* 17 (4): 418–40.

Alesina, Alberti, and Eliana La Ferrara. 2002. "Who Trusts Others?" *Journal of
Public Economics* 85:207–34.

Anderson, Elijah. 1990. *Streetwise: Race, Class, and Change in an Urban
Community.* Chicago: University of Chicago Press.

———. 1999. *Code of the Street: Decency, Violence, and the Moral Life of the Inner
City.* New York: W.W. Norton.

Anderson, Steven G. 2001. "Welfare Recipient Views about Caseworker
Performance: Lessons for Developing TANF Case Management
Practices." *Family in Society: The Journal of Contemporary Human Services* 82
(2): 165–75.

———. 2002. "Ensuring the Stability of Welfare-to-Work Exits: The Importance of Recipient Knowledge about Work Incentives." *Social Work* 47 (2): 162–70.

Anthony, Denise. 2005. "Cooperation in Microfinance Borrowing Groups: Identity, Sanctions, and Reciprocity in the Production of Collective Goods." *American Sociological Review* 70 (3): 496–515.

Appelbaum, Eileen, Annette Bernhardt, and Richard J. Murnane, eds. 2003. *Low-Wage America: How Employers Are Reshaping Opportunity in the Workplace.* New York: Russell Sage Foundation.

Asch, Solomon E. 1951. "Effects of Group Pressure upon the Modification and Distortion of Judgment." In *Groups, Leadership, and Men,* edited by H. Guetzknow, 177–90. Pittsburgh, PA: Carnegie Press.

Bane, Mary Jo. 2012. "Who Will Speak for the Poor? The Silence at the Center of Our Politics." *Commonweal,* September 23, 10–11.

Bane, Mary Jo, and David T. Ellwood. 1994. *Welfare Realities: From Rhetoric to Reform.* Cambridge, MA: Harvard University Press.

Bazeley, Patricia. 2007. *Qualitative Data Analysis with NVivo.* Thousand Oaks, CA: Sage.

Bell, Stephen H. 2001. "Why Are Welfare Caseloads Falling?" Working Paper DP 01–02, Urban Institute, Washington, DC.

Bitler, Marianne P., Jonah B. Gelbach, and Hilary Hoynes. 2001. "The Impact of Welfare Reform on Living Arrangements." Seminar paper, Harvard Kennedy School, Inequality and Social Policy Multidisciplinary Program. www.hks.harvard.edu/inequality/Seminar/Papers/Hoynes.pdf.

———. 2006. "What Mean Impacts Miss: Distributional Effects of Welfare Reform Experiments." *American Economic Review* 96 (4): 988–1012.

Blank, Rebecca M. 2001. "What Causes Public Assistance Caseloads to Grow?" Working Paper 6343, National Bureau of Economic Research, Cambridge, MA.

———. 2002. "Evaluating Welfare Reform in the United States." *Journal of Economic Literature* 40 (4): 1105–66.

Blank, Rebecca M., Sheldon H. Danziger, and Robert F. Schoeni, eds. 2006. *Working and Poor: How Economic and Policy Changes Are Affecting Low-Wage Workers.* New York: Russell Sage Foundation.

Bloom, Daniel, Mary Farrell, and Barbara Fink, with Diana Adams-Ciardullo. 2002. "The Implementation of Time Limits." Ch. 4 of *Welfare Time Limits: State Policies, Implementation, and Effects on Families.* July 2002. Administration for Children and Families Archives. http://archive.acf.hhs.gov/programs/opre/welfare_employ/approach_tlimits/reports/welfare_timelimits/welfare_tl_chp4.html.

Bobo, Lawrence. 1991. "Social Responsibility, Individualism, and Redistributive Policies." *Sociological Forum* 6:71–92.

Bos, Johannes, Aletha Huston, Robert Granger, Greg Duncan, Tom Brock, and Vonnie McLoyd. 1999. "New Hope for People with Low Incomes: Two-Year Results of a Program to Reduce Poverty and Reform Welfare." Report to Manpower Demonstration Research Corporation. April. www.mdrc.org/publications/60/execsum.html.

Bourdieu, Pierre. 1977. *Outline of a Theory of Practice.* Cambridge: Cambridge University Press.

———. 1983/1986. "The Forms of Capital." In *Handbook of Theory and Research for the Sociology of Education,* edited by John G. Richardson, 241–58. Westport, CT: Greenwood Press.

Bourgois, Philippe. 1995. *In Search of Respect: Selling Crack in El Barrio.* New York: Cambridge University Press.

Bourgois, Philippe, and Jeffrey Schonberg. 2009. *Righteous Dopefiend.* Berkeley: University of California Press.

Braithwaite, Valerie, and Margaret Levi, eds. 1998. *Trust and Governance.* New York: Russell Sage Foundation.

Brickman, Philip, Lawrence J. Becker, and Sidney Castle. 1979. "Making Trust Easier and Harder through Two Forms of Sequential Interaction." *Journal of Personality and Social Psychology* 37 (4): 515–21.

Briggs, Xavier de Souza. 1998. "Brown Kids in White Suburbs: Housing Mobility and the Many Faces of Social Capital." *Housing Policy Debate* 9 (1): 177–221.

Brodkin, Evelyn Z. 1986. *The False Promise of Administrative Reform: Implementing Quality Control in Welfare.* Philadelphia: Temple University Press.

———. 1997. "Inside the Welfare Contract: Discretion and Accountability in State Welfare Administration." *Social Service Review* 71 (1): 1–33.

———. 2011. "Policy Work: Street-Level Organizations under New Managerialism." *Journal of Public Administration Research and Theory* 21:253–77.

Brodkin, Evelyn Z., and Malay Majmundar. 2010. "Administrative Exclusion: Organizations and the Hidden Costs of Welfare Claiming." *Journal of Public Administration Research and Theory* 20 (4): 827–48.

Bromer, Juliet, and Julia R. Henly. 2009. "The Work-Family Support Roles of Child Care Providers across Settings." *Early Childhood Research Quarterly* 24 (3): 271–88.

Brush, Lisa Diane. 2011. *Poverty, Battered Women, and Work in U.S. Public Policy.* New York: Oxford University Press.

Burt, Ronald S. 2000. "The Network Structure of Social Capital." *Research in Organizational Behavior* 22:345–423.

Burton, Linda, Andrew J. Cherlin, Judith Francis, Robin Jarrett, James Quane, Constance Williams, and N. Michelle Stem Cook. 1998. *What Welfare Recipients and the Fathers of Their Children Are Saying about Welfare Reform.* Report from the project "Welfare, Children, and Families: A Three-City

Study." June. Baltimore: Johns Hopkins University. http://web.jhu.edu/
threecitystudy/images/publications/01_june1998.pdf.
Burton, Linda M., Andrew J. Cherlin, Donna-Marie Winn, Angela Estacion, and
Clara Holder-Taylor. 2009. "The Role of Trust in Low-Income Mothers'
Intimate Unions." *Journal of Marriage and Family* 71:1107–24.
Burton, Linda M., Diane Purvin, and Raymond Garrett-Peters. 2009.
"Longitudinal Ethnography: Uncovering Domestic Abuse in Low-Income
Women's Lives." In *The Craft of Life Course Research,* edited by Glen H. Elder
and Janet Z. Giele, 70–92. New York: Guilford Press.
Camasso, Michael J., and Susan E. Roche. 1991. "The Willingness to Change to
Formalized Child Care Arrangements: Parental Considerations of Cost and
Quality." *Journal of Marriage and the Family* 53 (4): 1071–82.
Carlson, Marcia, Sara S. McLanahan, and Paula England. 2004. "Union
Formation in Fragile Families." *Demography* 41:237–61.
Chase-Lansdale, P. Lindsay, Robert A. Moffitt, Brenda J. Lohman, Andrew J.
Cherlin, Rebekah Levine Coley, Laura D. Pittman, Jennifer Roff, and
Elizabeth Votruba-Drzal. 2003. "Mothers' Transitions from Welfare to
Work and the Well-Being of Preschoolers and Adolescents." *Science*
299:1548–52.
Chaudry, Ajay. 2004. *Putting Children First: How Low-Wage Working Mothers
Manage Child Care.* New York: Russell Sage Foundation.
Cherlin, Andrew J. 2009. *The Marriage-Go-Round: The State of Marriage and the
Family in America Today.* New York: Alfred A. Knopf.
Cherlin, Andrew J., Karen Bogen, James M. Quane, and Linda Burton. 2002.
"Operating within the Rules: Welfare Recipients' Experiences with Sanctions
and Case Closings." *Social Service Review* 76 (3): 387–405.
Clampet-Lundquist, Susan, Kathryn Edin, Andrew S. London, Ellen Scott, and
Vicki Hunter. 2004. "'Making a Way Out of No Way': How Mothers Meet
Basic Family Needs while Moving from Welfare to Work." In *Work-Family
Challenges for Low-Income Parents and Their Children,* edited by Ann C. Crouter
and Alan Booth, 203–41. Mahway, NJ: Lawrence Erlbaum Associates.
Coleman, James S. 1988. "Social Capital in the Creation of Human Capital."
American Journal of Sociology 94:S95–S120.
———. 1990. *Foundations of Social Theory.* Cambridge, MA: Harvard University
Press.
Coley, Rebekah Levine, P. Lindsay Chase-Lansdale, and Christine P. Li-Grining.
2001. *Child Care in the Era of Welfare Reform: Quality, Choices, and Preferences.*
Policy Brief 01–4. Report from the project "Welfare, Children, and Families:
A Three-City Study." Baltimore: Johns Hopkins University.
Cook, Karen S. 2001. "Trust in Society." In *Trust in Society,* vol. 2, edited by
Karen S. Cook, xi–xxviii. New York: Russell Sage Foundation.

————. 2005. "Networks, Norms, and Trust: The Social Psychology of Social Capital." *Social Psychology Quarterly* 68:4–14.

Cook, Karen S., Russell Hardin, and Margaret Levi. 2005. *Cooperation without Trust?* New York: Russell Sage Foundation.

Cook, Karen S., and Margaret Levi, eds. 1990. *The Limits of Rationality.* Chicago: University of Chicago Press.

Cook, Karen S., Margaret Levi, and Russell Hardin, eds. 2009. *Whom Can We Trust?: How Groups, Networks, and Institutions Make Trust Possible.* New York: Russell Sage Foundation.

Courtney, Mark E., Amy Dworsky, Irving Piliavin, and Andrew Zinn. 2005. "Involvement of TANF Applicant Families with Child Welfare Services." *Social Service Review* 79 (1): 119–57.

Crosby, Danielle A., Lisa Gennetian, and Aletha C. Huston. 2005. "Child Care Assistance Policies Can Affect the Use of Center-Based Care for Children in Low-Income Families." *Applied Developmental Science* 9 (2): 86–106.

Cyert, Richard M. 1988. *The Economic Theory of Organization and the Firm.* New York: New York University Press.

Danziger, Sandra K., Elizabeth Oltmans Ananat, and Kimberly G. Browning. 2004. "Childcare Subsidies and the Transition from Welfare to Work." *Family Relations* 53 (2): 219–28.

Danziger, Sandra K., Marcia J. Carlson, and Julia R. Henly. 2001. "Post-Welfare Employment and Psychological Well-Being." *Women's Health* 32 (1–2): 47–78.

Danziger, Sandra, Mary Corcoran, Sheldon Danziger, Coleen Heflin, Ariel Kalil, Judith Levine, Daniel Rosen, Kristin Seefeldt, Kristine Siefert, and Richard Tolman. 2000a. "Barriers to the Employment of Welfare Recipients." In *Prosperity for All? The Economic Boom and African Americans,* edited by Robert Cherry and William M. Rodgers, 245–78. New York: Russell Sage.

Danziger, Sandra, Mary E. Corcoran, Sheldon Danziger, and Colleen M. Heflin. 2000b. "Work, Income, and Material Hardship after Welfare Reform." *Journal of Consumer Affairs* 34 (1): 6–30.

Danziger, Sheldon, Colleen M. Heflin, Mary E. Corcoran, Elizabeth Oltmans, and Hui-Chen Wang. 2002. "Does It Pay to Move from Welfare to Work?" *Journal of Policy Analysis and Management* 21 (4): 671–92.

DeLeire, Thomas, Judith A. Levine, and Helen Levy. 2006. "Is Welfare Reform Responsible for Low-Skilled Women's Declining Health Insurance Coverage in the 1990s?" *Journal of Human Resources* 41 (3): 495–528.

DeNavas-Walt, Carmen, Bernadette D. Proctor, and Jessica C. Smith. 2011. *Income, Poverty, and Health Insurance Coverage in the United States: 2010.* U.S. Census Bureau, Current Population Reports P60–239. Washington, DC: Government Printing Office.

DeParle, Jason. 2004. *American Dream: Three Women, Ten Kids, and a Nation's Drive to End Welfare*. New York: Viking.

———. 2012. "Welfare Limits Left Poor Adrift as Recession Hit." *New York Times*, April 7.

Domínguez, Silvia, and Celeste Watkins. 2003. "Creating Networks for Survival and Mobility: Social Capital among African-American and Latin-American Low-Income Mothers." *Social Problems* 50:111–35.

Duncan, Greg J., and Jeanne Brooks-Gunn. 2000. "Family Poverty, Welfare Reform and Child Development." *Child Development* 71 (1): 188–96.

Duncan, Greg J., Aletha C. Huston, and Thomas Weisner. 2006. *Higher Ground: New Hope for the Working Poor and Their Children*. New York: Russell Sage Foundation.

Edelman, Peter, Harry J. Holzer, and Paul Offner. 2006. *Reconnecting Disadvantaged Young Men*. Washington, DC: Urban Institute.

Edin, Kathryn. 2000a. "Few Good Men: Why Poor Mothers Don't Marry or Remarry." *American Prospect* 11 (4): 26–31.

———. 2000b. "What Do Low-Income Single Mothers Say about Marriage?" *Social Problems* 47 (1): 112–33.

Edin, Kathryn, and Maria Kefalas. 2005. *Promises I Can Keep: Why Poor Women Put Motherhood before Marriage*. Berkeley: University of California Press.

Edin, Kathryn, and Laura Lein. 1997. *Making Ends Meet: How Single Mothers Survive Welfare and Low-Wage Work*. New York: Russell Sage Foundation.

Ehrenreich, Barbara. 2001. *Nickel and Dimed: On (Not) Getting By in America*. New York: Henry Holt.

Ehrle, Jennifer Macomber, Gina Adams, and Kathryn Tout. 2001. *Who's Caring for Our Youngest Children? Child Care Patterns of Infants and Toddlers*. Occasional Paper No. 42. Washington, DC: Urban Institute. www.urban.org/UploadedPDF/310029_occa42.pdf.

Ellwood, David T. 1988. *Poor Support: Poverty in the American Family*. New York: Basic Books.

Ellwood, David T., and Christopher Jencks. 2004a. "The Spread of Single-Parent Families in the United States since 1960." In *The Future of the Family*, edited by Daniel P. Moynihan, Timothy M. Smeeding, and Lee Rainwater, 25–65. New York: Russell Sage Foundation.

———. 2004b. "The Uneven Spread of Single-Parent Families: What Do We Know? Where Do We Look for Answers?" In *Social Inequality*, edited by Kathryn M. Neckerman, 3–77. New York: Russell Sage Foundation.

England, Paula. 2000. "Marriage, the Costs of Children, and Gender Inequality." In *The Ties That Bind: Perspectives on Marriage and Cohabitation*, edited by Linda Waite, Christine Bachrach, Michelle Hindin, Elizabeth Thomson, and Arland Thornton, 320–42. New York: Aldine de Gruyter.

England, Paula, and Kathryn Edin, eds. 2007. *Unmarried Couples with Children.* New York: Russell Sage Foundation.

———. 2010. "Unmarried Couples with Children: Why Don't They Marry? How Can Policy-Makers Promote More Stable Relationships?" In *Families as They Really Are,* edited by Barbara Risman, 307–12. New York: W. W. Norton.

England, Paula, and Emily Fitzgibbons Shafer. 2007. "Everyday Gender Conflicts in Low-Income Couples." In *Unmarried Couples with Children,* edited by Paula England and Kathryn Edin, 55–83. New York: Russell Sage Foundation.

Estacion, Angela, and Andrew Cherlin. 2010. "Gender Distrust and Intimate Unions among Low-Income Hispanic and African-American Women." *Journal of Family Issues* 31 (4): 475–98.

Farrell, Henry. 2004. "Trust, Distrust, and Power." In *Distrust,* edited by Russell Hardin, 85–105. New York: Russell Sage Foundation.

Folk, Karen Fox, and Yunae Yi. 1994. "Piecing Together Child Care with Multiple Arrangements: Crazy Quilt or Preferred Pattern for Employed Parents of Preschool Children?" *Journal of Marriage and Family* 56:669–80.

Fraser, Nancy. 1987. "Women, Welfare, and the Politics of Need Interpretation." *Hypatia: A Journal of Feminist Philosophy* 2 (1): 103–21.

———. 1994. "After the Family Wage: Gender Equity and the Welfare State." *Political Theory* 22:591–618.

Fraser, Nancy, and Linda Gordon. 1994. "A Genealogy of *Dependency:* Tracing a Keyword of the U.S. Welfare State." *Signs* 19 (2): 309–36.

Frogner, Bianca, Robert Moffitt, and David Ribar. 2009. "How Families Are Doing Nine Years after Welfare Reform: 2005 Evidence from the Three-City Study." In *Welfare Reform and Its Long-Term Consequences for America's Poor,* edited by James Ziliak, 140–71. Cambridge: Cambridge University Press.

———. 2010. "Leaving Welfare: Long-Term Evidence from Three Cities." Working Paper 10–01. Report from the project "Welfare, Children, and Families: A Three-City Study." Baltimore: Johns Hopkins University. https://orchid.hosts.jhmi.edu/wfp/files/WP10 01_Leaving%20Welfare.pdf.

Fukuyama, Francis. 1999. *The Great Disruption: Human Nature and the Reconstitution of Social Order.* New York: Free Press.

Fuller, Bruce, Sharon L. Kagan, Gretchen L. Caspary, and Christiane A. Gauthier. 2002. "Welfare Reform and Child Care Options for Low-Income Families." *The Future of Children* 12 (1): 96–119.

Gambetta, Diego, and Heather Hamill. 2005. *Streetwise: How Taxi Drivers Establish Their Customers' Trustworthiness.* New York: Russell Sage Foundation.

Gennetian, Lisa A., Aletha C. Huston, Danielle A. Crosby, Young Eun Chang, Edward D. Lowe, and Thomas S. Weisner. 2002. *Making Child Care Choices:*

How Welfare and Work Policies Influence Parents' Decisions. New York: Manpower Demonstration Research Corporation.

Gerson, Kathleen. 2010. *The Unfinished Revolution: How a New Generation Is Reshaping Family, Work, and Gender in America*. Oxford: Oxford University Press.

Glaeser, Edward, David I. Liabson, José A. Scheinkman, and Christine L. Soutter. 2000. "Measuring Trust." *Quarterly Journal of Economics* 115 (3): 811–46.

Glanville, Jennifer L. and Pamela Paxton. 2007. "How Do We Learn to Trust? A Confirmatory Tetrad Analysis of the Sources of Generalized Trust." *Social Psychology Quarterly* 70 (3): 230–42.

Goffman, Erving. 1963. *Stigma: Notes on the Management of Spoiled Identity*. Englewood Cliffs, NJ: Prentice-Hall.

Goldsmith, Andrew. 2005. "Police Reform and the Problem of Trust." *Theoretical Criminology* 9 (4): 443–70.

Gordon, Linda, ed., 1990. *Women, the State, and Welfare*. Madison: University of Wisconsin Press.

Graefe, Deborah Roempke, and Daniel T. Lichter. 2008. "Marriage Patterns among Unwed Mothers: Before and After PRWORA." *Journal of Policy Analysis and Management* 27 (3): 479–97.

Granovetter, Mark. 1974. *Getting a Job: A Study of Contacts and Careers*. Cambridge, MA: Harvard University Press.

———. 1985. "Economic Action and Social Structure: The Problem of Embeddedness." *American Journal of Sociology* 91 (3): 481–510.

Greenhouse, Steven. 2004. "Workers Assail Night Lock-Ins by Wal-Mart." *New York Times*, January 18.

Grogger, Jeffrey. 2002. "The Behavioral Effects of Welfare Time Limits." *American Economic Review* 92:385–89.

Grogger, Jeffrey, and Lynn A. Karoly. 2005. *Welfare Reform: Effects of a Decade of Change*. Cambridge, MA: Harvard University Press.

Handler, Joel F., and Yeheskel Hasenfeld. 1991. *The Moral Construction of Poverty: Welfare Reform in America*. Newbury Park, CA: Sage Publications.

———. 1997. *We the Poor People: Work, Poverty, and Welfare*. New Haven: Yale University Press.

Haney, Lynne, and Miranda March. 2003. "Married Fathers and Caring Daddies: Welfare Reform and the Discursive Politics of Paternity." *Social Problems* 50 (4): 461–81.

Hansen, Karen V. 2005. *Not So Nuclear Families: Class, Gender, and Networks of Care*. New Brunswick: Rutgers University Press.

Hardin, Russell. 1993. "The Street-Level Epistemology of Trust." *Politics and Society* 21:505–29.

———. 2001. "Conceptions and Explanations of Trust." In *Trust in Society*, vol. 2, edited by Karen S. Cook, 3–39. New York: Russell Sage Foundation.

———. 2002. *Trust and Trustworthiness*. New York: Russell Sage Foundation.

———, ed. 2004. *Distrust*. New York: Russell Sage Foundation.

———. 2006. *Trust*. Cambridge, UK: Polity Press.

Harding, David. 2010. *Living the Drama: Community, Conflict, and Culture among Inner-City Boys*. Chicago: University of Chicago Press.

Harding, David J., Michèle Lamont, and Mario Luis Small, eds. 2010. "Reconsidering Culture and Poverty." Special issue. *Annals of the American Academy of Political and Social Science* 629 (1).

Harknett, Kristen. 2006. "The Relationship between Private Safety Nets and Economic Outcomes among Single Mothers." *Journal of Marriage and Family* 68 (1): 172–91.

Harris, Kathleen Mullan. 1993. "Work and Welfare among Single Mothers in Poverty." *American Journal of Sociology* 99 (2): 317–52.

Hawkins, Alan J., and Tamara A. Fackrell. 2010. "Does Relationship and Mrriage Education for Lower-Income Couples Work? A Meta-Analytic Study of Emerging Research." *Journal of Couple and Relationship Therapy* 9:181–91.

Hawkins, Alan J., and Theodora Ooms. 2010. "What Works in Marriage and Relationship Education? A Review of Lessons Learned with a Focus on Low-Income Couples." Research Report, National Healthy Marriage Resource Center. www.healthymarriageinfo.org/download.aspx?id=389.

Hays, Sharon. 2003. *Flat Broke with Children: Women in the Age of Welfare Reform*. Oxford: Oxford University Press.

Hearn, Frank. 1997. *Moral Order and Social Disorder: The American Search for Civil Society*. New York: Aldine de Gruyter.

Heimer, Carol A. 1988. "Social Structure, Psychology, and the Estimation of Risk." *Annual Review of Sociology* 14:491–519.

———. 2001. "Solving the Problem of Trust." In *Trust in Society*, vol. 2, edited by Karen S. Cook, 40–88. New York: Russell Sage Foundation.

Henly, Julia R. 2002. "Informal Support Networks and the Maintenance of Low-Wage Jobs." In *Laboring below the Line: The New Ethnography of Poverty, Low-Wage Work, and Survival in the Global Economy*, edited by Frank Munger, 179–203. New York: Russell Sage Foundation.

Henly, Julia R., Sandra K. Danziger, and Shira Offer. 2005. "The Contribution of Social Support to the Material Well-Being of Low-Income Families." *Journal of Marriage and Family* 67 (1): 122–40.

Henly, Julia R., and Susan Lambert. 2005. "Nonstandard Work and Child-Care Needs of Low-Income Parents." In *Work, Family, Health, and Well-Being*, edited by Suzanne M. Bianchi, Lynne M. Casper, and Rosalind B. King, 469–88. Mahwah, NJ: Lawrence Erlbaum Associates.

Henly, Julia R., and Sandra Lyons. 2000. "The Negotiation of Child Care and Employment Demands among Low-Income Parents." *Journal of Social Issues* 56 (4): 683–706.

Henly, Julia R., H. Luke Shaefer, and Elaine Waxman. 2006. "Nonstandard Work Schedules: Employer- and Employee-Driven Flexibility in Retail Jobs." *Social Service Review* 80:609–34.

Herdt, Gilbert, ed. 2009. *Moral Panics, Sex Panics: Fear and the Fight over Sexual Rights.* New York: New York University Press.

Hill, Heather D. 2007. "Steppin' Out: Infidelity and Sexual Jealousy among Unmarried Parents." In *Unmarried Couples with Children,* edited by Paula England and Kathryn Edin, 104–32. New York: Russell Sage Foundation.

Holzer, Harry J., Julia I. Lane, David B. Rosenblum, and Fredrik Andersson. 2011. *Where Are All the Good Jobs Going? What National and Local Job Quality and Dynamics Mean for U.S. Workers.* New York: Russell Sage Foundation.

Huston, Aletha. C. 2004. "Child Care for Low-Income Families: Problems and Promises." In *Work-Family Challenges for Low-Income Parents and Their Children,* edited by Ann C. Crouter and Alan Booth, 139–64. Mahwah, NJ: Lawrence Erlbaum Associates.

Iceland, John. 2003. *Poverty in America: A Handbook.* Berkeley: University of California Press.

Illinois Department of Human Services. 2011a. "Market Rate Survey of Licensed Child Care Programs in Illinois FY10." www.dhs.state.il.us/page.aspx?item=56055#a_toc7.

———. 2011b. "06.05.01—Rate Chart, 07/01/11." www.dhs.state.il.us/page.aspx?item=55964.

Jarrett, Robin L. 1994. "Living Poor: Family Life among Single Parent, African-American Women." *Social Problems* 41 (1): 30–49.

Jarrett, Robin L., Kevin M. Roy, and Linda M. Burton. 2002. "Fathers in the 'Hood: Qualitative Research on Low-Income African American Men." In *Handbook of Father Involvement: Multidisciplinary Perspectives,* edited by Catherine Tamis-LeMonda and Natasha Cabrera, 211–48. New York: Lawrence Erlbaum Associates.

Jencks, Christopher. 2002. "Liberal Lessons from Welfare Reform." *American Prospect,* July, A9–12.

Jencks, Christopher, Joseph Swingle, and Scott Winship. 2006. "Welfare Redux." *American Prospect* 17 (3): 36–40.

Kalil, Ariel, Kristin S. Seefeldt, and Hui-Chen Wang. 2002. "Sanctions and Material Hardship under TANF." *Social Service Review* 76 (4): 642–62.

Katz, Michael B. 1986. *In the Shadow of the Poorhouse: A Social History of Welfare in America.* New York: Basic Books.

Kilty, Keith M., and Elizabeth A. Segal, eds. 2006. *The Promise of Welfare Reform: Political Rhetoric and the Reality of Poverty in the Twenty-First Century.* Binghamton, NY: Haworth Press.

Kirschenman, Joleen, and Kathryn M. Neckerman. 1991. "'We'd Love to Hire Them, But . . .': The Meaning of Race for Employers." In *The Urban Underclass,* edited by Christopher Jencks and Paul E. Peterson, 203–32. Washington, DC: Brookings Institute.

Klerman, Jacob Alex. 2005. "Family Structure." In *Welfare Reform: Effects of a Decade of Change,* by Jeffrey Grogger and Lynn A. Karoly, 173–98. Cambridge, MA: Harvard University Press.

Kluegel, James R., and Eliot R. Smith. 1986. *Beliefs about Inequality: Americans Views of What Is and What Ought to Be.* New York: DeGruyter.

Kollock, Peter. 1994. "The Emergence of Exchange Structures: An Experimental Study of Uncertainty, Commitment, and Trust." *American Journal of Sociology* 100 (2): 313–45.

Kramer, Roderick M. 2004. "Collective Paranoia: Distrust between Social Groups." In *Distrust,* edited by Russell Hardin, 136–66. New York: Russell Sage Foundation.

Kramer, Roderick M., and Karen S. Cook, eds. 2004. *Trust and Distrust in Organizations: Dilemmas and Approaches.* New York: Russell Sage Foundation.

Lambert, Susan J. 2008. "Passing the Buck: Labor Flexibility Practices That Transfer Risk onto Hourly Workers." *Human Relations* 61 (9): 1203–27.

Lambert, Susan J., Anna Haley-Lock, and Julia R. Henly. 2012. "Schedule Flexibility in Hourly Jobs: Unanticipated Consequences and Promising Directions." *Community, Work and Family* 15 (3): 293–315.

Lambert, Susan J., and Julia R. Henly. 2012. "Frontline Managers Matter: Labour Flexibility Practices and Sustained Employment in Hourly Retail Jobs in the U.S." In *Are Bad Jobs Inevitable? Trends, Determinants and Responses to Job Quality in the Twenty-First Century,* edited by Chris Warhurst, Francoise Carré, Patricia Findlay, and Chris Tilly, 143–59. Basingstoke: Palgrave Macmillan.

Lambert, Susan J., and Julia R. Henly. Forthcoming. "Double Jeopardy: The Misfit between Welfare-to-Work Requirements and Job Realities." In *Work and the Welfare State: The Politics and Management of Policy Change,* edited by Evelyn Brodkin and Gregory Marston. Washington, DC: Georgetown University Press.

Lens, Vicki, and Susan Elizabeth Vorsanger. 2005. "Complaining after Claiming: Fair Hearings after Welfare Reform." *Social Service Review* 79 (3): 430–53.

Levi, Margaret. 1998. "A State of Trust." In *Trust and Governance,* edited by Valerie Braithwaite and Margaret Levi, 77–101. New York: Russell Sage Foundation.

Levine, Judith A. 2009. "It's a Man's Job, or So They Say: The Maintenance of Sex Segregation in a Manufacturing Plant." *Sociological Quarterly* 50:257–82.

Lewis, Dan, Laura Amsden, Kristen Shook Slack, Bong Joo Lee, Paul Kleppner, James Lewis, Stephanie Riger, and Robert Goerge. 2004. "The Two Worlds of Welfare Reform in Illinois: Fourth Annual Report from the Illinois Families Study." University Consortium on Welfare Reform, report to the Illinois General Assembly. www.ipr.northwestern.edu/publications/papers/IFSyear4.pdf.

Lewis, J. David, and Andrew Weigert. 1985. "Trust as Social Reality." *Social Forces* 63:967–85.

Lewis, Oscar. 1966. *La Vida*. New York: Random House.

Liebow, Elliot. 1967. *Tally's Corner: A Study of Negro Streetcorner Men*. Boston: Little, Brown.

Lin, Nan. 2001. *Social Capital: A Theory of Social Structure and Action*. Cambridge: Cambridge University Press.

Lindhorst, Taryn, and Julianna D. Padgett. 2005. "Disjunctures for Women and Frontline Workers: Implementation of the Family Violence Option." *Social Service Review* 79 (3): 405–29.

Lipsky, Michael. 1980. *Street-Level Bureaucracy: Dilemmas of the Individual in Public Services*. New York: Russell Sage Foundation.

Lloyd, Susan E. 1997. "The Effects of Domestic Violence on Women's Employment." *Law and Policy* 19 (2): 139–67.

London, Andrew S., Ellen K. Scott, Kathryn Edin, and Vicki Hunter. 2004. "Welfare Reform, Work-Family Tradeoffs, and Child Well-Being." *Family Relations* 53 (2): 148–58.

Loprest, Pamela. 1999. *Families Who Left Welfare: Who Are They and How Are They Doing?* Discussion Paper 99–02. Washington, DC: Urban Institute.

Lowe, Edward D., and Thomas S. Weisner. 2004. "'You Have to Push It—Who's Gonna Raise Your Kids?': Situating Child Care and Child Care Subsidy Use in the Daily Routines of Lower Income Families." *Children and Youth Services Review* 26 (2): 143–271.

Macy, Michael W., and John Skvoretz. 1998. "The Evolution of Trust and Cooperation between Strangers: A Computational Model." *American Sociological Review* 63 (5): 638–60.

March, James G. 1994. *A Primer on Decision Making: How Decisions Happen*. New York: Free Press.

March, James G., and Herbert A. Simon. 1958. *Organizations*. New York: Wiley.

Matthews, Hannah, and Danielle Ewen. 2005. "Child Care Assistance in 2004: States Have Fewer Funds for Childcare." Pub. No. 05–52, Center for Law and Social Policy, Washington, DC. www.clasp.org/publications.php?id=3&year=2005#0.

McLanahan, Sara. 2011. "Family Instability and Complexity after a Nonmarital Birth: Outcomes from Children in Fragile Families." In *Social Class and*

Changing Families in an Unequal America, edited by Marcia J. Carlson and Paula England, 108–33. Stanford: Stanford University Press.

McLaughlin, Heather, Christopher Uggen, and Amy Blackstone. 2012. "Sexual Harassment, Workplace Authority, and the Paradox of Power." *American Sociological Review* 77:625–47.

Menjívar, Cecilia. 2000. *Fragmented Ties: Salvadoran Immigrant Networks in America.* Berkeley: University of California Press.

Mink, Gwendolyn. 1990. "The Lady and the Tramp: Gender, Race, and the Origins of the American Welfare State." In *Women, the State, and Welfare,* edited by Linda Gordon, 92–122. Madison: University of Wisconsin Press.

Moffitt, Robert. 1999. "The Effect of Pre-PRWORA Waivers on AFDC Caseloads and Female Earnings, Income, and Labor Force Behavior." Working paper, Johns Hopkins University.

———. 2003. "The Role of Non-Financial Factors in Exit and Entry in the TANF Program." *Journal of Human Resources* 38: 1221–254.

Molm, Linda D., Nobuyuki Takahashi, and Gretchen Peterson. 2000. "Risk and Trust in Social Exchange: An Experimental Test of a Classical Proposition." *American Journal of Sociology* 105 (5): 1396–1427.

Mowday, Richard T., Lyman W. Porter, and Richard M. Steers. 1982. *Employee-Organization Linkages: The Psychology of Commitment, Absenteeism and Turnover.* New York: Academic Press.

Murray, Charles. 1984. *Losing Ground: American Social Policy, 1950–1980.* New York: Basic Books.

National Child Care Information Center. 2005. *CCDF Report of State Plans, Fiscal Year 2004–2005.* Washington, DC: U.S. Department of Health and Human Services.

Nee, Victor, and Jimy Sanders. 2001. "Trust in Ethnic Ties: Social Capital and Immigrants." In *Trust in Society,* vol. 2, edited by Karen S. Cook, 374–92. New York: Russell Sage Foundation.

Newman, Katherine S. 1999. *No Shame in My Game: The Working Poor in the Inner City.* New York: Alfred Knopf.

Norušis, Marija. 2010. *SPSS Statistics 17.0 Guide to Data Analysis.* Upper Saddle River, NJ: Prentice Hall.

Oliker, Stacey J. 1995a. "The Proximate Contexts of Workfare and Work: A Framework for Studying Poor Women's Economic Choices." *Sociological Quarterly* 36 (2): 251–72.

———. 1995b. "Work Commitment and Constraint among Mothers on Workfare." *Journal of Contemporary Ethnography* 24 (2): 165–94.

———. 2000. "Examining Care at Welfare's End." In *Care Work: Gender, Labor and the Welfare State,* edited by Madonna Harrington Meyer, 167–85. New York: Routledge.

Ostrom, Elinor, and James Walker, eds. 2003. *Trust and Reciprocity: Interdisciplinary Lessons from Experimental Research.* New York: Russell Sage Foundation.

Patterson, James T. 2000. *America's Struggle against Poverty in the Twentieth Century.* Cambridge, MA: Harvard University Press.

Pavetti, LaDonna. 1993. "The Dynamics of Welfare and Work: Exploring the Process by Which Women Work Their Way off Welfare." PhD diss., Harvard University.

Peel, Mark. 1998. "Trusting Disadvantaged Citizens." In *Trust and Governance,* edited by Valerie Braithwaite and Margaret Levi, 315–42. New York: Russell Sage Foundation.

Piven, Frances Fox, and Richard A. Cloward. 1993. *Regulating the Poor: The Functions of Public Welfare.* New York: Vintage.

Portes, Alejandro. 1998. "Social Capital: Its Origins and Applications in Modern Sociology." *Annual Review of Sociology* 24:1–24.

Putnam, Robert D. 2000. *Bowling Alone: The Collapse and Revival of American Community.* New York: Simon and Schuster.

Quadagno, Jill S. 1994. *The Color of Welfare: How Racism Undermined the War on Poverty.* New York: Oxford University Press.

Quane, James M., Jessica Su, and Pamela Joshi. 2009. "'It's Not Business As Usual Any More': Workers' Reflections on Discretion, Trust and Power Dynamics at the Frontlines of Welfare Reform." Working Paper 09–04. Report from the project "Welfare, Children, and Families: A Three-City Study." Baltimore: Johns Hopkins University. https://orchid.hosts.jhmi.edu/wfp/files/WP%20 09–04%20It's%20Not%20Business%20As%20Usual%20Any%20More.pdf.

Randles, Jennifer. 2009. *Parenting in Poverty and the Politics of Commitment: Promoting Marriage for Poor Families through Relationship Education.* Working Paper, Institute for the Study of Social Change, University of California, Berkeley. www.escholarship.org/uc/item/0tp2b2xm.

Reed, Joanna. 2007. "Anatomy of the Breakup: How and Why Do Unmarried Couples with Children Break Up?" In *Unmarried Couples with Children,* edited by Paula England and Kathryn Edin, 133–56. New York: Russell Sage Foundation.

Reese, Ellen. 2005. *Backlash against Welfare Mothers: Past and Present.* Berkeley: University of California Press.

Ribar, David C., Marilyn Edelhoch, and Qiduan Liu. 2008. "Watching the Clocks: The Role of Food Stamp Recertification and TANF Time Limits in Caseload Dynamics." *Journal of Human Resources* 43:208–39.

Robinson, Sandra L. 1996. "Trust and Breach of the Psychological Contract." *Administrative Science Quarterly* 41 (4): 574–99.

Roschelle, Anne R. 1997. *No More Kin: Exploring Race, Class, and Gender in Family Networks.* London: Sage Publications.

Ross, Catherine E., John Mirowsky, and Shana Pribesh. 2001. "Powerlessness and the Amplification of Threat: Neighborhood Disadvantage, Disorder, and Mistrust." *American Sociological Review* 66:568–91.

Rotter, Julian B. 1980. "Interpersonal Trust, Trustworthiness, and Gullibility." *American Psychologist* 35:1–7.

Roy, Kevin M. 1999. "Low-Income Single Fathers in an African American Community and the Requirements of Welfare Reform." *Journal of Family Issues* 20:432–57.

———. 2004. "You Can't Eat Love: Constructing Provider Role Expectations for Low-Income and Working-Class Fathers." *Fathering: A Journal of Theory, Research and Practice about Men as Fathers* 2:253–76.

Roy, Kevin M., and Natasha Cabrera. 2009. "Not Just Provide and Reside: Engaged Fathers in Low-Income Families." In *Families As They Really Are,* edited by Barbara J. Risman, 301–6. New York: W.W. Norton.

Rubinowitz, Leonard S., and James E. Rosenbaum. 2000. *Crossing the Class and Color Lines: From Public Housing to White Suburbia.* Chicago: University of Chicago Press.

Sampson, Robert J. 2000. "The Neighborhood Context of Investing in Children: Facilitating Mechanisms and Undermining Risks." In *Securing the Future: Investing in Children from Birth to College,* edited by Sheldon Danziger and Jane Waldfogel, 205–27. New York: Russell Sage Foundation.

———. 2012. *Great American City: Chicago and the Enduring Neighborhood Effect.* Chicago: University of Chicago Press.

Sampson, Robert J., Jeffrey D. Morenoff, and Felton Earls. 1999. "Beyond Social Capital: Spatial Dynamics of Collective Efficacy for Children." *American Sociological Review* 64 (5): 633–60.

Sampson, Robert J., Jeffrey D. Morenoff, and Thomas Gannon-Rowley. 2002. "Assessing 'Neighborhood Effects': Social Processes and New Directions in Research." *Annual Review of Sociology* 28:443–78.

Sandfort, Jodi R., Ariel Kalil, and Julie A. Gottschalk. 1999. "The Mirror Has Two Faces: Welfare Clients and Front-Line Workers View Policy Reforms." *Journal of Poverty* 3 (3): 71–91.

Sapiro, Virginia. 1990. "The Gender Basis of American Social Policy." In *Women, the State, and Welfare,* edited by Linda Gordon, 36–54. Madison: University of Wisconsin Press.

Sarkisian, Natalia. 2005. "The Cultural Contradictions of Welfare." *Contemporary Sociology* 34 (5): 473–76.

Sarkisian, Natalia, Mariana Gerena, and Naomi Gerstel. 2006. "Extended Family Ties among Mexicans, Puerto Ricans, and Whites: Superintegration or Disintegration?" *Family Relations* 55 (3): 331–44.

————. 2007. "Extended Family Integration among Euro and Mexican Americans: Ethnicity, Gender, and Class." *Journal of Marriage and Family* 69 (1): 40–54.

Sarkisian, Natalia, and Naomi Gerstel. 2004. "Kin Support among Blacks and Whites: Race and Family Organization." *American Sociological Review* 69 (6): 812–37.

Schoeni, Robert F., and Rebecca M. Blank. 2000. *What Has Welfare Reform Accomplished? Impacts on Welfare Participation, Employment, Income, Poverty, and Family Structure.* Working Paper No. 7627. Cambridge, MA: National Bureau of Economic Research. www.nber.org/papers/w7627.pdf.

Schott, Liz, and Ife Finch. 2010. "TANF Benefits Are Low and Have Not Kept Pace with Inflation: Benefits Are Not Enough to Meet Families' Basic Needs." Center for Budget and Policy Priorities, Washington, DC. www.cbpp.org/cms/index.cfm?fa=view&id=3306.

Scott, Ellen K., Kathryn Edin, Andrew S. London, and Rebecca Joyce Kissane. 2004. "Unstable Work, Unstable Income: Implications for Family Well-Being in the Era of Time-Limited Welfare." *Journal of Poverty* 8:61–88.

Scott, Ellen K., Andrew London, and Allison Hurst. 2005. "Instability in Patchworks of Child Care When Moving from Welfare to Work." *Journal of Marriage and Family* 67:370–86.

Seefeldt, Kristin S. 2008. *Working after Welfare: How Women Balance Jobs and Family in the Wake of Welfare Reform.* Kalamazoo, MI: W. E. Upjohn Institute for Employment Research.

Sewell, William H. 1992. "A Theory of Structure: Duality, Agency, and Transformation." *American Journal of Sociology* 98:1–29.

Sidel, Ruth. 2006. *Unsung Heroes: Single Mothers and the American Dream.* Berkeley: University of California Press.

Sinkewicz, Marilyn, and Irwin Garfinkel. 2009. "Unwed Fathers' Ability to Pay Child Support: New Estimates Accounting for Multiple-Partner Fertility." *Demography* 46 (2):247–64.

Skocpol, Theda. 1992. *Protecting Soldiers and Mothers: The Political Origins of Social Policy in the United States.* Cambridge, MA: Harvard University Press.

Small, Mario Luis. 2009. *Unanticipated Gains: Origins of Network Inequality in Everyday Life.* New York: Oxford University Press.

Small, Mario Luis, David J. Harding, and Michèle Lamont. 2010. "Reconsidering Culture and Poverty." *Annals of the American Academy of Political and Social Science* 629:6–27.

Smith, Rebekah J. 2006. "Family Caps in Welfare Reform: Their Coercive Effects and Damaging Consequences." *Harvard Journal of Law and Gender* 29:151–200.

Smith, Sandra Susan 2007. *Lone Pursuit: Distrust and Defensive Individualism among the Black Poor.* New York: Russell Sage Foundation.

Spalter-Roth, Roberta M., Heidi I. Hartmann, and Linda Andrews. 1992. "Combining Work and Welfare: An Alternative Anti-Poverty Strategy." Report to the Ford Foundation, Institute for Women's Policy Research, Washington, DC.

Stack, Carol. 1974. *All Our Kin: Strategies for Survival in a Black Community.* New York: Harper and Row.

Swidler, Ann. 1986. "Culture in Action: Symbols and Strategies." *American Sociological Review* 51:273–86.

Talbot, Margaret. 2001. "The Lives They Lived: 01–07–01: Peggy McMartin Buckey, b. 1926; The Devil in the Nursery." *New York Times Magazine,* January 7.

Tyler, Tom R. 2001. "Why Do People Rely on Others? Social Identity and Social Aspects of Trust." In *Trust in Society,* vol. 2, edited by Karen S. Cook, 285–306. New York: Russell Sage Foundation.

Uttal, Lynet. 1999. "Using Kin for Child Care: Embedment in the Socioeconomic Networks of Extended Families." *Journal of Marriage and the Family* 61:845–57.

Vobejda, Barbara, and Judith Havemann. 1996. "2 HHS Officials Quit over Welfare Changes." *Washington Post,* September 12.

Wacquant, Loïc. 2002. "Scrutinizing the Street: Poverty, Morality, and the Pitfalls of Urban Ethnography." *American Journal of Sociology* 107 (6): 1468–1532.

———. 2009. *Punishing the Poor: The Neoliberal Government of Social Insecurity.* Durham: Duke University Press.

Waite, Linda, Christine Bachrach, Michelle Hindin, Elizabeth Thomson, and Arland Thornton, eds. 2000. *The Ties That Bind: Perspectives on Marriage and Cohabitation.* New York: Aldine Transaction.

Waite, Linda J., and Maggie Gallagher. 2000. *The Case for Marriage: Why Married People Are Happier, Heathier, and Better Off Financially.* New York: Random House.

Wallace, Geoffrey, and Rebecca M. Blank. 1999. "What Goes Up Must Come Down? Explaining Recent Changes in Public Assistance Caseloads." In *Economic Conditions and Welfare Reform,* edited by Sheldon H. Danziger, 49–89. Kalamazoo, MI: W. E. Upjohn Institute for Employment Research Institute.

Waller, Maureen R. 2002. *My Baby's Father: Unmarried Parents and Paternal Responsibility.* New York: Cornell University Press.

———. 2010. "Viewing Low-Income Fathers' Ties to Families through a Cultural Lens: Insights for Research and Policy." *Annals of the American Academy of Political and Social Science* 629:102–24.

Watkins-Hayes, Celeste. 2009. *The New Welfare Bureaucrats: Entanglements of Race, Class, and Policy Reform.* Chicago: University of Chicago Press.

Western, Bruce. 2006. *Punishment and Inequality in America.* New York: Russell Sage Foundation.

Wilson, William J. 1987. *The Truly Disadvantaged: The Inner City, the Underclass, and Public Policy.* Chicago: University of Chicago Press.

———. 2009. *More Than Just Race: Being Black and Poor in the Inner City.* New York: Norton.

Wrigley, Julia, and Joanna Dreby. 2005. "Fatalities and the Organization of Child Care in the United States, 1985–2003." *American Sociological Review* 70:729–57.

Yamagishi, Toshio. 2001. "Trust as a Form of Social Intelligence." In *Trust in Society,* vol. 2, edited by Karen S. Cook, 121–47. New York: Russell Sage Foundation.

Young, Louise, and Kerry Daniel. 2003. "Affectual Trust in the Workplace." *International Journal of Human Resource Management* 14 (1): 139–55.

Zedlewski, Shelia R., Sandi Nelson, Kathryn Edin, Heather L. Koball, Kate Pomper, and Tracy Roberts. 2003. *Families Coping without Earnings or Government Cash Assistance.* Occasional Paper No. 64. Washington, DC: Urban Institute.

Ziliak, James P., David N. Figlio, Elizabeth E. Davis, and Laura S. Connolly. 2000. "Accounting for the Decline in AFDC Caseloads: Welfare Reform or Economic Conditions?" *Journal of Human Resources* 35 (3): 570–86.

Zimbardo, Philip G. 2008. *The Lucifer Effect: Understanding How Good People Turn Evil.* New York: Random House.

Index

The letter *t* following a page number denotes a table.